D0172569

Cyber-Investing

Cyber-Investing

Cracking Wall Street with Your Personal Computer

David L. Brown
Kassandra Bentley

John Wiley & Sons, Inc.

New York • Chichester • Weinheim • Brisbane • Singapore • Toronto

This text is printed on acid-free paper.

Copyright © 1997 by David L. Brown and Kassandra Bentley
Published by John Wiley & Sons, Inc.

All rights reserved. Published simultaneously in Canada.

Reproduction or translation of any part of this work beyond
that permitted by Section 107 or 108 of the 1976 United
States Copyright Act without the permission of the copyright
owner is unlawful. Requests for permission or further
information should be addressed to the Permissions Department,
John Wiley & Sons, Inc.

This publication is designed to provide accurate and authoritative
information in regard to the subject matter covered. It is sold
with the understanding that the publisher is not engaged in
rendering legal, accounting, or other professional services. If
legal advice or other expert assistance is required, the services
of a competent professional person should be sought.

Library of Congress Cataloging-in-Publication Data:

Brown, David L., 1940–
    Cyber-investing : cracking Wall Street with your personal computer
    David L. Brown, Kassandra Bentley. — 2nd ed.
      p.   cm.
    Includes index.
    ISBN 0-471-16987-0 (cloth : alk. paper). — ISBN 0-471-16986-2
    (pbk. : alk. paper)
      1. Investments—Data processing. 2. Investments—United States—
    Data processing. 3. Stocks—United States—Data processing.
    4. Investment analysis—Computer programs. 5. Portfolio management—
    Computer programs. 6. Investments—Databases. 7. Database
    searching. 8. Investments—Computer network resources.
    I. Bentley, Kassandra. II. Title.
    HG4515.5.B77   1997
    332.6′0285′416—dc21   96-47737

Printed in the United States of America

10 9 8 7 6 5 4 3

This book is dedicated to Dr. Richard K. Carlin,
who, as the founder of Telescan, pioneered the tools
that make cyber-investing so powerful, and to all
the employees of Telescan who help bring to life
Richard's seemingly endless fountain of ideas.

PREFACE

Since the first edition of this book was published two years ago, opportunities for computerized investing have continued to grow. Many of the products we dubbed "tools of tomorrow" in that book did in fact arrive. Global investing has in fact become an arena for the individual investor. Perhaps most impressive has been the virtual explosion of investing information on the Internet. Two years ago, few Web sites were devoted to investing. Now there are dozens with content that is impressive both in quality and quantity. Two years ago, we covered the Internet in a couple of paragraphs; in this edition we have given it a full chapter, and that barely scratches the surface. The potential of the Internet for investors is overwhelming.

The stock market itself has continued to advance. In the past two years the Dow climbed to the top of its long-term price trend, then abruptly pulled back in July 1996 with a breathtaking 200-point drop. This correction gave us added confidence in the cyber-investing tools in this book because it was clear that the market was then dangerously extended. But during the extraordinary bull market of 1995, it had not been extended, as we clearly demonstrated in the first edition of this book. In early 1995 when the Dow pushed through the 4000 barrier and timid investors were hanging back in fear, we wrote (and demonstrated with one of the technical tools described in Chapter 13) that the market was merely at the midpoint of its long-term trend. Those who paid attention would have had the courage to stay invested as the Dow broke through one new high after another, and, based on the same cyber-investing tool, would have been able to foresee the major market correction in the summer of 1996.

Our personal experience over the past two years has also increased our confidence in the cyber-investing process and tools described in this book. The Cyber-Investing Newsletter, which is based on the investing concept and tools described in this book, had a return of 26.5 percent in 1995; this, despite the fact that only 50 percent of the portfolio was invested as the market moved into dangerous territory late in the year. More important, others who have completely different investing philosophies but use a process similar to the one we describe have done even better.

The cyber-investing process works. It works in any kind of market, be it bullish, bearish, or sideways. It works with international stocks as well as domestic stocks. The process itself is a discipline, and once you are confident of the process, you can use it in any investing arena. After all, it doesn't matter how deep the water is if you know how to swim.

This book will teach you to swim.

DAVID L. BROWN
KASSANDRA BENTLEY
http://www.cyberinvest.com

Houston, Texas
November 1996

ACKNOWLEDGMENTS

There are many who made valuable contributions to the Second Edition of this book. First, we want to thank our editor at John Wiley & Sons, Jacqueline Urinyi, for her enthusiasm and support in bringing out a second edition. We want to thank Mark Draud for his research and invaluable assistance; Tom Melton for his diligent editing of the manuscript; Luiz Alvim, for his contribution of the Alvim Stochastics; Neil Waldman and Greg Gensemer for putting together the Cyber-Investing Kit; Craig Carlin for his help on the Internet chapter; Paul Alvim for his general assistance; Doug Graham of Macro*World Investment Corporation for his gracious assistance with Chapter 11; and Kim Nir for her meticulous copyediting. Those who assisted with the first edition—Mark Arnold, Scott Brown, James Castillo, Scott LaRoche, Chris Meyers, Alex Waugh, Marlon Wells, and others—are *ipso facto* valuable contributors to this edition.

As always, we are indebted to Geri Fries, for her help in scheduling our time, and we are continually grateful to Carolyn Brown without whose support and encouragement we could not have completed the first or the second edition.

The stock graphs and serach reports were supplied by Telescan, Inc.

D.L.B.
K.B.

ABOUT THE AUTHORS

David L. Brown is the Chairman and CEO of Telescan, Inc., a leading information and technology provider, and editor of the Cyber-Investing Newsletter. He has taught courses in corporate finance and security analysis at the University of Houston and has served as Chairman of the U.S. Science and Technology Commission for a series of conferences with the former USSR. Mr. Brown began his career at NASA where he was instrumental in the design of the landing gear for the first lunar module.

Kassandra Bentley is a writer who specializes in financial and computer topics. She is currently writing her second book with Mr. Brown, *Wall Street City: Your Guide to the Hottest Investment Sites on the Web*.

CONTENTS

INTRODUCTION

The personal computer revolution of the past twenty years has shattered a lot of barriers, including the one between Wall Street and Main Street. A decade ago Wall Street had a lock on the kind of information needed to make a truly informed decision about trading stocks. It took a lot of manpower to research a stock and enormous computing power to manipulate that research into usable data. Few individual investors could afford to do it. Instead, they relied on stockbrokers at major brokerage houses who had access to large research staffs and mainframe computers. The PC and the information explosion of the past few years have changed all that.

Today, from Sioux City, Iowa to San Antonio, Texas, from Portland, Oregon to Portland, Maine, the information superhighway leads directly to Wall Street. With cyber-investing you can retrieve in seconds price and volume information for virtually any listed stock. You can plot intraday stock graphs or historical graphs for one week or one month, one year or twenty. You can see a company's earnings the minute they're released. You can obtain earnings estimates made by independent analysts for the next quarter, the next year, the next five years. You can read research reports written by professional analysts and inspect corporate financial statements filed with the Securities and Exchange Commission (SEC). You can consult forecasts by experts on where they think a stock is headed. You can even learn which corporate insiders are buying or selling their company's stock, how many shares they bought or sold, the price they paid, and the size of their current holdings!

This is cyber-investing.

Cyber-investing levels the playing field and makes it possible for an individual investor with a PC to do as well in the stock market as the experts on Wall Street. If you doubt this, listen to what Peter Lynch, the former manager of Fidelity Magellan Mutual Fund, has to say in his best-selling book, *One Up On Wall Street:*[1]

> The amateur investor has numerous built-in advantages that, if exploited, should result in his or her outperforming the experts, and also the market in general.

What might that performance be? The stock market in general has generated annual returns of 10 to 12 percent for the past 70 years. All growth-oriented mutual funds have averaged more than 10 percent per year for the past 35 years with the top 25 funds averaging more than 18 percent per year over the past 15 years. Mr. Lynch himself generated annual returns of over 26 percent during his 15-year reign at Fidelity Magellan. So, when he says that an amateur investor—that's you sitting in front of your PC—should be able to beat the experts by using the "normal 3 percent of the brain," he is implying you should be able to make more than 10 to 12 percent per year.

Anything over 15 percent is very good, but we believe a cyber-investor can do better than that. The purpose of this book is to introduce you to a powerful arsenal of computerized tools that can help you generate annualized returns of 15 to 20 percent or more a year!

How do you know this book is for you? It is if:

- You have been toying with the idea of investing in stocks but don't know how to start.

- You own stocks through a company investment plan but want to start investing on your own.

- You are retired and looking for ways to supplement your income.

- You have been using your personal computer to follow stocks and have made an occasional trade.

- You regularly trade stocks but are tired of relying on tips from brokers and the media.

---

[1] Peter Lynch, with John Rothchild, *One Up on Wall Street: How to Use What You Already Know to Make Money in the Market* (New York: Penguin Books USA, 1989, p. 14).

- You're a seasoned investor who wants to add 2 to 5 percent to your returns.

Whatever your level of interest in the stock market, you should find something of value in this book.

Here's a sampling of the powerful tools you'll find in these pages:

- Stock search tools that can search through more than 9,000 stocks *in seconds* and present you with a list of stocks that best match your unique investment goals.
- Evaluation tools to help you narrow a large list of stocks to the best of the best.
- Fundamental tools that can reveal the underlying strength or weakness of a company.
- Technical charting tools that can instantaneously draw price-and-volume stock graphs and plot dozens of technical indicators.
- Technical timing tools that can detect the likely reversal of an uptrend or downtrend, allowing you to time your trades to minimize risk and maximize reward.
- Technical analysis tools that can reveal trading patterns, which can turn an ordinary stock into a high-return investment.
- Industry group tools that can reveal the industries favored by institutional investors, which helps you increase your profit potential by buying stocks in the favored groups.
- Company research tools that offer a wide variety of information on public companies.
- Portfolio management tools to update and monitor your portfolio.
- Mutual fund search and analysis tools for the conservative investor.
- Options search and analysis tools for the more speculative investor.
- Advanced trading tools that can find speculative opportunities through pending mergers and acquisitions.

As you will see, we will talk frequently about Telescan products because they are the ones we know best. But don't expect a mere catalog of software. We will show the tools *in action* by implementing a number of investing strategies and techniques. Although we favor strategies that minimize risk and maximize reward, we're not trying to convert you to our investing philosophy. We will also demonstrate strategies, such as momentum investing and option speculation. You may tailor these to meet your needs, if you wish, or develop strategies of your own, once you master the tools. You may also adapt the strategies and techniques to other cyber-investing products, many of which are listed in the Source List at the end of this book.

The cyber-investing process underlying any strategy consists of five simple steps:

1. Identify stocks that have the best price growth potential.

2. Analyze them in a systematic way.

3. Time each purchase to minimize risk and maximize reward.

4. Manage your portfolio to stay abreast of changes that might affect your stocks.

5. Sell each stock when the time is right.

This process is essentially the process of successful investing. It is a systematic process that can make you financially independent over time. All it takes to be a successful investor is a willingness to learn how to use the tools, a few hours a week to build and manage your portfolio, and the discipline to stick with a system.

We decided to write this book after seeing the eagerness with which people flock to investing seminars. They come to learn more about how to use computerized tools. They come to learn the secrets of successful strategies. They come to learn how to increase their returns, even if those returns are already above average. That's what we want to demonstrate in this book. One of us (David Brown) is the author of two successful market newsletters, a well-known speaker at investment seminars, and chief executive officer of Telescan, Inc., a publicly traded company that is one of the leading producers of investment products and online financial services. The other (Kassandra Bentley) is a writer who has written extensively on computer products and investment software. We have been part of the computerized investing field almost since it began. We know the market and we know the products.

FREE CYBER-INVESTING KIT

The publisher has included with this book a Cyber-Investing Kit that lets you experiment with many of the investing tools mentioned in these pages. The kit includes free software (in the back of this book) and free online access for 30 days to the Telescan 3.0 system. An upgrade to the Windows version is available at a discounted price. The software features a stock search program, a charting and analysis program, and search programs for options and mutual funds. The kit provides free access for 30 days to research tools such as earnings estimates, news, and corporate profiles. It also includes free or discounted admission to Telescan investing seminars held throughout the country and access during the free trial to more than 20 online newsletters. One of these is the Cyber-Investing Newsletter, which is co-edited by David Brown who uses the investing tools and techniques described in this book. A complete description of the contents of the Cyber-Investing Kit appears at the end of the book.

HOW TO USE THIS BOOK

The best way to use this book is to read the first three chapters and then install the Telescan software. (Hardware requirements, installation procedures, and operating instructions appear in the Quick Start Guide at the end of the book.) We urge you to use your free online time to follow along with the examples in the book. This will shed much light on the points we try to make in each chapter. If you don't have a computer yet, read the book first; then reread the pertinent chapters as you begin to use the computerized tools to build your portfolio.

Here's a recap of what you'll find in the rest of the book.

Chapters 1 and 2 set the stage for the rest of the book with a discussion about why to invest in the stock market and what makes stocks go up.

Chapters 3, 4, and 5 introduce the computerized investing process and a stock search tool. Chapter 6 shows you how to test search strategies on past market periods, and Chapters 7 and 8 describe a two-stage process for evaluating a list of stocks from a search.

Chapters 9, 10, 11, and 12 present technical analysis and timing tools for buying and selling stocks, and for managing a portfolio. We discuss technical buy and sell signals, targets and stops, electronic trading, monitoring a portfolio, and how to use market indexes and mutual funds to evaluate your performance.

Chapters 13, 14, and 15 describe advanced strategies and tools for the more sophisticated investor. Topics include market analysis, industry group analysis, and a brief look at options. In Chapter 15, we also show you a way to identify low-cost speculative opportunities.

Chapter 16 describes investing opportunities on the Internet, and Chapter 17 provides a glimpse into the future of cyber-investing, including a brief assessment of global investing.

Finally, at the end of the book you'll find a description of the Cyber-Investing Kit, a Quick Start Guide for installing and using the Telescan software, and a Source List for a variety of computerized investing tools and services.

YOU MUST REMEMBER THIS . . .

As you read this book, keep these points in mind:

- Cyber-investing tools and techniques can help you outperform the market, which has produced average returns of 10 to 12 percent per year over the past 70 years.

- The cyber-investing process is essentially the process of successful investing. You can apply it to any investing philosophy or use it in any kind of market.

- The amateur status of the individual investor has built-in advantages, according to Peter Lynch, author and legendary money manager. Cyber-investing can help you exploit those advantages.

Now is the time to become a cyber-investor because in the 21st Century, there won't be any other kind.

Cyber-Investing

1

WHY INVEST
IN STOCKS?

The stock market continues to be one of the few places where an ordinary person can legitimately accumulate a great deal of money. When we wrote the first edition of this book in late 1994, the Dow was around 3700. In 1995, it broke through the 4000 and 5000 barriers, and then took just ten months to push past the 6000 level. During this two-year period, Nasdaq stocks gained an average of 70 percent. The S&P 500 gained 58 percent. The New York Stock Exchange index gained 55 percent.

Where were you during this record-setting market?

At this writing, the Dow is comfortably above 6000 and climbing. Whether or not the bull run continues, now is a good time to get acquainted with some cyber-investing tools that can help you penetrate the mystique of the market and turn it to your advantage.

To whet your appetite, let's take a look at some companies that have had extraordinary returns during the past three years, and then we will show you how cyber-investing tools can turn ordinary stocks into top performers.

Exhibit 1.1 shows 14 stocks with an average return of more than 1,810 percent over the past two years. Ten thousand dollars invested in these stocks in May 1993 would have grown to more than $175,000 by

Exhibit 1.1   Superstars: Over a three-year period, these stocks gained an average of more than 1,810%—an averaged annualized return of over 160%. (Many of the stocks have since split.)

Company	May 1993	May 1996	% Gain	Annualized Return
Iomega Corp. (IOMG)	1.25	63.37	4,970	265%
Zoltek Companies, Inc. (ZOLT)	3.50	80.00	2,186	182
Colonial Data Tech Corp. (CDTX)	1.00	20.75	1,975	174
Wireless Telecom Group (WTT)	1.00	17.62	1,662	163
J L G Industries (JLGI)	3.50	61.50	1,657	163
Stratacom Inc. (STRM)	3.00	52.50	1,650	162
Hologic Inc. (HOLX)	2.25	38.25	1,600	160
America Online (AMER)	3.75	62.75	1,573	158
Presstek, Inc. (PRST)	9.00	146.00	1,522	152
Chesapeake Energy Corp. (CHK)	4.00	62.50	1,463	149
U.S. Robotics Corp. (USRX)	12.00	177.25	1,377	145
PrePaid Legal Services, Inc. (PPD)	1.30	18.75	1,342	144
Medic Computer Systems, Inc. (MCSY)	6.50	91.75	1,312	140
Tellabs, Inc. (TLAB)	5.00	57.62	1,052	124

May 1996. It is unlikely that anyone would have been fortunate enough to have bought *all* these stocks in May of 1993 or smart enough to have held them for exactly three years, even with the powerful computerized tools in this book. But there is nothing magic about those dates. Exhibit 1.2 shows another list of companies for other time periods with even more spectacular returns.

We are not saying that this book will help you make these kinds of returns, but we can show you how to find stocks with the *potential* for extraordinary returns. We will show you how to use cyber-investing tools to generate annual returns of 15 to 20 percent *or more* from a portfolio of seemingly ordinary stocks.

Exhibit 1.2 More superstars: These stocks gained from 126% in 9 weeks to 4,100% over 5 years.

Company	Purchase Date	Purchase Price	Sell Date	Sell Price	% Gain	Time Period
HBO & Co. (HBOC)	6/28/91	1.50	6/13/96	63.00	4,100	5 years
Cisco Systems (CSCO)	6/21/91	2.00	6/13/96	56.25	2,713	5 years
Clear Channel Comm. (CCU)	6/28/91	4.00	13/96	85.25	2,031	5 years
Newbridge Networks (NN)	6/28/91	3.25	6/18/96	65.00	1,900	5 years
Diana Corp. (DNA)	6/9/95	5.00	6/7/96	96.00	1,820	1 year
General Datacomm. (GDC)	1/28/91	2.30	6/21/93	14.20	1,637	29 months
Micron Technology (MU)	11/12/90	7.50	3/14/94	84.50	1,027	28 months
Corrections Corp. (CXC)	11/25/94	8.00	5/24/96	83.50	944	18 months
Newbridge Networks (NNCXF)	9/14/92	8.50	8/26/93	74.00	770	11 months
DSC Communications (DIGI)	8/31/92	8.50	10/15/93	67.50	694	13½ months
J L G Industries (JLGI)	1/21/95	10.00	6/13/96	74.12	641	5 months
California Amplifier (CAMP)	8/4/95	6.00	6/7/96	43.50	625	10 months
Synoptics Comm. (SNPX)	4/29/92	7.00	5/26/93	41.00	486	13 months
Safeguard Scientifics (SFE)	7/29/94	9.00	9/29/95	49.00	444	14 months
Trimedyne, Inc. (TMED)	9/27/93	6.50	3/4/94	15.95	437	5 months
Software Toolworks (TWRX)	10/8/92	3.30	10/19/93	16.80	409	12 months
Integrated Device (IDTI)	11/16/92	6.50	3/14/92	30.50	369	4 months
Grumman Corp. (GQ)	11/12/90	16.75	3/14/94	65.00	288	4 months
Inter Tel, Inc. (INTL)	1/6/95	7.25	5/31/96	27.50	279	17 months
QVC Network (QVCN)	10/22/72	21.00	6/1/93	72.00	243	7 months
Kelley Oil Corp. (KOIL)	4/12/93	9.50	6/3/93	27.70	192	7 weeks
President Riverboat (PREZ)	2/24/93	12.70	5/27/93	32.30	154	12 weeks
Mextel Communications (CALL)	11/3/92	11.75	1/4/93	27.00	130	8 weeks
Echo Bay Mines (ECO)	3/11/93	5.35	5/18/93	12.10	126	9 weeks

FROM SUPER-BORING TO SUPERSTAR

A stock does not have to be a "tenbagger" to generate high returns.[1] Take Delta Airlines, for example. Delta is thought of as a solid (some would say boring) company. Its stock price has a compounded average gain of about 7 or 8 percent per year for the past 20 years. Had you bought Delta 20 years ago and held on to it, you would have made a total return of 9 or 10 percent per year, including dividends. A nice average investment, but certainly not anything to get excited about. With cyber-investing tools,

---

HOW TO READ A STOCK GRAPH

Stock graphs are constructed with minor variations, depending on the software used. If you're not used to looking at stock graphs, you may want to take a moment to get acquainted with the ones in this book, which were produced by the Telescan Investment Platform for Windows®.

The date of the graph, the name of the company with stock symbol in parentheses, and the stock price appear at the top of the graph. The price is the last trade (if the graph is printed during the trading day) or the closing price.

On a one-year graph, each bar represents the high and low range for one day's trading. The close for that day is represented by the horizontal line or "lip" on the bar. The daily volume is plotted on the bottom of the graph. The status line below the graph shows the open, high, low, last trade, change, and volume for the date of the graph. If a technical indicator is plotted on the graph, the status line may show the parameters of that indicator instead.

On graphs of two years or more, prices are compressed, because there is room for only so much data. One bar may represent two days to several weeks, depending on the time span of the graph.

All prices are adjusted for stock splits.

---

[1] A "tenbagger" is a stock that is sold for ten times what is paid for it.

Exhibit 1.3   Delta's long-term trading channel shows the fluctuations in the stock price over 20 years.

however, that 9 or 10 percent could theoretically be turned into almost 60 percent per year! Here's how.

We have overlaid long-term trading channels on Delta's stock graph in Exhibit 1.3. These channels measure the range of the stock price to the high side and low side of the long-term price trend. As you can see, Delta did not make a smooth climb from $14 to $80 a share over the past 20 years.[2] Instead, it rose and fell, advanced and retreated, on its way up. If you had bought Delta each time it neared the bottom of the lower channel and sold it each time it neared the top of the upper channel (to use an oversimplified strategy for illustration), your annualized return on this average stock would have been nearly 60 percent per year. There's nothing average about that.

Making 60 percent a year on a single stock is not that simple or that predictable, of course. Nevertheless, one of the safest investing strategies

---

[2] All stock graphs in this book reflect any splits that may have occurred in the stock during the period shown.

is to buy solid, predictable, long-term performers when they are under-valued and sell them when they become overvalued.

There is and there always will be an abundance of undervalued stocks. Benjamin Graham, author of *The Intelligent Investor,* attributes this continuous over/undervaluation of stocks to the "miscalculation and excesses of optimism and pessimism [with which] the public has valued its shares."[3] Warren Buffett, who is called the world's most successful investor, puts it this way:

> The most common cause of low prices is pessimism—sometimes pervasive, sometimes specific to a company or industry. We want to do business in such an environment, not because we like pessimism but because we like the prices it produces. It's optimism that is the enemy of the rational buyer.[4]

In other words, the market will continue to overvalue and undervalue common stocks because of the human emotion that drives it. This pattern can be exploited to your great advantage with modern computerized tools that can sort through thousands of stocks and zero in on the ones that are the most undervalued.

Undervalued stocks are not the only way to go. There is another powerful way to boost your returns, and that too is made possible by computerized investing tools. Buy stocks in industries favored by institutional investors, and buy them early.

Institutional investors dominate the market, accounting for over 70 percent of all trading. This domination gave rise to the concept of industry group rotation. When an industry group moves into favor with institutional investors, the influx of large amounts of institutional money tends to create a wave of rising stock prices. Likewise, the exodus of the institutions from an industry group tends to create falling prices. Cyber-investing tools let you discern this ebb and flow of institutional money. With practice, you can jump on the wave as an industry group begins to move into favor, ride it to the crest, and (hopefully) jump off before the group falls out of favor and dashes you on the rocks.

This is again an oversimplification. But the point is, cyber-investing tools can transform a group of ordinary stocks into an extraordinary portfolio.

---

[3] Benjamin Graham, *The Intelligent Investor* (New York: Harper & Row, 1973), p. 106.
[4] Robert G. Hagstrom, *The Warren Buffett Way* (New York: John Wiley & Sons, 1994), p. 54.

MONKEY SEE, MONKEY DO

It is commonly said that anyone can make an average return of 10 percent by throwing darts at a newspaper's stock tables to make their picks. This is based on the fact that over the past 70 years the market has averaged a return of about 10 percent compounded annually, including dividends. If you concentrate on secondary stocks (those outside the largest 1,000 to 2,000 companies), the return is about 12 percent. This means that you could have chosen stocks at random—even by throwing darts at stock tables—and made 10 to 12 percent over time.

Occasionally, this is put to the test, often by pitting a monkey against stock experts. In 1994, a chimpanzee in Sweden named Ola actually threw darts at a newspaper's stock tables tacked to the wall and outperformed five stock analysts, increasing his original investment 13 percent in one month. In the same year, NBC's news program *Dateline* sponsored a stock-picking contest between a monkey and a professional money manager. Casey, the chimp, made his picks by yanking cards from a Rolodex; the money manager made his after careful research. One year later, Casey's stocks had gained 9 percent, the expert's only 1 percent. After two years, the chimp was still ahead, with a gain of 39 percent versus the expert's 35 percent!

If a monkey can make these kinds of returns, you might ask, who needs this book? Consider this. If you could do that well with random selections, how much better might you do with computerized tools? Tools that can identify stocks that have the greatest chance of growth. Tools that can find industry groups favored by the institutions. Tools that show you how to buy stocks at a point of minimum risk and sell them at a point of maximum reward. Doesn't it make sense that you can do better with computerized investing tools than a monkey with darts?

We are not saying that it's easy to make above-average returns. But today's cyber-investing tools allow you to implement a straightforward, methodical, disciplined process, and that can make the difference between success and failure in the stock market.

MUTUAL FUNDS DO IT, TOO!

If you're still not convinced that annual returns of 15, 20, or 30 percent are possible, consider mutual funds.

When mutual fund managers find a stock they like, they buy hundreds of thousands of shares of the stock, not the few hundred shares the small investor buys in an average trade. Money managers must patiently accumulate the shares, often over several months, so as not to drive up the stock price before they can acquire a position. The same thing happens in reverse when they want to sell. They have to dispose of their shares gradually so as not to drive the price down before they can unload the fund's shares. We, on the other hand, can sell our few hundred shares the minute we sense a reversal in the wind.

Nevertheless, mutual funds have done well. Despite their cumbersome size *and* a welter of government regulations that the small investor does not have, the top 25 growth-oriented funds had an average annualized return of 17.3 percent over the past 15 years. All growth-oriented mutual funds together—the good, the bad, and the mediocre—managed to average over 15.4 percent over the past 20 years.[5] Peter Lynch, who managed the gigantic Fidelity Magellan mutual fund, averaged over 26 percent a year for 15 years.

It was Mr. Lynch who said that amateur investors have the advantage over the professionals in our ability to move in and out of the market quickly. Add to this advantage the power of computerized tools, and you have the makings for outstanding returns in the stock market.

LIFESTYLES OF THE RICH AND NOT YET FAMOUS

David Brown, who is a recognized expert on cyber-investing, regularly speaks at conferences where investors gather to learn more about computerized investing. The audiences are made up mostly of individual investors, and he has heard story upon story of ordinary people making extraordinary returns.

In the fall of 1993 Brown spoke at a conference of computerized investors in Orlando, Florida. About 150 individuals had come to the conference to learn how to improve their returns. Yet when he asked for a show of hands of those who had averaged more than a 20 percent return over a number of years, more than a third of the audience raised their

---

[5] These figures are from Morningstar, Inc., as of August 31, 1996. The return of 15.4% for all growth-oriented funds is for 20 years and 8 months.

hands. Many of them, he was surprised to learn, were averaging more than 40 percent per year.

Afterwards, several of the 40+ percent investors talked about their investing success. Two stories were especially remarkable. A retired 70-year-old dentist from Connecticut had averaged an annual compounded return of 43.6 percent over the past six years. He used some of the tools described in this book and a strategy developed from the one Brown had been using in his newsletter. In a nutshell, this investor used a cyber-investing stock search tool to generate two lists. One list was based on Brown's undervalued growth strategy and the other on a popular momentum strategy (both strategies are described in this book). Then he bought the stocks that appeared on both lists. Simple, but effective.

The other investor started with an initial investment of $50,000 and built his portfolio to $1.6 million over seven years. (He had broker confirmations for every trade.) That's an annualized return of more than 60 percent per year. He declined to share his strategies, because he planned to start managing money for others. He did reveal, however, that he used the stock search tool described in Chapters 4 and 5 to find the stocks that generated his spectacular returns.

ANY PLAN IS BETTER THAN NO PLAN

All these successful investors have one thing in common: a disciplined, methodical approach to investing. They use a variety of strategies, search tools, and trading rules, but each follows his own methods, whatever they are, rigorously and faithfully.

Discipline, in fact, is the one thing most successful traders have in common. Jack D. Schwager, who interviewed a number of supertraders for his book *Market Wizards*, writes:

> Each trader had found a methodology that worked for him and remained true to that approach. It is significant that discipline was the word most frequently mentioned.[6]

Discipline, no doubt, had something to do with the success stories reported by *Newsweek* in December 1991. The star performer was a 68-year-old retired schoolteacher who averaged a 37 percent annual return over

---

[6] Jack Schwager, *Market Wizards: Interviews with Top Traders* (New York: New York Institute of Finance, a division of Simon & Schuster, 1989), p. 439.

four years. According to the same article, 62 percent of the investment clubs surveyed by the National Association of Investors Corporation beat the S&P 500 over an average of nine years. These same investment clubs (made up of individual investors) outperformed 79 percent of mutual funds that invest in stocks.

One of the best known investment clubs is a group of 16 women in Beardstown, Illinois who came to prominence in 1994 with *The Beards-town Ladies' Common-Sense Investment Guide.*[7] The Beardstown ladies averaged an annual return of 23.4 percent over 10 years, twice the return of the S&P 500.[8]

Another example of spectacular returns through cyber-investing comes to us from Mark W. Arnold, a former vice president of a major Wall Street brokerage firm. His published returns averaged 58.5 percent over the past three years compared with 12.6 percent for the S&P 500.[9] His secret? The insider trading tool described in Chapter 4.

Perhaps you read about Anne Scheiber of New York who invested $5,000 in stocks in 1944 and built it to $20 million by the time she died in January 1996. Her annualized return (17.5%) matched that of market expert Benjamin Graham (17.4%) and was not far behind Warren Buffett's 22.7 percent.

The experience of David Brown lends further credence to the power of cyber-investing. In early 1990, Brown began publishing two newsletters. One was a long-term, very conservative stock portfolio based on a strategy called undervalued growth investing. That portfolio averaged almost 18 percent per year, compounded annually, over six years. There were some wide variances in performance from year to year, but the portfolio never had a negative year, and in 1995 it was up nearly 27 percent. The second newsletter was aimed at speculators and concentrated almost exclusively on high-risk options. This portfolio averaged nearly 20 percent per year over four years, with extremely wide variations from year to year. During two of the years, returns exceeded 100 percent; in the other two, there were significant losses.

---

[7] The Beardstown Ladies Investment Club with Leslie Whitaker, *The Beardstown Ladies' Common-Sense Investment Guide* (New York: A Seth Godin Production, 1994).
[8] *The New York Times,* Thursday, March 2, 1995, p. C1.
[9] For the year ended March 1994: Arnold 68.2%; S&P 0.7%. For the year ended March 1995: Arnold 19.8%; S&P 8.5%. For the year ended March 1996: Arnold 87.4%; S&P 31.3%. Source: *Trading on Tomorrow's Headlines,* by Mark Arnold.

It is important to point out that when we talk about making returns of 15 to 20 percent per year, we're talking about average compounded returns *over time*. You may make 50 percent one year and lose 10 percent the next, but your annualized compounded return over the two years would be a little over 16 percent.

A WORD OF CAUTION

We are very optimistic about the excellent returns that are possible with cyber-investing. Nevertheless, you must know that investing in common stocks, by its very nature, involves risk. Even if you should average 15 percent or more a year, there could be times when your portfolio will be down 10 or 20 percent or more. Should this occur at a time when you need the underlying cash, it could create a hardship. Although the kinds of returns we talk about in this book are based on the experience of the market in general, on the experience of others, and on our own experience, there can be no assurance that you will generate a positive return even if the tools and techniques described in this book are applied successfully.

Frankly, there are no guaranteed returns of any kind on any investment. Bank certificates of deposits, which come the closest to having a guaranteed return, provide no assurance that their returns will protect the purchasing power of your dollar. In fact, there have been times when CDs have suffered annual losses of purchasing power for long periods. Treasury bonds, one of the most conservative investments, have substantial risks during periods of rising interest rates. For example, during 1994, long-term investors in treasury bonds faced a net loss of nearly 20 percent in their portfolios.

In the end, it comes down to a matter of risk versus reward. History has shown that no other investment has outperformed stocks in the long run. But you must make your own assessment about the risk and rewards of the stock market. Our job in this book is to furnish you with the tools and help you learn the skills you need to invest successfully in the stock market. Your job, if you wish to be an investor, is to choose your investment tools carefully and wield them as skillfully as you can. Despite these words of caution, however, we believe that investing in stocks judiciously over time can generate handsome returns.

Not everyone makes spectacular returns in the market, of course. Perhaps you have friends or acquaintances who have frequently tallied up losses instead of gains. It would be interesting to know if they had a plan or if they bought on tips and sold on rumors. If they had a plan, did they have the discipline to stick to it? Did they diversify? Did they rotate with industry groups? Did they try to break even on a losing stock by buying more of it (called *down-averaging*)? Whatever they did or did not do, it is almost certain they did not have and use all the cyber-investing tools described in this book.

Our point is this: If a random selection of stocks can yield a 10 to 12 percent return, think how much better you can do with the abundance of information, the powerful tools, and the disciplined approach that are now possible through cyber-investing.

ONE PERCENT WORTH A MILLION BUCKS?

Cyber-investing will no doubt take some time and effort. It could, depending on your level of computer literacy, take a couple of weekends to learn how to use the tools. Once you've mastered the tools, it may take two to three hours a week to build and manage your portfolio. Is it worth it, to make 15 to 20 percent a year?

Consider this. On an investment of $10,000 over 20 years, the difference between a return of 7.5 percent and a return of 15 percent is not double, it is almost quadruple! Why? Because of the value of compounding. At 7.5 percent, $10,000 will grow to $42,479 over 20 years; at 15 percent, it will grow to $163,665.

With higher rates of return, compounding is even more impressive. For example, an annual return of 30 percent for 20 years transforms that $10,000 into more than $1.9 million, which means that a 30 percent return is *eleven* times better than 15 percent! You can see, compounding makes it incredibly worthwhile to aim for the higher returns.[10]

In fact, adding even one percentage point to your returns is more than worthwhile. The table in Exhibit 1.4 shows the difference that one percent can make on an initial investment of $10,000 for 20 years. The

---

[10] For those who are less mathematically inclined, there is the old "Rule of 72": To get the number of years it will take to double your money, divide the return into 72. For example, at 8 percent, your money will approximately double in 9 years; at 12 percent, it will double in approximately 6 years; at 18 percent, it will double in approximately 4 years.

Exhibit 1.4   This table shows the difference that one additional percentage point can make on a $10,000 investment over 20 years.

Rate	$10,000 Grows To	Difference Between:
15%	$ 163,665	
16%	194,608	15% and 16% = $30,943
20%	383,380	
21%	452,590	20% and 21% = $69,210
25%	867,362	
26%	1,017,211	25% and 26% = $149,849
30%	1,900,500	
31%	2,215,270	30% and 31% = $314,770

difference between 15 percent and 16 percent is $30,943, a year's salary for some people. The difference between 20 percent and 21 percent is almost $70,000, enough to put a child through college. The difference between 30 percent and 31 percent is over $300,000, enough to buy a small yacht or a fine retirement home. If you were to start with an initial investment of $30,000, one extra percentage point could be worth almost one million dollars!

A SINGLE TOOL CAN ADD THREE PERCENT

Let us put this whole chapter into perspective: Just *one* of the tools you'll learn about in this book could make a difference of three percentage points in your returns. It did for David Brown.

In 1993, he backtested a technical search tool called the MACD indicator on 15 different 25-day periods between July 1991 and April 1993.[11] (Backtesting allows you to run a search on historical stock data and then compare the selected stocks with their current prices to see what the return would have been for that group of stocks.) He used the same search strategy he had used in his published newsletter. The results? This *single*

---

[11] The MACD is the moving average convergence/divergence indicator that is discussed in Chapter 9.

Exhibit 1.5   This table shows the difference that three additional percent-age points can make on a $10,000 investment over 20 years.

Rate	$10,000 Grows To	Difference Between:
15%	$ 163,665	
18%	273,930	15% and 18% = $110,265
20%	383,376	
23%	628,206	20% and 23% = $244,830
25%	867,362	
28%	1,393,797	25% and 28% = $526,435
30%	1,900,496	
33%	2,999,389	30% and 33% = $1,098,893

computerized tool would have improved his annualized returns by three percentage points. Exhibit 1.5 shows what this could mean in dollars and cents.

Looking at it from another perspective, if you are 20 years old as you read this, you could conceivably be a millionaire before you're 40 by fol-lowing the investing process in this book. If you are already 40, it is still possible to retire a millionaire. If you're near retirement age, well, remem-ber that 70-year-old dentist who is gilding his golden years with annual re-turns of 43 percent. He is living proof that it is never too late to start.

YOU MUST REMEMBER THIS . . .

Investing in stocks is one of the few ways an ordinary person can turn a modest nest egg into a fortune. It isn't easy and it isn't certain, but it is absolutely possible. To keep things in perspective:

- Remember Ola and Casey, the stock-picking chimps.
- Remember the mutual funds that averaged nearly 20 percent per year, despite their cumbersome size.
- Remember the amateur investors who have had annualized re-turns over 40 percent, using some of the cyber-investing tools and strategies described in this book.

- Remember that cyber-investing tools can turn ordinary stocks into extraordinary performers by revealing their patterns of under- and over-valuation.

- Remember that cyber-investing tools can reveal the industries favored by institutional investors and help you profit from this knowledge.

- Remember that a single cyber-investing tool can add from one to three percent to your returns.

- Remember that a 20-percent return per year can make you a millionaire, if you start early enough. Fifteen percent per year can result in significant wealth over time.

If you're tempted to forget any of this, revisit the tables in Exhibits 1.4 and 1.5 from time to time for inspiration! And remember, we present the tools and techniques in a simple, straightforward fashion. You may use them in the same way. Start with one or two tools, and add more as your comfort level increases. It is well worth your time and effort to master the art of cyber-investing.

Now is the time to start.

2

WHAT MAKES STOCKS GO UP?

History tells us a random selection of stocks will return 10 to 12 percent a year over time. Logic tells us, given today's powerful computerized tools, we should be able to do much better than that.

In this book we will show you how to use a wide range of computerized tools that can help you generate returns of 15 to 20 percent or more per year. We will take you step-by-step through a cyber-investing process that will simplify and unify the whole approach to investing in stocks.

To illustrate the investing process, we need an investing strategy. One of our favorites is based on undervalued growth stocks (stocks with high expected earnings growth and low price-to-earnings ratios that have a good chance of rising). To set the stage for all that follows, we are going to spend some time talking about price-to-earnings (P/E) ratios and what makes stocks go up. Understanding this is essential to using many of the cyber-investing tools that we will be talking about.

If you are grounded in a completely different investment philosophy, please bear with us. You'll find that once you learn the tools, you can apply them with ease to your own strategies.

THE POSITIVE PRESSURE OF P/E

There are various reasons why stock prices go up. Changes in ownership, such as a merger, a takeover, or a new investor who takes a major position in the stock, can drive a stock price up. For example, if IBM were to announce its intentions to acquire XYZ Software Corporation, you can bet XYZ's stock price would rise close to IBM's offer. But changes in ownership are anomalous events that are almost impossible for nonprofessionals to predict.

There are more rational reasons why a company's stock price goes up. Its earnings could actually increase, its P/E ratio could rise, or both these events could happen.[1] This is what we are going to talk about in this chapter: earnings expectations and P/E ratios and how they affect a company's stock price.

It should be fairly obvious why the stock price goes up when earnings increase. When we buy a stock, we are basically paying a company to earn money for us, as its shareholders. The more money a company earns, in general, the more the market will pay for its stock. It is less obvious why a stock's P/E ratio goes up and how it affects the stock price.

Simply stated, P/E ratio is the price of the stock divided by its current earnings per share. But P/E is more than that. It is the price the market is willing to pay for a company's earnings, and that price is more influenced by earnings *potential* and market *perception* than by actual earnings. In other words, the market's perception of a company's future earnings potential drives the stock's price and, hence, its P/E ratio. Thus, one company with steady earnings may have a P/E of 5 or 6 whereas another with small current earnings but huge potential may have a P/E over 100. In short, high expectations lead to increased P/E; lowered expectations lead to decreased P/E.

These expectations are fed by two sources. One source is the Wall Street analysts who publish earnings estimates for the companies they follow. The other is institutional investors who employ specialists to make projections about a company's earnings. Either way, when the market reacts to news of increased earnings potential, money begins to flow into the stock, and the stock price and P/E ratio start to rise.

---

[1] Throughout this book, when we talk about earnings we are talking about earnings-per-share (EPS)—a company's after-tax earnings divided by the number of outstanding shares. Earnings should not be confused with dividends, which are sometimes paid to sharcholders out of a company's profits.

This focus on future earnings potential is responsible for the wide variance of P/E ratios among companies. Nothing is more important in investing than understanding how P/E ratios change and what happens when they do. That has everything to do with whether or not you make money in the stock market.

COMPARING P/E RATIOS

The best way to understand P/E ratios is to examine companies that have a low P/E and a high P/E.

Let's look at Paine Webber and America Online (Exhibit 2.1). In early May 1996, Paine Webber had a P/E of 7.6, based on a stock price of $20⅜ and fiscal 1996 estimated earnings of $2.69. America Online's P/E was 133, based on a stock price of $62¾ and fiscal 1996 estimated earnings of $0.47. Paine Webber's estimated earnings for the current fiscal year are almost six times higher than America Online's. Why then is the market willing to pay almost three times as much for America Online? To put it another way: Why would an investor pay only $7.60 for one dollar of Paine Webber's earnings but a staggering $133 for a dollar of America Online's earnings? The reason is *expectation* of future earnings.

Exhibit 2.2 shows what Wall Street analysts think of the short-term earnings potential of America Online and Paine Webber.[2] (Such estimates are available through many online services and the Internet.) The analysts think that America Online's earnings will double from 1996 to 1997 whereas Paine Webber's are expected to increase only about 6 percent. But that still would result in Paine Webber's 1997 earnings being almost two dollars higher than America Online's 1997 earnings. So what is going on?

The fact is, investors—particularly, institutional investors—look further than one or two years into the future. Institutional investors usually acquire a substantial position in a stock, several hundred thousand shares or more; thus, they may take several months to build a position, so as not to unduly affect the stock price. This forces them to be long-term investors, and as such, they often look as far as five or more years down

---

[2] All earnings estimates and earnings growth-rate projections in this book have been obtained from Zacks Investment Research. Zacks reports are available through Telescan and directly from Zacks through its Internet Web site (see Chapter 16 and the Source List at the end of the book).

Exhibit 2.1 A comparison of P/E ratios for America Online and Paine Webber.

	May 1996 Stock Price	Fiscal 1996 Est. Earnings*	Fiscal 1996 P/E
America Online	$62¾	$0.47	133.5
Paine Webber	$20⅜	$2.69	7.6

*Source: Zacks Investment Research, May 1996.

the road. With that perspective, it is easier to understand why the market is willing to pay more for America Online than for Paine Webber: They see a five-year growth rate of nearly 50 percent for America Online and only about 9 percent for Paine Webber.

If the two companies achieve their projected growth rates, the gap between them will continue to widen (Exhibit 2.3). By the year 2002, America Online's earnings would be almost 50 percent higher than Paine Webber's. Does that justify paying almost three times as much for America Online *now* than for Paine Webber? Maybe not, but many institutional investors believe in the higher end of the estimated growth rate for America Online (66 percent) based on its performance history. If the higher rate is achieved, America Online will earn almost *three times* more than Paine Webber in the year 2002, even if Paine Webber also achieves its more optimistic growth rate of 10.5 percent.

Exhibit 2.2 A consensus of analysts' earnings estimates for America Online and Paine Webber as of May 1996.

	Year End	Estimated Average Earnings per Share
America Online	1995	−$0.49 actual
	1996	0.47
	1997	.94
	Projected 5-year growth rate	46%
Paine Webber	1995	$0.54 actual
	1996	2.69
	1997	2.85
	Projected 5-year growth rate	9.25%

Source: Zacks Investment Research, Inc., May 1996.

Exhibit 2.3   Projected earnings for America Online and Paine Webber, based on the consensus of analysts' 5-year growth rates.

	5-Year Growth Rate	1996	1997	1998	1999	2000	2001	2002
AMER	46.0% (mean)	$0.47	$0.94	$1.37	$2.00	$2.93	$4.27	$ 6.24
PWJ	9.25% (mean)	2.69	2.85	3.11	3.40	3.72	4.06	4.44
AMER	66.0% (high)	0.51	1.20	1.99	3.31	5.49	9.11	15.13
PWJ	10.5% (high)	3.05	3.12	3.45	3.80	4.21	4.65	5.14

Source: 1996 and 1997 figures are estimates obtained from Zacks Investment Research in May 1996. Figures for 1998 through 2002 are the authors' projections based on the 5-year growth rate obtained from Zacks.

Consider this: When we wrote the first edition of this book in the summer of 1994, America Online was selling at $71.[3] Paine Webber was selling at $15½. So back in 1994, this same divergence of price and P/E existed. During the next two years, America Online's price increased sixfold whereas Paine Webber increased only 33 percent. So, the rationale of betting on the future paid off. During that period, it *was* worth paying more for America Online than for Paine Webber.

Only time will tell where these two companies will be by the year 2000. But are you beginning to see the logic to this process? The great gap between the P/E ratios of the two companies is mirrored by the gap the market sees between their expected earnings far into the future.

As we said earlier, there are other reasons why stocks go up, such as changes of ownership. But rising P/Es are somewhat easier to predict and find, and they are one of the best ways to make money *systematically* in the stock market. Keep in mind, however, that stocks do not always live up to expectations, which brings us to the risk of high P/Es.

---

[3] America Online had three 2-for-1 stock splits since the summer of 1994. Seventy-one dollars is a presplit price. Based on today's number of shares, that price would be around $9.

HIGH P/Es: RISKY BUSINESS

You might conclude, based on the discussion so far, that you should look for companies like America Online, with high P/Es and 50 percent growth rates. After all, this would assure you of a 50 percent per year return, if the P/E stays the same. Therein lies the rub. P/Es fall, as well as rise. Negative expectations lead to falling P/Es, and the higher the P/E, the harder the fall—and the greater the risk to the investor.

Take a stock with a P/E of 100 or more. There is not a lot of room for it to rise, considering that the historical average P/E for stocks is about 14. But it does have a long, long way to fall. Why would it fall? Because it is exceedingly difficult for a company to continue to grow at 50 percent or more, year after year after year. Too many things can happen to make a company stumble. Competition could put a squeeze on its profit margins; some unforeseen event could adversely affect the whole industry and impact the company as well.

A falling P/E, like a rising P/E, is based on expectations of future earnings—pessimistic expectations rather than optimistic. Rumors and fears about a specific company or an entire industry can get out of hand, and the P/E (and stock price) may fall precipitously before you can sell your shares. In fact, when fears about an industry set in, a company's P/E often falls even though its earnings continue to increase. This happened to America Online as we were writing this book. The stock price fell from $62¾ in mid-May 1996 to $26 in late July, with the P/E falling from 224 to 93 (based on reported fiscal 1996 earnings of 28 cents, which was 19 cents less than estimated earnings of 47 cents).

U.S. SURGICAL: GOING BOTH WAYS

U.S. Surgical Corporation offers another instructive example of a rising P/E based on high expectations and a falling P/E based on fear.[4]

U.S. Surgical began as a manufacturer of surgical staplers. In the early 1990s, it introduced laparoscopic products and entered a period of

---

[4] Short sellers may have played a role in creating some of the upward surge in U.S. Surgical (and in America Online). Short sellers sell stock they don't own (by borrowing it from a brokerage firm) with the expectation that the stock price will fall and they will be able to cover their positions at a much lower price and pocket the difference. If the stock goes up instead of down, they are forced to cover their positions at a higher price. This can help drive up the stock price, which may have happened with U.S. Surgical and America Online. Nonetheless, their earnings histories and P/Es still prove our basic point.

extraordinary growth. Earnings went from $0.38 in 1988 to $2.32 in 1992, a growth rate well in excess of 50 percent per year. They had one positive earnings surprise after another. As analysts began raising their earnings growth rate estimates from 20 percent to 30, 40, and 50 percent, U.S Surgical's P/E rose from 12 to 67, causing the stock price to climb from $7 a share to $126 a share.

In this euphoric atmosphere, U.S. Surgical introduced its first line of synthetic sutures in 1991 and promptly captured an impressive market share. By the end of 1992, these products represented about half of the company's revenues. The future looked bright. But during the first half of 1992, the stock price leveled. In mid-1992 it took a steep dive, losing almost 40 percent of its value (Exhibit 2.4)—even though 1992 earnings were 47 percent higher than the previous year's. The reason? Competitive pressures and fears about the industry.

The main cause, no doubt, was the specter of health-care reform that was spooking all medical stocks in 1992, even before the presidential election that year. In addition, head-on competition from Johnson & Johnson,

Exhibit 2.4   U.S. Surgical moved sharply on expectations and fell even more sharply on fear.

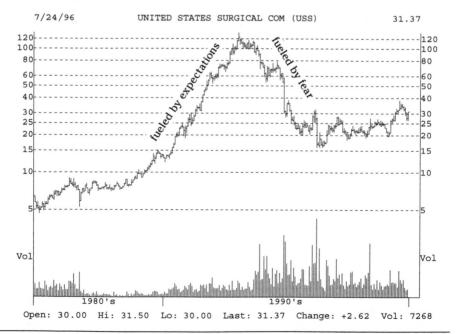

who entered the synthetic sutures market, forced U.S. Surgical to cut prices, which created margin pressure. Reduced profit margins created doubt on Wall Street that the company could continue to grow at 50 percent a year, even though current earnings continued to grow due to revenue growth. Analysts revised their earnings growth rate estimates downward, and U.S. Surgical's stock price began to fall. By the first quarter of 1993, it had lost 57 percent from its 1991 high, tumbling from $126 to $54 while its P/E dropped from 67 to 23. Later, the earnings did fall apart (with a loss of $2.48 in 1993), and the stock dropped all the way to $17! Incidentally, there was a clue at the time that earnings were not going to do well: Insiders were dumping the stock in unprecedented amounts. (We will talk more about the importance of insiders in Chapter 4.)

The moral of this story is: Beware of extraordinarily high P/Es. If the P/E should drop by more than the earnings growth rate, it could wipe out an entire year's gain, and more, in stock price.

RISING P/Es: TAKING CARE OF BUSINESS

It should occur to you by now that the greatest reward and least risk may lie in buying stocks with relatively low P/Es that are expected to rise. Where do you find such stocks? We look for companies that have been out of favor with investors for some reason but are expected to turn around. Let's return to Paine Webber and consider what might happen *if* the company should revitalize its earnings growth.

Let's say Paine Webber develops some exciting new products, begins a great new advertising campaign, and hires the top salespeople away from its competitors. How do you think the market would react? For one thing, Wall Street analysts might become more optimistic about Paine Webber's earning potential. They might begin to project a 5-year growth rate of 15 to 20 percent, instead of the current 9.25 percent. A 20 percent growth rate would elevate Paine Webber's earnings estimates to $5.58 by the year 2000 and to $8.03 by 2002 (Exhibit 2.5). The market would undoubtedly take notice of this enhanced earnings growth, and as awareness set in, investors might be willing to pay 10 to 20 times earnings for Paine Webber's stock, instead of the current 7.6 times earnings.

Exhibit 2.6 shows what *could* happen to Paine Webber's stock price if this imaginary scenario were to take place. If analysts were to perceive an accelerated earnings growth rate of 20 percent, the P/E ratio would likely rise. If it were to reach even 10 by the end of 1996, the stock price

Exhibit 2.5 This table compares Paine Webber's earnings based on the analysts' estimates to an imaginary growth rate of 20 percent.

5-Year Growth Rate	1996	1997	1998	1999	2000	2001	2002
9.25%	$2.69	$2.85	$3.11	$3.40	$3.72	$4.06	$4.44
20.0%	2.69	3.22	3.87	4.64	5.58	6.69	8.03

Source: 1996 and 1997 figures (for the 9.25% growth rate) are estimates obtained from Zacks Investment Research in May 1996. Figures for 1998 through 2002 are the authors' projections based on the 5-year growth rate obtained from Zacks. All 20 percent figures are projections based on the Zacks 1996 estimate.

would increase to $27. Anyone who had the foresight to buy Paine Webber at $20⅜ in May 1996 would have made over 35 percent by the end of the year. Let us emphasize that this is a fictitious and oversimplified situation. But if this kind of growth were to take place, things could be much better than we have described. If the market were truly to believe in an earnings growth rate of 20 percent, it would more likely drive the P/E to 20, not 10. Should that happen, the stock price in our imaginary scenario would jump to $54, and the smart investor who had bought the stock at $20⅜ would make over 150 percent!

Exhibit 2.6 This table shows what Paine Webber's stock price *could be* if its P/E ratio went to 10 or 20, based on an imaginary 20 percent earnings growth rate.

Year	EPS if Growth Rate were 20%	Projected Stock Price with a 10 P/E	Projected Stock Price with a 20 P/E
1996	$2.69	$27	$ 54
1997	3.22	32	64
1998	3.87	39	77
1999	4.64	46	93
2000	5.58	56	112
2001	6.69	67	134
2002	8.03	80	161

Too theoretical? What do you think caused the meteoric growth of the superstar stocks listed in Chapter 1? Rising earnings coupled with rising P/Es. What fueled U.S. Surgical's initial climb? Rising earnings and a rising P/E. We are not suggesting, however, that you rush right out and buy stocks with low P/Es and high estimates of earnings growth. Wait until there is solid evidence that the earnings growth is going to materialize. Some of the clues (which we will talk about later) are heavy insider buying, upward revision of earnings estimates, increased volume, and industry group momentum. These events often precede rising P/Es.

A rising P/E ratio was responsible for one of the best examples of profit that we made on a single stock: Computer Associates. But we waited for evidence of improved earnings growth before we plunged in.

Computer Associates: The Case of the Rising P/E

Computer Associates once designed software primarily for mainframe computers. For several years, the company went through a period of sluggish earnings due to a stagnant mainframe computer market (well known to any long-time holder of IBM stock). In late 1991, the stock was selling at $7½ with earnings of $0.89 and a P/E ratio of 8 (Exhibit 2.7). (NOTE: These prices are *before* the 2-for-1 stock split in late 1995.) Then in 1992, the company announced, among other things, aggressive plans to enter the PC software market. Earnings began to materialize almost immediately, climbing to $1.95 in fiscal 1993. The stock price rose to $43, sending the P/E to 22. Thus, while earnings more than doubled, the P/E almost tripled, boosting the stock price almost 500 percent over a two-year period!

The important point is this: Rising earnings and rising P/Es create geometric increases in stock prices, and that could mean spectacular returns for you.

The Risk of Extremes

Extremes at either end of the P/E scale carry significant risk. High P/E stocks got that way because of market sentiment, and what the market gives, the market can take away. If earnings do not materialize as expected or if the stock gets caught in a firestorm of industry fears and rumors, high P/Es have a long way to fall.

Low P/E ratios are not necessarily the answer either. A low P/E is not always just the result of pessimistic expectations about earnings (a condition that can change). Often a low P/E reflects the market's concern

Exhibit 2.7   Computer Associates' earnings doubled between 1991 and 1993, but the stock price increased by about 500 percent.

about the basic health and continued viability of the company itself. If this is the case, the stock may never get off the ground. That is why we are cautious about low P/Es. Under normal market conditions, we would view a P/E ratio below 5 or so as a red flag raised by the many keen minds that analyze such things. You would be wise to follow their lead and steer clear of stocks with very low P/Es.

The key word, then, when talking about P/E ratios, is *rising.* And the crystal ball for determining whether or not a P/E will rise is expected earnings growth. But crystal balls can be wrong. Nothing in the stock market is certain, and there is no *absolute* cause and effect between earnings growth and P/E. Sometimes earnings materialize but the P/E doesn't rise. What happens then? You'd still make money as long as the earnings roll in and the P/E doesn't fall too much.

Say you bought a stock at $20, with current earnings of $2 (which makes the P/E 10) and expected earnings growth of 20 percent. If earnings should increase by 20 percent, the stock price would increase to $24, even if the P/E stayed at 10, so you would still make a 20 percent return on your investment. Should the P/E fall, you would still be cushioned somewhat by the earnings. In fact, the P/E could fall 20 percent, and *if* the earnings growth held steady at 20 percent, your loss would be minimal.

Of course, you could be wrong about the earnings growth as well. Even with sophisticated computerized tools, you will sometimes be wrong. Still, your best bet may be a stock with a relatively low P/E and good expectations of earnings growth. If worse comes to worst, you will have a much shorter distance to fall.

YOU MUST REMEMBER THIS . . .

As we move on to the rest of the book, we hope you will take these points with you:

- P/E ratio is one of the most important considerations when buying a stock.
- P/Es vary enormously from stock to stock because of expectations of future earnings.
- An extremely high P/E is dangerous because of the poor risk/reward ratio: It has much farther to fall than to rise.
- An unusually low P/E can signal a weak company with poor prospects for growth.
- The smart move is to buy stocks with rising P/Es. These are companies that are selling at a relatively low P/E at the moment but have high expectations of earnings growth.

Keep in mind, we are trying to illustrate the cyber-investing process. If you disagree with the P/E philosophy we have expressed, at least consider the process.

Now we are going to show you how to find potential winners.

3

THE CYBER-INVESTING PROCESS

Venturing into cyberspace without a plan is like trying to drive from New York to San Francisco without a roadmap. You might enjoy the scenery as you meander across the country, but you will never reach your destination until you find the right highway and stay on it. In cyberspace you can wander the information superhighway and try out all the investing tools, but unless you have a plan—and procedures for implementing it—you will never accomplish your goal.

That goal, we assume, is to generate long-term annual returns of 15 to 20 percent or more on a portfolio of carefully chosen stocks. Our mission in this book is to introduce you to the cyber-investing tools and techniques that will help you achieve your goal. The plan we offer is a five-step computerized investing process that may be used in its entirety or adapted to your own investing preferences. The procedures for implementing the plan are described throughout the rest of the book.

THE PLAN: A FIVE-STEP CYBER-INVESTING PROCESS

Here is an overview of the cyber-investing process shown in Exhibit 3.1.

Exhibit 3.1   The cyber-investing process.

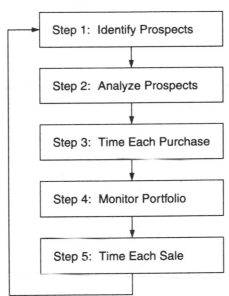

Step 1: Identify Prospects

The first step in the cyber-investing process is to identify stocks for possible purchase. In Chapters 4 and 5, we will introduce you to a powerful stock search tool and four different investing strategies for finding stocks. The first strategy is based on insider buying; the second is based on undervalued growth stocks like those discussed in Chapter 2; the third uses special ranking indicators to find the top stocks in specific categories; and the fourth is based on momentum investing. After you understand how to create these searches, you should be able to build dozens of others that reflect your unique goals and investing style.

Step 2: Analyze Prospects

The second step in the cyber-investing process is a two-stage evaluation of the stocks found by the search. We will show you how to retrieve supplementary information during a search that may be used to quickly evaluate the stocks and generate a short list for stage two of the evaluation. Then we will use a variety of technical charting tools and online information tools to evaluate the short list and reduce it to an even shorter list of stocks for possible purchase.

Step 3: Time Each Purchase

Step 3 shows you how to maximize potential profits by using technical buy signals to time your stock purchases. The more fundamental investors may view this as some sort of technical voodoo, but our experience says otherwise (and we are about three-quarters fundamentalist ourselves). In a number of tests against historical markets, we have proven to our satisfaction that technical timing can add from one to three percent annually to our returns. If you remember from Chapter 1 how much an additional three percent means in dollars and cents, you will not want to bypass this step.

Step 4: Manage Your Portfolio

The fourth step in the cyber-investing process is managing your portfolio. It begins with the purchase of your first stock and continues as long as you own a stock. Portfolio management includes managing diversification, monitoring holdings, and reviewing your performance. It also includes staying aware of market conditions that might dictate a review of how you allocate your assets. This could lead to converting certain stocks into cash at market highs or investing more aggressively at market lows. As you will see, however, the five-step cyber-investing process itself should make you relatively independent of market conditions, much more so than most investing programs.

Step 5: Time Each Sale

Step 5 has to do with timing the sale of a stock to your best advantage. There are positive and negative reasons to sell a stock, both of which have to do with its risk/reward relationship. As in buying stocks, you can enhance your returns by using technical indicators to find the most propitious time to sell. This should also help you avoid many disasters!

YOU MUST REMEMBER THIS . . .

This five-step process can be used as a roadmap for your first venture into cyber-investing. With it you can:

- Find a list of stocks that most closely match your major investment goals.
- Narrow the list to a few top stocks.
- Maximize your profit potential with technical buy signals.
- Implement good portfolio management procedures.
- Reduce risk and enhance profits by a continual assessment of each stock's risk/reward relationship.

In the following chapters, you will see this process in action. Once you've learned how to use it, you may adapt it to fit your own goals and investing style.

4

A HIGH-TECH DIVINING ROD

In movies about the Old West there was often a grizzled prospector waving a three-pronged stick over the ground expecting it to vibrate whenever it sensed the presence of gold. This so-called divining rod never really worked, but the old guys kept using it anyhow and every now and then someone would strike gold. Well, if they could see us now . . . .

Today's gold mines are on Wall Street, and the modern prospector can sit in front of a computer screen with a high-tech divining rod that would have made those celluloid prospectors weep for joy. Because this one can, in fact, find gold!

The modern divining rod is a computerized search tool that can sort through thousands of stocks in seconds to find the ones that best match your specific investment goals. All you need is a personal computer, a modem, and a computerized search product that uses an online database.[1] If the data is online, as opposed to being delivered via diskettes or CD ROM, it is updated on a continual basis—every few minutes, hourly, or daily—and is, therefore, timely. Nothing is more critical than timeliness

---

[1] An online database is a reservoir of data maintained at a central location and connected to users through a modem in their PCs. (A modem uses an ordinary telephone line to transmit data.) An online database may or may not be accessible through the Internet.

when you are prospecting for stocks. (Imagine making an investment decision with month-old stock prices!)

A COMPUTERIZED DIVINING ROD

Computerized search products have been around for more than a decade, but they have come a long way in the past few years. The early ones were very simplistic; their primary purpose was to eliminate companies that did not meet a specific requirement. You could, for example, eliminate companies with P/E ratios lower than 5 and higher than 50 and end up with a list of stocks, in no particular order, that had P/Es between 5 and 50. Such a list had limited use. Search products have improved steadily over the years, but as you are about to see, the most modern one has taken a giant leap forward.

The search product we will use to demonstrate the search process is ProSearch™, which is produced by Telescan, Inc. It is the search tool we know best and one of the best on the market. In addition, it is included with this book as part of the Cyber-Investing Kit, and you may use it without charge for a trial period in order to practice and apply the strategies we describe. Many of these search strategies, however, can be adapted to other programs.

We call ProSearch a search tool, but it is more like a computerized toolkit that has over 200 separate tools (called indicators) with which to screen Telescan's online database. Each tool may be used separately or combined in myriad ways to create thousands of different search strategies. Like its predecessors, ProSearch can eliminate companies that do not meet your basic requirements, but it can do much, much more. It can take a universe of stocks that meet your basic requirements and then score and rank those stocks so that the very best (according to your specifications) will rise like cream to the top of the list. For instance, if you ask for stocks with the highest historical earnings, the first stock on your list will have *the* highest historical earnings of over 9,000 stocks in the search universe. If you ask for stocks that had the largest percentage gain today, the biggest gainer would be listed first, with the rest of the stocks in descending order.

However, a single indicator is rarely used alone in a search. Many different objectives may be combined into a powerful search strategy by selecting up to 40 indicators (out of a possible 300). ProSearch would then find the stocks that best meet the *combined* goals.

In this chapter, we will start with a simple but effective search, and add to it one piece at a time. (In Chapter 5 we'll create more sophisticated searches.) We suggest you use part of your free online time to duplicate the searches as we go along. Searches may be constructed offline, but you must go online to submit the search.

THE INSIDE SCOOP

One of the simplest ways to find stocks with excellent potential for growth is to follow the insiders. Insiders should know better than anyone else whether a company's earnings are likely to increase.

Corporate insiders are defined by the Securities and Exchange Commission as the officers, directors, and major shareholders who own more than 10 percent of a company's shares. These people are at or near the controls. They know the topics of the yet-to-be-released news, the contents of the currently unpublished annual report, the figures on the not-yet-public bottom line. They usually know what's going to happen before it happens, and when they see a rosy future they often start buying their company's stock.

INSTALLING PROSEARCH

ProSearch 4.0 for DOS is included on the free Telescan diskette. To use it, install the program as described in the Quick Start Guide at the end of the book. (The Quick Start Guide also has hardware requirements, log-on information, and a section on using the program.)

Please note that the searches in this book were created with the Windows-based ProSearch 5.0. The main difference between the Windows 5.0 version and the DOS 4.0 version is the number of indicators: Version 5.0 has 300 indicators, whereas version 4.0 has 200 indicators, but all searches except the ranking search in Chapter 5 can be created with version 4.0.

To activate ProSearch, you must log on to the database and then select PROSEARCH from the program menu. As a book purchaser, you will have 30 days of free searches and free online time. The Cyber-Investing Kit has more details.

Twenty years ago, the individual investor had great difficulty finding insider trading data. Requirements for reporting insider trades were not as strict in those days, and even if you could find (and afford) the printed monthly reports that were available, much of the immediacy was lost. Now, insiders are required to disclose their activity within 10 days after the first of the month following the trade, and the information is available quickly and cheaply from an online service as soon as it is published by the SEC.

One of the strongest advocates of following the insiders is Mark W. Arnold, former vice president of a major Wall Street brokerage firm, whom we mentioned earlier. "No one," he says, "has shown me an approach which generates consistently better results than following the lead of corporate insiders." In *Trading on Tomorrow's Headlines,* he reveals his 1993 study of stock performance based on insider buying activity. As a group, these stocks outperformed the market by 31 percentage points: a return of 38.71 percent versus 7.1 percent for the S&P 500.[2]

Mr. Arnold is not the only one who believes in following the lead of insiders. Former Fidelity Magellan guru Peter Lynch wrote, "There's no better tip-off to the probable success of a stock than that people in the company are putting their own money into it."[3] In his book *Winning on Wall Street,* market wizard Marty Zweig quotes his 1974–1976 study on stocks with insider buying.[4] He found that stocks with heavy insider buying outperformed the S&P 500 by almost 200 percent (45.8 percent compared with 15.8 percent). Dr. Zweig also documents four other academic studies that confirm his findings.

Our own research substantiates the value of insider trading. Over a 12-month period (4/1/92 through 3/31/93), our insider buying search had a higher return (40.4 percent) than all other searches tested during that period.[5]

Exhibit 4.1 provides a graphic demonstration of the foresight of insiders. As you can see, there was very heavy insider buying in the months that preceded the 10-point run-up of A Plus Network's stock in the spring of 1996. As the stock neared $20 insider selling began, and within two months the stock had plunged to a new low. Of course, insiders don't always know what's going to happen. Sometimes, they buy simply because

---

[2] Mark W. Arnold, *Trading on Tomorrow's Headlines* (Houston: Telescan, Inc., 1995).
[3] Lynch, *One Up on Wall Street,* p. 134.
[4] Martin Zweig, *Winning on Wall Street* (New York: Warner Books, 1986).
[5] David Brown and Mark Draud, *ProSearch Strategy Handbook* (Houston: Telescan, 1993).

Exhibit 4.1   This is a graphic demonstration of the wisdom of following the lead of insiders. ACOM stock dropped sharply at the beginning of June. Two months later it had plummeted all the way to $9.

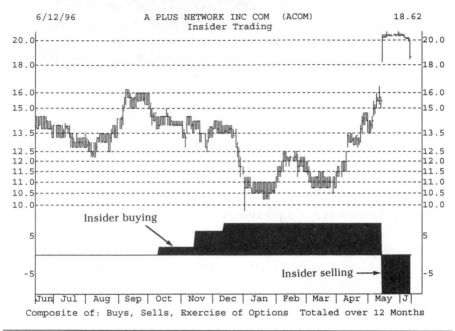

they think the stock is undervalued, and unless the public agrees, the stock is unlikely to move. Still, it is often profitable to follow their early lead.

If we had the space, we could show you dozens and dozens of stock graphs that reveal heavy insider buying just before a stock takes off. But we can do better than that. We can show you how to profit *legally* from such insider activity with an insider buying search.

SEARCH 1: A SIMPLE INSIDER SEARCH

Our first search will be a simple search that uses only one indicator because it has only one goal: to find stocks with high insider buying. There are four basic steps in creating a search with ProSearch. All except the fourth step may be done offline.

1. Select the indicators you want to use to find and rank stocks and specify the desired action. We will select *insider trading* from a list of nearly 300 indicators and tell the computer to search for the *highest* net insider buying.[6]

2. Specify the number of stocks you want to see on the search report. In the interest of space, we'll ask for 10. (ProSearch will return from 10 to 200 stocks; in ProSearch 5.0 the maximum is 250.)

3. Select the universe of stocks you want to search. We'll use "all stocks," which includes the entire database of over 9,000 stocks. We could, if we wished, limit the search to optionable stocks or some other portion of the database.

4. Submit the search to the online database. We'll save the search first—a critical step if you create the search offline—and then log on to submit the search.

Within seconds, ProSearch will return a search report that ranks companies according to the number of insiders buying the stock: The more insiders buying, the higher the company will be ranked.

It's as simple as that.

There are just two differences between this simplest of searches and the most complex search you can create. In the more complex searches, you will use more indicators (up to 40) and additional search modes, both of which we will address shortly.

Search Results: They Must Know Something We Don't

Let's take a look at the results of our simple insider buying search (Exhibit 4.2). We asked for the top 10 stocks that had the highest net insider buying. The search program totaled the net insider buying for each of more than 9,000 stocks, ranked them from highest to lowest, and returned a list of the 10 top-ranked stocks. Keep in mind these were the companies

---

[6] To arrive at net insider buying, Telescan subtracts the number of insiders selling stock from the number of insiders buying stock and totals it over a three-month period. A figure of 3, for example, means that there are 3 more insiders buying than there are insiders selling during the three-month period.

Exhibit 4.2   Search 1 lists the top 10 stocks with the highest insider buying on July 26, 1996.

ProSearch Top Stock Report
7/26/96

Indicator	Action
Insider trading	Rank stocks by highest scores

Rank	Symbol	Stock Name	Percentile Rank	Industry Group Symbol
1>	MDSN	MADISON GAS & ELEC CO COM		.UDI
		Insider Trading = 26.0	99	
2>	CFB	COMMERCIAL FEDERAL CORP COM		.BSB
		Insider Trading = 17.0	99	
3>	BNK	C N B BANCSHARES INC COM		.BAN
		Insider Trading = 17.0	99	
4>	STA	STARTER CORP COM		.TAM
		Insider Trading = 15.0	99	
5>	TAP	TRAVELERS AETNA P&C CL A CL A		.IPC
		Insider Trading = 14.0	99	
6>	PRJ	PROVIDENCE JOURNAL CO CL A		.BRO
		Insider Trading = 14.0	99	
7>	SMGS	SOUTHEASTERN MICH GAS ENT COM		.UGA
		Insider Trading = 11.0	99	
8>	GSFC	GREEN STREET FNCL CORP COM		.BSL
		Insider Trading = 11.0	99	
9>	TLCM	TELCOM SEMICONDUCTOR INC COM		.ESE
		Insider Trading = 10.0	99	
10>	GSBI	GRANITE ST BANKSHARES INC COM		.BAN
		Insider Trading = 10.0	99	

This report is based on mathematical calculations and, as such, no investment decision should be based solely on its conclusions.

Source: ProSearch 5.0, courtesy of Telescan, Inc.

with the most insider buying on the date of the report. Tomorrow the list may be different. Next week it certainly will.

The number 1 stock on our report is Madison Gas & Electric Company, with a net of 26 insiders buying the stock; the tenth ranked company, Granite State Bankshares, had a net of 10 insiders buying the stock. The *percentile rank* shows where the stock ranks for the indicator compared with all other stocks.[7] All the stocks on this list are ranked in the 99th (the highest) percentile. We will put this feature to good use later.

Who's Buying and How Much?

In cyberspace, information is nothing if not abundant. Not only can we find out the number of insiders buying their company's stock, we can also learn their names, the number of shares they bought, the price they paid, and the total number of shares they now own. All this information can be obtained with a couple of keystrokes from Telescan and from other on-line services. (A sample insider text report is shown in Exhibit 4.3.)

Why do you care about these details? Because it is important to know who is buying or selling, whether they are selling all or a small fraction of their shares, and whether they are exercising low-priced stock options or trading at the market price. Such information can help you assess the importance of the inside trade. One anomaly to watch for is a large group of insiders buying small quantities of stock. This could be part of a company stock purchase plan, which would negate to some extent the importance of the insider trading.

SEARCH 2: INSIDERS + WALL STREET EXPERTS

In the previous search, we found stocks that had received a vote of confidence from corporate insiders. This is an interesting list, but it would not be prudent to rush out and buy any of these stocks just yet. We need more evidence that something potentially profitable (to us!) is going on in these companies. The vote of confidence from insiders, as mentioned above, could be due to the exercise of stock options or employee stock purchase plans. What we need is another, perhaps more important, opinion. Let's see what Wall Street analysts think about the earnings potential of companies with high insider buying.

---

[7] As part of its scoring and ranking process, ProSearch places each stock in a percentile ranking from zero to 99 for the selected indicator. In other words, it takes all the stocks in the database and places 1/100 of them in each of 100 percentiles.

Exhibit 4.3 This is a list of insider trading in Travelers Aetna P&C as of July 26, 1996.

TAP Insider Trading—7/26/96

SEC	Sym	Pos	Name	Type	Date	Shares	Price	Holdings
06/96	TAP	DIR	BYRNE JOHN J	P	04/02/96	3,142,906	15.90	3,142,906
06/96	TAP	CB	LIPP ROBERT I	P	04/22/96–04/23/96	40,100	23.81–27.12	40,100
06/96	TAP	CB	RESTREPO ROBERT P JR	P	04/22/96	1,500	23.81	1,500
06/96	TAP	CB	SILBERSTEIN ALAN M	P	04/22/96	16,000	23.81	16,000
06/96	TAP	CB	KIERNAN JOSEPH P	P	04/22/96	4,000	23.81	4,000
05/96	TAP	CFO	HANNON WILLIAM P	P	04/22/96–04/23/96	4,100	23.81–27.12	4,100
05/96	TAP	CFO	HANNON WILLIAM P	P	04/22/96	300	25.00	300
05/96	TAP	OFF	MEAD CHRISTINE B	P	04/22/96	1,000	23.81	1,000
05/96	TAP	DIR	MECUM DUDLEY C	P	04/22/96	1,750	23.81	1,750
05/96	TAP	DIR	TASCO FRANK J	P	04/22/96	2,625	23.81	2,625
05/96	TAP	DIR	WEILL SANFORD I	P	04/22/96–04/23/96	4,100	23.81–27.12	4,100
05/96	TAP	DIR	ZANKEL ARTHUR J	P	04/22/96	4,000	23.81	4,000
05/96	TAP	DIR	BIALKIN KENNETH J	P	04/22/96	4,375	23.81	4,375
05/96	TAP	DIR	DIMON JAMES	P	04/22/96	2,000	23.81	2,000
05/96	TAP	VCB	FISHMAN JAY S	P	04/22/96	3,000	23.81–25.00	3,000

SEC = SEC release date

Type = P:open market purchase S:open market sale X:exercise options; PS:Private Sale PB:Private Buy JS:Gift Sale JB:Gift Buy
(O)wnership = D:direct I:Indirect

Position = AF:AFFILATE AF:AFFILATE of Investment Advisor B,BC,BT:Beneficial Owner of 10%+ CB:Chairman CEO:Chief Executive Officer CFO:Chief Financial Officer COO:Chief Operating Officer CP:Controlling Person D:Director DO:Director & Owner DS:Indirect Shareholder GP:General Partner H:Officer Director & 10%+ Owner IA:Investment Advisor LP:Limited Partner MC:Member Advisory Board O:Officer OB:Officer & 10%+ Owner OD:Officer & Director OP:Officer of Parent Co. OS:Subsidiary Officer OT:Officer and Treasurer OX:Divisional Officer PT:Partner P:President R:Retired, Deceased, Resigned Sec:Secretary SH:Shareholder T:Trustee TR:Treasurer UT:Unknown VP:Vice President VT:Voting Trust X:Former (with first 2 letters of relation)

Source: Telescan, Inc.

When the Analysts Speak . . .

Analysts are men or women employed by brokerage firms (usually) to re-search specific companies and write reports on their findings. They be-come experts on the companies they follow, learning the business, studying the industry, reading trade publications. They usually visit the company, talk with corporate officials, analyze conditions inside and out-side the company.

In short, they take the company's temperature on a regular basis. Then they make projections about the company's quarterly and annual earnings. In most cases, they also make a projection of the company's annualized 5-year growth rate of earnings per share (sometimes called a secular forecast). A large company may have a following of 30 or more analysts; a small company, one or two. Collectively, they are referred to as Wall Street analysts, research analysts, or industry analysts. When these analysts speak, the market (usually) listens!

Never does the market listen more intently than when analysts change their minds and raise or lower their projections. Such revisions are measured by an indicator called the *one-month change in consensus analysts' estimates*. That's a mouthful, but the indicator is really very sim-ple: It measures the average increase (or decrease) during the past 30 days in the analysts' earnings estimates for the current fiscal year.

Usually, an upward revision in estimates signals that something pos-itive is happening in the company. It may be gaining more market share; it may have a new product that is doing exceptionally well; it may be doing an outstanding job of cutting costs. It could be any event that points to in-creased growth for the company. When such an event is acknowledged by an upward revision in analysts' estimates, it can give a big boost to the company's stock price. A downward revision would obviously have the reverse impact.

Our own research has shown that, over a large number and different types of market periods, an upward revision in earnings estimates is the single best indicator for predicting stock price increases. Using this indi-cator with the insider buying indicator increases the power of a search. Together, they will find companies that have received thumbs up from the two groups that know them best: the insiders and the analysts. What bet-ter prospecting list could you have?

For our second search, we'll re-select the insider trading indicator and add the one-month change indicator, and ask for the highest combined scores on both.

IS TIMELINESS AN ISSUE?

Research analysts publish their earnings projections in-house before they are released to the general public. That means the customers of those firms—usually institutional investors—have first crack at the stocks. Does this reduce the impact of any upward revision for individual investors? Apparently not, according to our testing of the one-month change indicator on historical data.

At the time of our tests, information about upward revisions would have been available to the public for an average of three weeks. (Currently, there is a lag of one to seven days from release of estimates to inclusion in most online databases.) Nevertheless, our tests on six market periods—including bullish, bearish, and sideways markets—showed that the one-month change indicator is the single best predictor of stock price increases.

It would appear, therefore, that the positive impact from upward revisions of earnings estimates continues for many weeks after the announcement. This may be because most users of this data have been institutional investors who typically take many weeks, even months, to acquire a position in a stock. After the information is released, institutions have to assess the possible impact of the revision and then spread their action over a period of time to avoid moving the stock prematurely. This gives online databases plenty of time to publish the information for use by individual investors. In time, the investing public will become aware of the factors that caused analyst optimism, as increased sales and earnings gradually materialize (or do not, as the case may be!).

For those who have to see something to believe it, we'll show you in Chapter 6 how to backtest this and other ProSearch indicators.

Search Results: Two Thumbs Up

This search (Exhibit 4.4) shows completely different results from the previous search. The top-ranked company, Standard Commercial Corp., has only four insiders buying but an impressive 36.2 percent upward revision of earnings estimates. In fact, none of the companies on this report are in the 99th percentile with regard to insider buying, but five are in the 99th

Exhibit 4.4   Search 2 lists the top 10 stocks on July 26, 1996 ranked by insider buying and upward revisions in earnings estimates.

ProSearch Top Stock Report
7/26/96

Indicator	Action
Insider buying	Rank stocks by highest scores
1-month change in earnings estimates	Rank stocks by highest scores

Rank	Symbol	Stock Name	Percentile Rank	Industry Group Symbol
1>	STW	STANDARD COMMERCIAL CORP COM		.TLS
		Insider Trading = 4.0	98	
		Upward Revision = 36.2	99	
2>	TPC	T P C CORP COM		.UPG
		Insider Trading = 4.0	98	
		Upward Revision = 10.5	98	
3>	TMR	TEXAS MERIDIAN RES CORP COM		.OCP
		Insider Trading = 3.0	98	
		Upward Revision = 10.5	98	
4>	MLG	MUSICLAND STORES CORP COM		.RSP
		Insider Trading = 2.0	97	
		Upward Revision = 19.0	98	
5>	TNL	TECHNITROL INC COM		.ECC
		Insider Trading = 3.0	98	
		Upward Revision = 5.6	96	
6>	FGAS	FORCENERGY INC COM		.OIL
		Insider Trading = 1.0	95	
		Upward Revision = 58.0	99	
7>	BORR	BORROR CORP COM		.BHO
		Insider Trading = 1.0	95	
		Upward Revision = 20.0	99	
8>	UCOR	UROCOR INC COM		.IIIC
		Insider Trading = 1.0	95	
		Upward Revision = 26.6	99	
9>	OS	OREGON STEEL MILLS INC COM		.STE
		Insider Trading = 2.0	97	
		Upward Revision = 6.2	96	
10>	TAC	TANDYCRAFTS INC COM		.RSP
		Insider Trading = 1.0	95	
		Upward Revision = 36.3	99	

This report is based on mathematical calculations and, as such, no investment decision should be based solely on its conclusions.

Source: ProSearch 5.0, courtesy of Telescan, Inc.

percentile on upward revision of earnings estimates. It is the combination of the two indicators that is important in this simple search. It gives us the best of two worlds, not necessarily the best of each.

SEARCH 3: NARROWING THE UNIVERSE

Despite two thumbs up from insiders and analysts, we would not consider buying the stocks from the previous search without additional information. First, the search is much too simple, and second, we have not evaluated any of the stocks with respect to their other merits. What we have is a working list of 10 candidates that seem ideal, based on two indicators. Normally, we would expand the search by adding a number of indicators to score and rank the stocks, but we are still in the get-acquainted stage with the search tool. For now, let's just narrow the universe of the search a bit.

Eliminate the Undesirable

Our next screening technique harks back to the earliest computerized search programs. These primitive tools could only screen out the undesirable: Enter a minimum goal, they eliminated all stocks below it; enter a maximum goal, they got rid of all stocks above it. This was a relatively crude technique, but it was useful then and it's still useful now. In fact, most search programs still work on this simple screening principle because it is useful for separating the wheat from the chaff.

Let's apply the elimination method to our previous search. Let's assume that, regardless of how many insiders are buying or how optimistic the analysts are, we don't want any stocks priced below $5 or above $100. Very low-priced stocks are saddled with a higher commission, percentage-wise, and they may not be marginable. (If you prefer low-priced stocks, however, you might wish to use 5 or 10 as the maximum.) Very high-priced stocks require either a larger dollar investment or a smaller incremental purchase; those who like to buy in 100 share increments may not want to put $10,000 or more in one position. Whatever the reasons, we are eliminating these stocks simply to illustrate the search tool.

We will add the *stock price indicator* to the previous search and tell the computer to eliminate all stocks below $5 and above $100. In other words, we are narrowing our universe of stocks to those that meet our minimum goal which, in this case, is a stock priced between $5 and $100. When we rerun the search, the program will not have to consider the lower-priced or higher-priced stocks. It will simply score the stocks in our designated universe for high insider buying and high upward revisions in Wall Street estimates, and rank them accordingly.

Search Results

The results of this expanded search are shown in Exhibit 4.5. Notice that the stock price is now listed for each stock. Notice also that two stocks from the previous search report, Musicland Stores Corp. and Borror Corp., are missing from the new report. They were eliminated because of their low prices, which allowed two lower-ranked stocks to move up into the top ten list.

Don't set impossible standards when you narrow your search universe. Eliminating stocks that do not meet your minimum requirements is an important step in the search process, but you can be overly zealous. If you use too many indicators to narrow the search universe, you may end up like the lover who is searching for the perfect mate: All possible candidates are eliminated because the standards are too high. Be careful not to put in too many restrictions. Use just a few indicators to narrow the search universe; then use the most important indicators—those that best define your investment goals—to score and rank the remaining stocks.

SEARCH 4: MAKING LISTS, SAVING TIME

So far we have shown you how to use search tools to score and rank stocks and to eliminate stocks from the search universe. There is yet another way to use these tools. You may simply list information about the stocks on the search report. Some of the information may be used to evaluate the stocks and narrow the list of candidates; other data may be needed when you are ready to place an order with your broker. Either way, listing information during the search saves you from having to look it up later.

To demonstrate the list-only feature, we will add the *P/E ratio indicator* to our previous search and tell the computer to list the information.

Exhibit 4.5   Search 3 lists the top 10 stocks on July 26, 1996 priced between $5 and $100 and ranked by insider buying and upward revision in earnings estimates.

ProSearch Report
7/26/96

Indicator	Action
Insider buying	Rank stocks by highest scores
1-month change in earnings estimates	Rank stocks by highest scores
Stock price	Eliminate stocks below $5 and above $100

Rank	Symbol	Stock Name	Percentile Rank	Industry Group Symbol
1>	STW	STANDARD COMMERCIAL CORP COM		.TLS
		Insider Trading = 4.0	98	
		Upward Revision = 36.2	99	
		Price = 13.6	58	
2>	TPC	T P C CORP COM		.UPG
		Insider Trading = 4.0	98	
		Upward Revision = 10.5	98	
		Price = 6.6	19	
3>	TMR	TEXAS MERIDIAN RES CORP COM		.OCP
		Insider Trading = 3.0	98	
		Upward Revision = 10.5	98	
		Price = 11.4	46	
4>	TNL	TECHNITROL INC COM		.ECC
		Insider Trading = 3.0	98	
		Upward Revision = 5.6	96	
		Price = 30.6	88	
5>	FGAS	FORCENERGY INC COM		.OIL
		Insider Trading = 1.0	95	
		Upward Revision = 58.0	99	
		Price = 18.8	74	
6>	TAC	TANDYCRAFTS INC COM		.RSP
		Insider Trading = 1.0	95	
		Upward Revision = 36.3	99	
		Price = 5.5	15	
7>	UCOR	UROCOR INC COM		.HHC
		Insider Trading = 1.0	95	
		Upward Revision = 26.6	99	
		Price = 10.9	43	
8>	OS	OREGON STEEL MILLS INC COM		.STE
		Insider Trading = 2.0	97	
		Upward Revision = 6.2	96	
		Price = 13.5	57	
9>	COX	COX COMMUNICATIONS CL A CL		.BCA
		Insider Trading = 1.0	95	
		Upward revision = 16.6	98	
		Price = 19.9	76	
10>	FAF	FIRST AMERN FNCL CORP CA COM		.IPC
		Insider Trading = 1.0	95	
		Upward Revision = 14.0	98	
		Price = 29.9	88	

This report is based on mathematical calculations and, as such, no investment decision should be based solely on its conclusions.

Source: ProSearch 5.0, courtesy of Telescan, Inc.

We will not concern ourselves here with low or high P/Es, as discussed in Chapter 2. We simply want to list the P/E ratio so we do not have to look it up when we make our purchase decision.

The results from this search are shown in Exhibit 4.6. Notice that the list of stocks is exactly the same as the previous search, because P/E ratio was not used to eliminate or rank the stocks. The computer simply retrieved the P/E ratio for each stock and listed it on the report.

You will notice that three of the stocks on this report are marked N/A for the P/E ratio. This means one of two things: Either the stocks do not have any current earnings or their total earnings for the year were negative. Their presence on this report apparently means that the analysts expect positive earnings this year. These are known as turn-around situations, which are good but fraught with risk. Not every company that is expected to turn the corner to positive earnings does so. Or, if it does, it may not do so in a timely fashion, as expected by the analysts. So beware. Although turn-around situations can produce some large stock gains, they can also produce huge disappointments.

If you are averse to this kind of risk, you can eliminate such companies from the search universe. That's the beauty of computerized search products. Simply add the earnings per share indicator to the search and require the company to have some minimum level of positive earnings, say, 5 cents. Then all the stocks found by your search will have at least one year of positive earnings.

An expanded version of this insider trading search is on the Telescan diskette. See the Quick Start Guide at the back of the book for instructions on using it.

YOU MUST REMEMBER THIS . . .

We have demonstrated in this chapter the tremendous power of computerized search tools. Even simple searches can narrow a playing field of more than 9,000 stocks to a handful that meet your stated goals. As we move forward to more complex searches, keep in mind that the basic search process will remain essentially the same.

- A limited number of indicators should be used to narrow the search universe to meet your minimum requirements.

Exhibit 4.6   Search 4 lists the P/E ratio for the top 10 stocks on July 26, 1996, with restricted stock price ranked by insider buying and upward revisions in earnings estimates.

ProSearch Report
7/26/96

Indicator	Action
Insider buying	Rank stocks by highest scores
1-month change in earnings estimates	Rank stocks by highest scores
Stock price	Eliminate stocks below $5 and above $100
P/E ratio	List only

Rank	Symbol	Stock Name	Percentile Rank	Industry Group Symbol
1>	STW	STANDARD COMMERCIAL CORP COM		.TLS
		Insider Trading = 4.0	98	
		Upward Revision = 36.2	99	
		Price = 13.6	58	
		P/E Ratio = N/A	—	
2>	TPC	T P C CORP COM		.UPG
		Insider Trading = 4.0	98	
		Upward Revision = 10.5	98	
		Price = 6.6	19	
		P/E Ratio = 82.7	94	
3>	TMR	TEXAS MERIDIAN RES CORP COM		.OCP
		Insider Trading = 3.0	98	
		Upward Revision = 10.5	98	
		Price = 11.4	46	
		P/E Ratio = 36.6	84	
4>	TNL	TECHNITROL INC COM		.ECC
		Insider Trading = 3.0	98	
		Upward Revision = 5.6	96	
		Price = 30.6	88	
		P/E Ratio = 14.5	43	
5>	FGAS	FORCENERGY INC COM		.OIL
		Insider Trading = 1.0	95	
		Upward Revision = 58.0	99	
		Price = 18.8	74	
		P/E = 1875.0	99	
6>	TAC	TANDYCRAFTS INC COM		.RSP
		Insider Trading = 1.0	95	
		Upward Revision = 36.3	99	
		Price = 5.5	15	
		P/E Ratio = N/A	—	

Exhibit 4.6   (continued)

Rank	Symbol	Stock Name	Percentile Rank	Industry Group Symbol
7>	UCOR	UROCOR INC COM		.HHC
		Insider Trading = 1.0	95	
		Upward Revision = 26.6	99	
		Price = 10.9	43	
		P/E Ratio = N/A	—	
8>	OS	OREGON STEEL MILLS INC COM		.STE
		Insider Trading = 2.0	97	
		Upward Revision = 6.2	96	
		Price = 13.5	57	
		P/E Ratio = 15.6	48	
9>	COX	COX COMMUNICATIONS CL A CL		.BCA
		Insider Trading = 1.0	95	
		Upward Revision = 16.6	98	
		Price = 19.9	76	
		P/E Ratio = 46.2	88	
10>	FAF	FIRST AMERN FNCL CORP CA COM		.IPC
		Insider Trading = 1.0	95	
		Upward Revision = 14.0	98	
		Price = 29.9	88	
		P/E Ratio = 11.8	27	

This report is based on mathematical calculations and, as such, no investment decision should be based solely on its conclusions.

Note: "N/A" means the data was not available or pieces of the data that make up the calculation, such as negative numbers, cause it to be invalid. The most likely reason for a P/E ratio of N/A is that the company had no earnings or had negative earnings at the time of the search. See comment in text.

Source: ProSearch 5.0, courtesy of Telescan, Inc.

- The indicators most important to your investment goals should be used to score and rank stocks from best to worst.

- Less important indicators may be used to list information for evaluating the stocks.

- Before purchasing any stock found by a search, we strongly suggest that it be put through the kind of evaluation described in Chapters 7 and 8.

The searches in this chapter clearly illustrate the underlying premise of this book: That there is an enormous amount of information available with which to make investing decisions—information that was not available to individual investors a decade or two ago. Today, you can use insider trading data and analysts' projections—and much, much more—with speed, ease, and economy. In cyberspace, you can do it from Main Street, USA, as easily as from Wall Street.

In the next chapter, we'll develop three completely different searches to show you a wide range of possibilities for modern computerized stock search tools.

5

PROSPECTING FOR STOCKS

In the previous chapter we used a few simple searches to introduce you to a powerful prospecting tool. Now we're going to create three more sophisticated searches to demonstrate the range and subtlety of this search tool. By the time you finish this chapter, you will be able to prospect on your own, designing searches that will find stocks to match *your* specific investment goals.

First, we'll develop a search based on value investing that will look for undervalued stocks, those with relatively low P/Es that are expected to rise. Next, we will create a *ranking search* that will find the highest ranked stocks, both fundamentally and technically. Finally, we'll design a search based on momentum investing, which should appeal to technicians.

All of these searches are ones we use in real life, yet they represent only a small fraction of what you can do with a computerized search tool. Our goal is not to sell you on a specific investing philosophy, but to give you practice in creating searches. Again, we'll be using Telescan's Pro-Search, mainly because the scoring and ranking method isn't available in other search products, nor are some of the indicators that we've found to be the most powerful. Nevertheless, many of the strategies can be adapted to other search products.[1]

We invite you to create the searches as we go along.

SEARCH 1: THE BARGAIN HUNTERS

Investors who look for fundamentally sound stocks that are selling for less than their intrinsic value are called value investors. They believe that, if their analysis is accurate, such stocks should move up for fundamental reasons. If this sounds vaguely familiar, it is because we talked about these kinds of stocks in Chapter 2. Value investors want stocks with relatively low P/E ratios that have a good chance of rising. Our first search then will be based on a classic value investing strategy: looking for undervalued growth stocks.

What exactly is an undervalued growth stock? We know what undervalued means: something that is selling for less than what it is worth, a bargain. We also know that a growth stock is one whose earnings and price have been growing steadily over a long period of time—3, 5, or 10 years, depending on the defined time horizon—and whose earnings and price are expected to continue to grow for a long time. An undervalued growth search then would identify stocks with high historical growth and high projected growth but which, for some reason, are selling at less than what appears to be their real value. This is the goal of our first search.

The Basic Search

In any search we need to do three things: Eliminate stocks that don't meet our basic standards; rank the remaining stocks in order of best to worst, according to the conditions we impose; and list information to aid us in our final selection. The latter will be addressed in Chapter 7 as a way to help you evaluate the results of this undervalued growth search. The current discussion will be restricted to the elimination and ranking functions.

---

[1] Investment newsletters are an alternative way to identify prospects. Online newsletters, like those in the Cyber-Investing Kit, are particularly helpful because the comments and advice are timely. Before you act on anyone's recommendation, however, put the stock through the Hot Stock Tip evaluation described in Chapter 8—at least until you are comfortable with the newsletter editor's strategy and techniques.

Our basic undervalued growth search has three requirements:

1. The long-term price trend must be high—the higher, the better.

2. Projected earnings for the next five years must be high—the higher, the better—and comparable to the past growth rate.

3. The stock must be priced low compared with its long-term price trend—the lower, the better.

To accomplish these basic objectives, we will use the three indicators discussed below. (The entire search strategy is shown in Exhibit 5.1.)

Bargains Only.   Value investors are basically bargain hunters. We want stocks that are selling apparently for less than they're worth, stocks that appear to be temporarily undervalued. The first thing we have to do is quantify our terms. The tool we'll use to quantify undervaluation is based on a trendline called a *least-squares (LSQ) line*.

Do not be put off by the term "least squares." It simply refers to a mathematical formula (transparent to the user) used to plot a line on a graph through a stock's historical prices so that roughly half the price activity is above the line and half below the line. In other words, an LSQ line tells you where the midpoint of all the data is. The current price is then established with relation to this line. (The LSQ line is the middle line on the graphs in this chapter. This concept is discussed at length in Chapter 8.)

ProSearch provides a very useful tool based on LSQ lines called the *LSQ deviation indicator*. This indicator tells you how far above or below the LSQ line the current stock price is, that is, how far it has deviated from the midpoint of its price action. To find undervalued stocks, we'll look for those that are, say, at least 10 percent below their LSQ line.

In this search, we'll use our most important indicator—the LSQ deviation indicator—in two different search modes. First, we'll use it to eliminate any stock that isn't at least 10 percent below its long-term LSQ line, because we've determined somewhat arbitrarily that is our minimum requirement. Then we'll use it to score and rank stocks according to where they fall below the LSQ line. The lower they are, the higher the ranking.[2] If you're using ProSearch, you will see that these two steps can be done at one time on the same screen.

---

[2] In ProSearch, use the *Absolute* search mode to eliminate stocks; use the *Relative* search mode to score and rank them.

Exhibit 5.1   Search request 1: Undervalued growth stocks.

Indicators (Abbreviation on Report)	Action: The Basic Search
10-year LSQ deviation (10LDv)	Eliminate stocks that are not at least 10% below their LSQ line Rank stocks by lowest scores
10-year price-growth rate (10$Gr)	Rank stocks by highest scores
5-year projected EPS growth rate (5yPEG)	Rank stocks by highest scores

Indicators	Action: Narrow the Universe
8/17/9 weekly MACD (Mc8wC)	Eliminate stocks that aren't technically positive
3-week relative performance (3-Wk)	Eliminate stocks that have not had a positive move over the past 3 weeks.
Group rank (GrpRk)	Eliminate stocks that have groups below 50% ranking

Indicators	Action: Seasoning
3-year LSQ deviation (3LDv)	Rank stocks by lowest scores
Quarter-over-quarter earnings—most recent quarter (%cELt)	Rank stocks by highest scores
Quarter-over-quarter earnings—second most recent quarter (%cE-2)	Rank stocks by highest scores
3-week price-rank change (c$-3)	Rank stocks by highest scores
6-week price-rank change (c$-6)	Rank stocks by highest scores
3-week group-rank change (cGRP3)	Rank stocks by highest scores
Stock price	List only

Note: The abbreviation shown in parentheses after the indicator name identifies the indicator on the search report.

Incidentally, if you don't want to use the LSQ line, you could use the relative P/E ratio indicator to find stocks selling at a low valuation with respect to *their* history. It should produce comparable results.

Track Records Count.   High growth stocks, by definition, have high historical growth rates. One way to quantify historical growth is to measure the increase in stock price over time. To this end, we'll use the *10-year price growth rate indicator* and ask for the highest scores. This will tell us how much the stock price has increased over the past 10 years; the greater the increase, the higher the score.

The Future of Earnings.   High earnings estimates are a positive sign for the continued price growth of the stock—especially if analysts are willing to stick their necks out and peer five years into the future. (If you recall from Chapter 2, high expectation of earnings is what makes P/Es rise rapidly.) The *5-year projected EPS growth rate indicator* uses the analysts' five-year annualized growth rate as the score for the stock. A stock with a 20 percent growth rate, for example, is expected to grow 20 percent per year over the next five years. We'll use this indicator and ask for the highest scores.

To summarize the basic search, we will eliminate all stocks that are not at least 10 percent below their 10-year LSQ line; then, within that universe, we will ask the computer to return stocks that are the farthest below their LSQ line (the most undervalued ones), which have the highest 10-year price growth rates and the highest 5-year projected-earnings growth rates.

Only Movers and Shakers Allowed

A computerized search program allows you to eliminate unacceptable stocks before you even begin the search. In the basic search above, the LSQ deviation indicator will eliminate stocks that don't meet our requirements for undervaluation. Now we'll add three more indicators to restrict the universe to stocks that are on an uptrend and have positive momentum. Otherwise, we would have to eliminate down-trending or low-momentum stocks later in the analysis stage.

Wanted: Stocks with Positive Attitude.   It doesn't do much good to find a bargain-priced stock if it is headed in the wrong direction. To make sure every stock in our search universe is technically positioned to move up, we will use a technical indicator that measures overbought and oversold conditions, namely, the *moving average convergence/divergence (MACD) indicator*. The MACD concept, which we'll discuss in a later chapter, answers two important questions: How strongly does the market feel about a stock? How likely is it that the current trend will continue?

The MACD indicator comes in daily and weekly versions; we'll use the longer-term weekly indicator and require it to have at least turned positive. This will tell us the stock has turned up, not down. (By the way, you don't have to understand the concept behind a technical indicator to use it; you just need to tell the computer what to do with it!)

Wanted: Stocks on the Move.   The MACD indicator makes sure that the stocks in our search universe are technically positioned to go up, not down. But undervalued stocks—those selling at low levels with respect to their history—frequently linger there a while. To make sure we're not the first skater on the pond, we need to look at the stock's recent performance. We'll use a *3-week relative performance indicator,* which measures the amount of movement in the stock price over the past three weeks, and tell the computer to eliminate stocks that haven't had an upward movement.

By the way, ProSearch 5.0 users may prefer to use the technical rank indicator and search for stocks ranked in the 60th percentile or higher.

Wanted: Stocks from Good Families.   A stock usually needs the support of its industry group to make any kind of big move in P/E ratio. Because rising P/Es are our ultimate goal, we should make sure the stock's industry group also has upward momentum. We will use the *group rank indicator* for this purpose and tell the computer to eliminate any stock whose industry group is not in the top half of all industry groups, with regard to price behavior over the past few months.

Our search universe is now restricted to stocks that are undervalued according to their long-term price trend, stocks that are in a positive technical position, stocks that have had a recent upward price movement, and stocks that are riding on industry group momentum.

Seasoning the Search

We have a good search, as far as it goes. The tools we've selected will eliminate stocks that do not meet our basic standards and will then rank the remaining stocks according to our primary investment objectives. But we still need more information. What about the stock's position in its short-term trading channel? What about earnings momentum and price momentum? Is the stock's industry group continuing to gain strength or is it running out of steam?

What we need is a little seasoning for our search. Something to bring out the flavor of the stocks and make the best ones even better. The seasoning will not change the nature of the search—if we started out with chicken soup, we'll end up with chicken soup—but it will coax to the top of the list those stocks that most closely match our requirements.

A Dash of Short-Term LSQ.   The 10-year LSQ indicator will make sure each stock is a bargain compared with its long-term history. But short-term patterns often look much different. We think the longer-term pattern is much more important, but it is wise to pay attention to the shorter term as well. Therefore, we will add a dash of short-term LSQ to intensify the undervalued flavor. We will ask for a low *3-year LSQ deviation* score, which means the computer will rank the stocks according to how far they are below their 3-year LSQ line.

A Pinch of Earnings Momentum.   We have already asked for stocks with a recent price move (with the MACD indicator and the 3-week relative strength indicator), but we would like reassurance that the stock is indeed on its way up. A pinch or two of earnings momentum would be nice. ProSearch has several tools that compare earnings for each of the last four quarters with the same quarter a year ago. What we want are stocks with the highest rate of change in quarter-over-quarter earnings growth, not necessarily the highest quarterly earnings. We will use two *quarterly rate of change indicators*—one for the most recent quarter and one for the second most recent quarter—and ask for the highest scores.

A Bit of Price Momentum.   Another way to confirm a stock is on its way up is to measure the rate of the change in stock price over time. ProSearch has an indicator that ranks stocks by stock price and several related indicators that measure the change in the price rank. We will use two of the latter—the 3-week and 6-week *price rank change indicators*—and ask for the highest scores.

A Touch of Industry Group Momentum.   We have already eliminated all below-average industry groups with the group rank indicator. But that doesn't tell us whether a group is on its way up or on its way down. An industry group ranked in the 75th percentile that used to be in the 90th percentile is going the wrong way. Unlike salmon, stocks don't swim well against the current. Even if the stock is moving upward, it is unlikely to get very far if the industry group is losing momentum. A touch of industry group momentum is needed to increase the chances that the industry group is headed in the right direction. We will use the *3-week group rank change indicator* and ask for the highest scores.

Weighty Matters

The indicators that we have used to score and rank stocks are not of equal importance to our goals, but they will be treated equally by the search unless we do something about it. Fortunately, ProSearch allows you to weight the indicators used for ranking stocks, and, thereby, emphasize their relative importance to your overall goals.

In the basic search we used weights of 100 percent for LSQ deviation and projected earnings growth and 80 percent for historical price growth. With the indicators used for "seasoning," we favored the more recent activity. The actual percentages are shown in Exhibit 5.2. Changing these percentages will change the results of the search.

THE WEIGHTING ISSUE

ProSearch allows you to emphasize your most important objectives by *weighting* the score-and-rank indicators. (These are the indicators used in the "relative" search mode.) There are five weights that can be assigned to an indicator: 20 percent, 40 percent, 60 percent, 80 percent, and 100 percent. These percentages tell the program how much of the indicator's score to use in the combined score that ranks the stocks. For example, if you have a search that includes high projected earnings, high historical earnings and low P/E ratio, you might weight the indicators 100 percent, 80 percent, and 40 percent, respectively. The program would then total the scores of the three indicators in the following manner:

High projected earnings	100% of the score
High historical earnings	80% of the score
Low P/E ratio	40% of the score

The combined total would become the overall score for the stock and be used to rank it. (This is a simplified explanation of the algorithm used in the program.)

Changing the weighting of even one indicator in a search will change the results of the search. Thus, weighting allows you to tailor a search precisely to your goals.

Search Results: Bargain Stocks with Room to Grow

Our search strategy for undervalued growth stocks (Exhibit 5.1) now includes 13 indicators. Three are used to create the basic search (one is used in two different search modes); three are used to further narrow the universe; six are used to help bring the most desirable stocks to the top of the list; and we added, as always, an indicator to list the stock price.

Exhibit 5.2 shows the 25 highest ranked stocks from our undervalued growth search. The number one stock on May 8 is Quanex Corporation. Its stock price has been growing at 15.6 percent over the past 10 years; earnings gains have been outstanding in the last two quarters at 30 percent and 60 percent, respectively, and are projected to grow at 28 percent per year over the next five years; and the stock is selling at 24.6 percent below its 10-year LSQ line and 3.5 percent below its 3-year LSQ. It appears to have good potential, but let's look at the rest of the list.

ECI Telecom showed up as the tenth most undervalued growth stock. Its price growth has indeed been exceptional over the past 10 years at 70 percent. So why is it now undervalued and priced almost 54 percent below its LSQ line? Probably because earnings are projected to grow at only 22 percent over the next five years. Not a bad growth rate, but well below its historical levels. It should not be surprising that it is selling well below its LSQ.

Take a look at Novell, ranked fifth. At 62 percent below its LSQ line, it would have to almost triple in price to get back to its long-term trend-line. Yet it has grown at more than 34 percent per year over the past 10 years. It you take a closer look, however, you will see one reason why it may be selling so far below its long-term trend. Earnings are projected to grow only at 18 percent per year for the next five years. Obviously, the 22 percent decrease last quarter over the comparable quarter a year ago would be disturbing to the market.

When you look closely at the figures, it becomes apparent why each stock is on the list. They all match the conditions set forth in our search criteria. All have had impressive ten-year growth rates; all are expected to have five more years of good earnings; and all are currently undervalued as measured by their long-term price trend. The problem becomes one of choosing among stocks with good potential.

We will solve that problem in Chapters 7 and 8 with a two-stage evaluation that uses a number of technical and fundamental evaluation tools. But even without further analysis, the stocks from this search—if you

Exhibit 5.2   Results of search 1: The top 25 undervalued growth stocks on May 8, 1996.

Criteria	Criteria Values		
EPS % CHG LAST QTR	High	80%	
LST-SQR DEVIATN 10YR	Low	100%	
LST-SQR DEVIATN 10YR	−99998	−10	a
EPS % CHG 2 QTR AGO	High	60%	
LST-SQR DEVIATN 3-YR	Low	60%	
MACD HST 8/17/9 WK	1	999998	a
PRICE RANK CHG 3-WK	High	80%	
ANNLZD 5-YR PROJ EPS	High	100%	
REL PERFORMANC 3-WK	101	999998	a
PRICE RANK CHG 6-WK	High	40%	
PRICE GROWTH 10-YR	High	80%	
GROUP RANK	50	999998	r
GROUP RANK CHG 3-WK	High	20%	
STOCK PRICE	List Only		

Prosearch Top Stock Report
5/08/96
All Stocks

1> NX   – QUANEX CORP COM   .SOS
    %cELt = 30.4   (70)   10LDv = −24.6   (8)   10LDv = −24.6   (8)
    %cE-2 = 60.0   (83)   3LDv = −3.5   (18)   Mc8wC = 24.0   (84)
    c$-3   = 2.7   (83)   5yPEG = 28.3   (85)   3-Wk   = 107.1   (81)
    c$-6   = −0.1   (64)   10$Gr = 15.6   (84)   GrpRk = 108.0   (72)
    cGRP3 = 1.0   (85)   Price = 22.6   (77)

2> OEA   – O E A INC COM   .APT
    %cELt = 20.0   (62)   10LDv = −16.3   (13)   10LDv = −16.3   (13)
    %cE-2 = 172.7   (95)   3LDv = 30.0   (88)   Mc8wC = 46.0   (91)
    c$-3   = 1.8   (80)   5yPEG = 26.1   (82)   3-Wk   = 103.2   (71)
    c$-6   = 1.8   (75)   10$Gr = 31.9   (97)   GrpRk = 106.2   (62)
    cGRP3 = 0.0   (78)   Price = 39.6   (91)

3> RADIF   – RADA ELECTRONICS INDS LTD COM   .EDE
    %cELt = 23.3   (65)   10LDv = −36.3   (3)   10LDv = −36.3   (3)
    %cE-2 = 4100.0   (99)   3LDv = 26.4   (86)   Mc8wC = 12.0   (75)
    c$-3   = 14.4   (96)   5yPEG = 40.0   (96)   3-Wk   = 121.6   (94)
    c$-6   = 8.9   (90)   10$Gr = 5.8   (45)   GrpRk = 105.2   (57)
    cGRP3 = −4.3   (15)   Price = 3.9   (10)

4> SPAR   – SPARTAN MOTORS INC COM   .APT
    %cELt = 66.6   (85)   10LDv = −66.4   (0)   10LDv = −66.4   (0)
    %cE-2 = −78.3   (4)   3LDv = −3.1   (18)   Mc8wC = 1.0   (52)
    c$-3   = 3.3   (85)   5yPEG = 19.0   (62)   3-Wk   = 105.1   (77)
    c$-6   = 1.4   (73)   10$Gr = 34.6   (98)   GrpRk = 106.2   (62)
    cGRP3 = 0.0   (78)   Price = 7.8   (21)

Exhibit 5.2   (continued)

5> NOVL   – NOVELL INC COM

				.DSO		
%cELt = –22.8	(24)	10LDv = –62.1	(0)	10LDv = –62.1	(0)	
%cE-2 = 166.6	(94)	3LDv = –0.5	(26)	Mc8wC = 41.0	(90)	
c$-3 = 4.1	(87)	5yPEG = 17.6	(57)	3-Wk = 109.9	(85)	
c$-6 = 5.3	(85)	10$Gr = 34.6	(98)	GrpRk = 107.1	(68)	
cGRP3 = –2.9	(26)	Price = 14.4	(57)			

6> HH   – HOOPER HOLMES INC COM

				.HHC		
%cELt = 100.0	(91)	10LDv = –17.5	(12)	10LDv = –17.5	(12)	
%cE-2 = 100.0	(91)	3LDv = 44.8	(92)	Mc8wC = 26.0	(85)	
c$-3 = 9.1	(93)	5yPEG = 15.8	(50)	3-Wk = 125.9	(95)	
c$-6 = 11.0	(92)	10$Gr = 9.9	(64)	GrpRk = 105.2	(57)	
cGRP3 = –7.0	(5)	Price = 10.6	(38)			

7> MAXE   – MAX & ERMAS RSTRS INC COM

				.FRS		
%cELt = –28.6	(21)	10LDv = –26.2	(7)	10LDv = –26.2	(7)	
%cE-2 = –8.4	(29)	3LDv = –0.2	(28)	Mc8wC = 22.0	(83)	
c$-3 = 6.8	(91)	5yPEG = 20.0	(68)	3-Wk = 117.9	(92)	
c$-6 = 7.6	(89)	10$Gr = 21.8	(92)	GrpRk = 113.3	(91)	
cGRP3 = –0.9	(55)	Price = 7.4	(19)			

8> QNTM   – QUANTUM CORP COM

				.DPE		
%cELt = 42.7	(77)	10LDv = –10.8	(17)	10LDv = –10.8	(17)	
%cE-2 = –62.2	(7)	3LDv = 3.8	(51)	Mc8wC = 72.0	(94)	
c$-3 = 4.3	(87)	5yPEG = 16.4	(52)	3-Wk = 117.9	(92)	
c$-6 = 0.3	(67)	10$Gr = 23.1	(93)	GrpRk – 114.9	(93)	
cGRP3 = 0.1	(79)	Price = 22.6	(77)			

9> CMFB   – CHEMFAB CORP COM

				.MIU		
%cELt = 41.1	(77)	10LDv = –16.6	(12)	10LDv = –16.6	(12)	
%cE-2 = 46.6	(78)	3LDv = –3.6	(17)	Mc8wC = 4.0	(62)	
c$-3 = –1.3	(37)	5yPEG = 20.0	(68)	3-Wk = 107.4	(82)	
c$-6 = –5.1	(13)	10$Gr = 14.4	(82)	GrpR k = 110.5	(85)	
cGRP3 = –2.4	(31)	Price = 12.6	(49)			

10> ECILF   – E C I TELECOM LTD COM

				.TES		
%cELt = 15.3	(57)	10LDv = –53.7	(1)	10LDv = –53.7	(1)	
%cE-2 = 16.0	(57)	3LDv = 32.9	(89)	Mc8wC = 17.0	(80)	
c$-3 = –0.1	(67)	5yPEG = 21.8	(72)	3-Wk = 116.7	(92)	
c$-6 = –2.6	(25)	10$Gr = 70.0	(99)	GrpRk = 108.2	(74)	
cGRP3 = 0.0	(78)	Price = 25.3	(80)			

11> DNAP   – D N A PLANT TECH CORP COM

				.MLR		
%cELt = 9.6	(50)	10LDv = –63.5	(0)	10LDv = –63.5	(0)	
%cE-2 = 16.0	(57)	3LDv = –10.8	(9)	Mc8wC = 4.0	(62)	
c$-3 = 7.9	(92)	5yPEG = 50.0	(99)	3-Wk = 115.3	(91)	
c$-6 = 4.0	(82)	10$Gr = –15.2	(3)	GrpRk = 109.0	(76)	
cGRP3 = 2.3	(91)	Price = 0.8	(1)			

12> NWL   – NEWELL CO COM

				.HSW		
%cELt = –8.7	(32)	10LDv = –22.5	(9)	10LDv = –22.5	(9)	
%cE-2 = 7.6	(48)	3LDv = 1.6	(40)	Mc8wC = 12.0	(75)	
c$-3 = 3.0	(84)	5yPEG = 14.1	(40)	3-Wk = 107.6	(82)	
c$-6 = 1.8	(75)	10$Gr = 24.3	(94)	GrpRk = 104.0	(52)	
cGRP3 = 1.0	(85)	Price = 28.3	(84)			

(continued)

Exhibit 5.2   (continued)

13> ELT	– ELSCINT LTD ORD SHS NEW			.SPE	
%cELt = 100.0	(91)	10LDv = –28.5	(6)	10LDv = –28.5	(6)
%cE-2 = 25.0	(66)	3LDv = 61.1	(95)	Mc8wC = 32.0	(87)
c$-3 = 0.6	(73)	5yPEG = 15.0	(48)	3-Wk = 110.1	(86)
c$-6 = 2.9	(79)	10$Gr = 9.8	(63)	GrpRk = 110.0	(82)
cGRP3 = –2.8	(29)	Price = 15.0	(60)		

14> IV	– MARK IV INDUSTRIES INC COM			.APT	
%cELt = 10.0	(51)	10LDv = –10.6	(17)	10LDv = –10.6	(17)
%cE-2 = 12.5	(53)	3LDv = 4.6	(54)	Mc8wC = 6.0	(65)
c$-3 = –0.2	(65)	5yPEG = 16.0	(51)	3-Wk = 101.2	(61)
c$-6 = –1.7	(36)	10$Gr = 22.9	(93)	GrpRk = 106.2	(62)
cGRP3 = 0.0	(78)	Price = 21.0	(75)		

15> VLO	– VALERO ENERGY CORP COM			.ORF	
%cELt = 1850.0	(99)	10LDv = –11.4	(17)	10LDv = –11.4	(17)
%cE-2 = 1050.0	(99)	3LDv = 22.0	(84)	Mc8wC = 38.0	(89)
c$-3 = –3.1	(16)	5yPEG = 17.7	(58)	3-Wk = 106.3	(80)
c$-6 = –0.4	(61)	10$Gr = 13.7	(80)	GrpRk = 111.8	(89)
cGRP3 = 2.0	(89)	Price = 27.3	(83)		

16> WMT	– WAL MART STORES INC COM			.RDI	
%cELt = –8.9	(32)	10LDv = –37.2	(3)	10LDv = –37.2	(3)
%cE-2 = 3.8	(43)	3LDv = 3.1	(47)	Mc8wC = 23.0	(83)
c$-3 = 3.3	(85)	5yPEG = 13.9	(39)	3-Wk = 103.8	(73)
c$-6 = 1.5	(73)	10$Gr = 19.5	(90)	GrpRk = 108.2	(74)
cGRP3 = 2.7	(94)	Price = 23.5	(78)		

17> RPOW	– R P M INC COM			.COA	
%cELt = 10.0	(51)	10LDv = –13.5	(15)	10LDv = –13.5	(15)
%cE-2 = –4.8	(32)	3LDv = –3.1	(18)	Mc8wC = 13.0	(76)
c$-3 = 2.5	(82)	5yPEG = 11.8	(27)	3-Wk = 104.1	(74)
c$-6 = 3.5	(81)	10$Gr = 11.3	(71)	GrpRk = 108.7	(75)
cGRP3 = 2.3	(91)	Price = 15.6	(62)		

18> MYE	– MYERS INDUSTRIES INC COM			.APT	
%cELt = 34.7	(73)	10LDv = –12.1	(16)	10LDv = –12.1	(16)
%cE-2 = –15.7	(25)	3LDv = 31.5	(88)	Mc8wC = 33.0	(88)
c$-3 = 7.7	(92)	5yPEG = 12.5	(32)	3-Wk = 120.7	(94)
c$-6 = 6.3	(87)	10$Gr = 22.0	(92)	GrpRk = 106.2	(62)
cGRP3 = 0.0	(78)	Price = 19.6	(72)		

19> HONI	– HON INDUSTRIES INC COM			.OFU	
%cELt = 34.1	(73)	10LDv = –16.5	(12)	10LDv = –16.5	(12)
%cE-2 = –51.8	(10)	3LDv = 11.6	(73)	Mc8wC = 102.0	(96)
c$-3 = 13.6	(96)	5yPEG = 12.5	(32)	3-Wk = 115.3	(91)
c$-6 = 20.3	(97)	10$Gr = 14.7	(82)	GrpRk = 108.9	(75)
cGRP3 = 11.3	(99)	Price = 28.3	(84)		

20> SCOR	– SYNCOR INTL CORP DEL COM			.DDW	
%cELt = 60.0	(84)	10LDv = –36.7	(3)	10LDv = –36.7	(3)
%cE-2 = 33.4	(72)	3LDv = 61.1	(95)	Mc8wC = 48.0	(91)
c$-3 = 4.4	(87)	5yPEG = 11.5	(25)	3-Wk = 113.1	(89)
c$-6 = 13.0	(94)	10$Gr = 9.7	(63)	GrpRk = 104.8	(54)
cGRP3 = –2.7	(30)	Price = 9.8	(31)		

Exhibit 5.2   (continued)

21> KNAP   – KNAPE & VOGT MFG CO COM   .HFU

%cELt = 0.0	(41)	10LDv = −20.9	(10)	10LDv = −20.9	(10)
%cE-2 = −28.0	(19)	3LDv = −11.3	(9)	Mc8wC = 12.0	(75)
c$-3 = 4.3	(87)	5yPEG = 15.0	(48)	3-Wk = 104.5	(75)
c$-6 = 2.7	(78)	10$Gr = 7.0	(51)	GrpRk = 103.9	(51)
cGRP3 = 0.5	(81)	Price = 14.1	(56)		

22> KWP   – KING WORLD PRODS INC COM   .FDI

%cELt = 16.2	(58)	10LDv = −11.5	(16)	10LDv = −11.5	(16)
%cE-2 = 56.0	(82)	3LDv = 7.2	(64)	Mc8wC = 2.0	(54)
c$-3 = −2.4	(22)	5yPEG = 16.3	(52)	3-Wk = 103.6	(72)
c$-6 = −0.5	(60)	10$Gr = 15.0	(83)	GrpRk = 106.6	(64)
cGRP3 = −1.3	(41)	Price = 43.0	(92)		

23> HOC   – HOLLY CORP COM   .ORF

%cELt = 41.6	(77)	10LDv = −25.8	(7)	10LDv = −25.8	(7)
%cE-2 = −16.0	(25)	3LDv = 20.1	(82)	Mc8wC = 42.0	(90)
c$-3 = 0.6	(73)	5yPEG = 12.5	(32)	3-Wk = 104.3	(75)
c$-6 = 3.0	(79)	10$Gr = 12.6	(76)	GrpRk = 111.8	(89)
cGRP3 = 2.0	(89)	Price = 27.0	(82)		

24> PSCX   – P S C INC COM   .EIC

%cELt = −81.9	(4)	10LDv = −19.1	(11)	10LDv = −19.1	(11)
%cE-2 = 60.8	(83)	3LDv = −19.9	(4)	Mc8wC = 36.0	(89)
c$-3 = −1.9	(28)	5yPEG = 24.3	(76)	3-Wk = 113.1	(89)
c$-6 = 4.1	(82)	10$Gr = 16.6	(86)	GrpRk = 108.4	(75)
cGRP3 = −1.2	(43)	Price = 9.8	(31)		

25> TAC   – TANDYCRAFTS INC COM   .RSP

%cELt = 10.8	(52)	10LDv = −43.6	(2)	10LDv = −43.6	(2)
%cE-2 = −126.3	(0)	3LDv = 5.9	(59)	Mc8wC = 14.0	(77)
c$-3 = 5.8	(90)	5yPEG = 15.2	(49)	3-Wk = 110.3	(86)
c$-6 = 6.2	(87)	10$Gr = 14.3	(81)	GrpRk = 110.2	(84)
cGRP3 = −1.9	(37)	Price = 6.6	(17)		

This report is based on mathematical calculations and, as such, no investment decision should be based solely on its conclusions.

Source: ProSearch 5.0, courtesy of Telescan, Inc.

bought them all—would most likely outperform the market over a reasonable length of time. We will put this to the test in the next chapter.

SEARCH 2: PULLING RANK

Our next search is one of the simplest searches to create. We will use a special group of indicators called *ranking indicators* to find top-ranked stocks in various categories.[3] These composite indicators, which were developed by experts, are based on heavily back-tested criteria. Essentially, they are composites of various criteria that represent some of the basic principles of investing.

The *fundamental rank indicator,* for example, is composed of low debt, high cash flow, and other items that indicate a very strong balance sheet. (This is one that probably would appeal to followers of Benjamin Graham or Warren Buffett.) Other ranking indicators represent momentum or value or technical strength.

One of the advantages of using ranking indicators is that you don't have to have a great deal of sophisticated financial knowledge.

The Basic Ranking Search

We constructed this ranking search in the summer of 1996, after the market had dropped precipitously from its late spring highs; in the case of Nasdaq, that drop was as much as 20 percent. This was a frightening period for many investors. After a pullback of this magnitude, one would look for stocks with exceptional value. The P/E ratio of such stocks would probably be very reasonable compared with their prospects, their price-to-book ratio should also be reasonable, and they sould be selling at a favorable position within their long-term trading channels. Moreover, we would like them to be relatively strong technically. (Consider that stocks that remained technically strong after a major market meltdown must surely be in favor with the investment community.)

Our basic search, then, will look for stocks that have significant value and good technical strength.

- To find the very best stocks from a value standpoint, we will use the *long-term value rank indicator* and request the highest scores.

- To find stocks that are still strong technically, we will use two *technical rank indicators,* one for short term and one for long term, and ask for the highest scores.

- We will give the most weight (100 percent) to the value indicator, because we insist on value at this point. We will give lesser

---

[3] Some of the ranking indicators are available only in the latest version of ProSearch 5.0, although many are in the version found on the enclosed diskette.

weights to the technical indicators, favoring the short term (80 percent) over the long term (20 percent).

Eliminating the Stragglers

The indicators just mentioned would accomplish our basic objective, which is finding stocks with good value and technical strength, but we want to eliminate some stocks right off the top.

- We don't want stocks in industry groups that are out of favor with institutional investors. To this end, we will use the *group rank indicator* and eliminate any stock below the 60th percentile.[4]

- We want our stocks to have had reasonable trading volume recently. As we pointed out earlier, stocks that are strong technically on good volume are better than those that are strong technically on low volume. Plus, we generally avoid stocks that are thinly traded. So we will use the *volume rank indicator* to eliminate the bottom half of all companies from a volume viewpoint. This indicator, by the way, combines the average daily trading volume with a comparison of recent volume to the 30-day average volume and to longer-term volume. Therefore, our stocks should reflect a reasonable volume level with the likelihood that volume is increasing.

- To find stocks that are performing well from an earnings, price, and group viewpoint, we will use the *ERG indicator*, which is a combination of earnings strength, price behavior, and industry group strength. We will eliminate stocks that are not in the top half of all stocks from an ERG viewpoint.

- Finally, because we rarely purchase stocks with a price below $5, we will use the *stock price indicator* to eliminate stocks below $5 in price.

---

[4] In ProSearch, use the rank search mode and enter minimum and maximum values.

Listing Information for the Final Decision

As we do in all searches, we will add a number of criteria that will simply retrieve information we can use to make our final decision. These will include:

- Analyst rank
- Fundamental rank
- Long-term growth rank
- Insider rank
- EPS rank
- Company growth ratio

Search Results: Top Ranked Stocks

Our ranking search request (Exhibit 5.3) now includes 13 indicators. Except for one performance indicator (the company growth ratio), we have used only composite rank indicators. Three are used to score and rank the stocks; four are used to eliminate stocks and narrow the search universe; and six used to retrieve information for the final decision.

The results of the ranking search are shown in Exhibit 5.4. A brief review would lead us to take a closer look at Sothebys, the number 1 stock on the list. It has higher percentile ranks in most of the important categories and it is cumulatively ranked first. Greentree Financial (No. 10) is also attractive, as is C COR Electronics (No. 19) and Countrywide Credit (No. 20). All of these stocks have an impressive growth ratio, which is one of our favorite indicators.

Keep in mind that all 25 stocks are good, as defined by our search request. They are the top one-quarter of one percent of all available stocks, and the number-1 stock is only marginally better than the number-25 stock. There are, however, ways to find the best of the best. One way is to look at the long-term and short-term price patterns. For example, the long-term chart for Countrywide Credit (Exhibit 5.5) shows excellent growth over the past 25 years. Furthermore, the stock is below its LSQ line and could increase nearly 50 percent before it reaches the top of the channel. The short-term chart (Exhibit 5.6) shows a trading pattern between $20 and $25, with the stock currently at $23. This leaves a little room for the short-term trader, but if the stock can break out of this trading range, there is an excellent opportunity for growth.

Exhibit 5.3   Search request 2: Ranking stocks.

Indicators (Abbreviation on Report)	Action: Score and Rank Stocks Weight
Long-term value rank (ValRk)*	Rank stocks by highest scores/100%
Short-term technical rank (STeRk)	Rank stocks by highest scores/80%
Long-term technical rank (LTeRk)	Rank stocks by highest scores/20%

Indicators	Action: Narrow the Universe
Group rank (GrpRk)	Eliminate stocks below 60 percentile
Volume rank (VolRk)	Eliminate stocks below 50 percentile
ERG rank (ERG)	Eliminate stocks below 60 percentile
Stock price (Price)	Eliminate stocks below $5

Indicators	Action: List Information
Analyst rank (AnaRk)	List only
Fundamental rank (FunRk)	List only
Long-term growth rank (LGrRk)	List only
Insider rank (InsRk)	List only
EPS rank (EPSRk)	List only
Company growth ratio (GrRat)	List only

Note: The abbreviation shown in parentheses after the indicator name identifies the indicator on the search report.

In actual trading, we would put this list of stocks through the two-stage evaluation described in Chapters 7 and 8. There might be some that are ripe for purchase in the wake of the mid-July market correction, and there might not. If there aren't, the investing process itself may be telling us to stay out of the market at this time.

SEARCH 3: STOCKS ON THE FAST TRACK

Now we're going to wipe the slate clean and pretend we're a whole different breed of investor. Let's imagine that we're no longer excited about insider buying or rising P/Es; nor are we overly concerned about value.

Exhibit 5.4   Results of search 2: The top 25 stocks on August 5, 1996, with highest combined ranking technical and fundamental values.

Criteria	Criteria Values	
LONG TERM VALUE RANK	High 100%	
SHORT TERM TECHNICAL RANK	High 80%	
LONG TERM TECHNICAL RANK	High 20%	
GROUP RANK	60.0–99.0	r
VOLUME RANK	50.0–99.0	r
ERG	50.0–99.0	r
STOCK PRICE	5.0–999998.0	a
ANALYST RANK	List Only	
FUNDAMENTAL RANK	List Only	
LONG TERM GROWTH RANK	List Only	
INSIDER RANK	List Only	
EPS RANK	List Only	
COMPANY GROWTH RATIO	List Only	

Prosearch Top Stock Report
08/05/96
Optionable Stocks

```
1> BID      – SOTHEBYS HOLDINGS INC CL A                    .SER
      ValRk  = 67.0    (87)   STeRk = 83.5   (97)    LTeRk  = 78.0   (94)
      GrpRk = 105.2    (78)   VolRk = 80.5   (86)    ERG    = 70.1   (75)
      Price  = 14.6    (60)   AnaRk = 41.0   (20)    FunRk  = 64.0   (95)
      LGrRk = 64.5     (84)   InsRk  = 70.0  (23)    EPSRk  = 65.0   (58)
      GrRat = 1.2      (55)
2> SKY      – SKYLINE CORP COM                              .MOB
      ValRk  = 73.0    (94)   STeRk = 70.0   (85)    LTeRk  = 62.0   (72)
      GrpRk = 105.4    (87)   VolRk = 68.5   (67)    ERG    = 89.6   (97)
      Price  = 25.3    (83)   AnaRk = 51.5   (36)    FunRk  = 68.0   (97)
      LGrRk = 54.5     (70)   InsRk  = 88.0  (86)    EPSRk  = 94.0   (90)
      GrRat = N/A      (  )
3> RIGS     – RIGGS NATIONAL CORP WASH COM                  .BAN
      ValRk  = 60.5    (78)   STeRk = 93.0   (99)    LTeRk  = 90.5   (98)
      GrpRk = 105.3    (83)   VolRk = 91.5   (97)    ERG    = 89.8   (97)
      Price  = 14.1    (58)   AnaRk = 38.5   (17)    FunRk  = N/A    (  )
      LGrRk = N/A      (  )   InsRk  = 48.5  (13)    EPSRk  = 98.0   (98)
      GrRat = N/A      (  )
4> BK       – BANK OF NEW YORK INC COM                      .BAN
      ValRk  = 56.0    (71)   STeRk = 91.5   (99)    LTeRk  = 88.0   (98)
      GrpRk = 105.3    (83)   VolRk = 74.5   (78)    ERG    = 83.3   (91)
      Price  = 54.1    (95)   AnaRk = 49.0   (32)    FunRk  = N/A    (  )
      LGrRk = 58.5     (77)   InsRk  = 4.0   ( 2)    EPSRk  = 77.0   (73)
      GrRat = 1.1      (49)
```

Exhibit 5.4   (continued)

```
 5> FDLNB   – FOOD LION INC CL B                              .RFS
      ValRk  = 64.0    (84)     STeRk = 62.0    (73)     LTeRk  = 82.0    (96)
      GrpRk  = 106.9   (94)     VolRk = 60.5    (53)     ERG    = 85.1    (93)
      Price  = 8.4     (24)     AnaRk = N/A     ( )      FunRk  = 47.5    (13)
      LGrRk  = 39.5    (41)     InsRk = 88.0    (86)     EPSRk  = 71.0    (66)
      GrRat  = 0.8     (26)
 6> GWF     – GREAT WESTERN FNCL CORP COM                     .BSL
      ValRk  = 55.5    (70)     STeRk = 82.0    (96)     LTeRk  = 84.0    (97)
      GrpRk  = 105.6   (89)     VolRk = 89.0    (95)     ERG    = 89.1    (96)
      Price  = 24.3    (81)     AnaRk = 35.5    (13)     FunRk  = N/A     ( )
      LGrRk  = 50.5    (62)     InsRk = 31.5    ( 8)     EPSRk  = 97.0    (95)
      GrRat  = 1.1     (49)
 7> CYN     – CITY NATIONAL CORP COM                          .BAN
      ValRk  = 55.5    (70)     STeRk = 74.0    (90)     LTeRk  = 77.5    (93)
      GrpRk  = 105.3   (83)     VolRk = 66.5    (63)     ERG    = 87.0    (95)
      Price  = 16.4    (66)     AnaRk = 70.0    (73)     FunRk  = N/A     ( )
      LGrRk  = N/A     ( )      InsRk = 70.0    (23)     EPSRk  = 94.0    (90)
      GrRat  = 1.5     (71)
 8> LTR     – LOEWS CORP COM                                  .IMU
      ValRk  = 55.0    (69)     STeRk = 74.5    (91)     LTeRk  = 83.5    (96)
      GrpRk  = 102.1   (62)     VolRk = 78.0    (83)     ERG    = 81.3    (89)
      Price  = 81.4    (97)     AnaRk = 61.5    (52)     FunRk  = N/A     ( )
      LGrRk  = 64.5    (84)     InsRk = 89.5    (89)     EPSRk  = 97.0    (96)
      GrRat  = 1.4     (66)
 9> PWJ     – PAINE WEBBER GROUP INC COM                      .SEC
      ValRk  = 54.5    (68)     STeRk = 78.5    (94)     LTeRk  = 66.0    (81)
      GrpRk  = 106.3   (92)     VolRk = 87.5    (93)     ERG    = 80.3    (88)
      Price  = 21.5    (77)     AnaRk = 62.0    (54)     FunRk  = N/A     ( )
      LGrRk  = 14.0    ( 1)     InsRk = 33.5    ( 8)     EPSRk  = 85.0    (78)
      GrRat  = 1.4     (66)
10> GNT     – GREEN TREE FNCL CORP DE COM                     .FCL
      ValRk  = 53.5    (66)     STeRk = 85.0    (98)     LTeRk  = 89.5    (98)
      GrpRk  = 107.6   (95)     VolRk = 73.0    (75)     ERG    = 91.5    (98)
      Price  = 35.5    (90)     AnaRk = 83.0    (98)     FunRk  = N/A     ( )
      LGrRk  = 74.5    (94)     InsRk = 88.0    (86)     EPSRk  = 93.0    (88)
      GrRat  = 1.5     (71)
11> COFI    – CHARTER ONE FINANCIAL INC COM                   .BSB
      ValRk  = 53.5    (66)     STeRk = 83.0    (97)     LTeRk  = 81.5    (95)
      GrpRk  = 106.1   (92)     VolRk = 76.5    (81)     ERG    = 86.1    (94)
      Price  = 37.1    (91)     AnaRk = 78.5    (92)     FunRk  = N/A     ( )
      LGrRk  = 35.5    (33)     InsRk = 31.5    ( 8)     EPSRk  = 79.0    (75)
      GrRat  = 1.2     (55)
12> ACF     – AMERICREDIT CORP COM                            .FCL
      ValRk  = 56.5    (72)     STeRk = 76.0    (92)     LTeRk  = 54.5    (55)
      GrpRk  = 107.6   (95)     VolRk = 68.0    (66)     ERG    = 92.5    (98)
      Price  = 14.4    (59)     AnaRk = 75.0    (82)     FunRk  = N/A     ( )
      LGrRk  = 73.5    (93)     InsRk = 55.5    (15)     EPSRk  = 98.0    (98)
      GrRat  = 2.2     (88)
```

(continued)

Exhibit 5.4   (continued)

13> RN	– R J R NABISCO HLDGS CORP COM			.TCI		
ValRk = 56.5	(72)	STeRk = 75.5	(92)	LTeRk = 54.0	(54)
GrpRk = 111.1	(98)	VolRk = 61.5	(55)	ERG = 67.1	(70)
Price = 31.4	(88)	AnaRk = 54.0	(40)	FunRk = 40.5	(6)
LGrRk = 19.5	(5)	InsRk = 33.5	(8)	EPSRk = 30.0	(23)
GrRat = 1.1	(49)				

14> BNL	– BENEFICIAL CORP COM			.FCL		
ValRk = 54.5	(68)	STeRk = 79.0	(94)	LTeRk = 58.5	(64)
GrpRk = 107.6	(95)	VolRk = 60.0	(52)	ERG = 85.0	(93)
Price = 55.4	(95)	AnaRk = 48.5	(30)	FunRk = 47.0	(13)
LGrRk = 30.0	(22)	InsRk = 57.5	(16)	EPSRk = 92.0	(85)
GrRat = 1.4	(66)				

15> BBC	– BERGEN BRUNSWIG CORP CL A CL			.DDW		
ValRk = 65.0	(85)	STeRk = 63.0	(74)	LTeRk = 49.5	(46)
GrpRk = 103.2	(66)	VolRk = 67.5	(65)	ERG = 73.6	(80)
Price = 26.6	(84)	AnaRk = 63.0	(56)	FunRk = 50.5	(17)
LGrRk = 49.0	(59)	InsRk = 91.5	(93)	EPSRk = 73.0	(68)
GrRat = 1.0	(41)				

16> PTEC	– PHOENIX TECHNOLOGIES LTD COM			.DSO		
ValRk = 54.0	(67)	STeRk = 79.5	(95)	LTeRk = 57.5	(62)
GrpRk = 105.4	(87)	VolRk = 61.5	(55)	ERG = 84.1	(92)
Price = 16.9	(68)	AnaRk = 80.0	(95)	FunRk = N/A	( )
LGrRk = 55.5	(72)	InsRk = 32.5	(8)	EPSRk = 77.0	(73)
GrRat = 1.2	(55)				

17> PIR	– PIER 1 IMPORTS INC COM			.RSP		
ValRk = 52.0	(62)	STeRk = 71.0	(87)	LTeRk = 77.5	(93)
GrpRk = 104.3	(74)	VolRk = 75.0	(78)	ERG = 71.0	(76)
Price = 15.8	(64)	AnaRk = 50.5	(34)	FunRk = 43.0	(7)
LGrRk = 32.0	(26)	InsRk = 29.5	(7)	EPSRk = 46.0	(38)
GrRat = 1.1	(49)				

18> RAL	– RALSTON-RALSTN PURINA GRP COM			.FOO		
ValRk = 50.5	(60)	STeRk = 89.5	(99)	LTeRk = 85.0	(97)
GrpRk = 102.8	(65)	VolRk = 71.0	(72)	ERG = 72.3	(78)
Price = 65.0	(96)	AnaRk = 61.5	(52)	FunRk = 40.0	(5)
LGrRk = 29.5	(21)	InsRk = 31.5	(8)	EPSRk = 67.0	(61)
GrRat = 0.8	(26)				

19> CCBL	– C COR ELECTRONICS INC COM			.BEQ		
ValRk = 67.0	(87)	STeRk = 79.5	(95)	LTeRk = 26.5	(15)
GrpRk = 105.9	(89)	VolRk = 68.5	(67)	ERG = 59.1	(58)
Price = 18.0	(71)	AnaRk = 55.0	(41)	FunRk = 62.0	(93)
LGrRk = 80.0	(97)	InsRk = 53.0	(14)	EPSRk = 74.0	(69)
GrRat = 2.5	(92)				

20> CCR	– COUNTRYWIDE CREDIT INDS COM			.FMB		
ValRk = 55.5	(70)	STeRk = 60.5	(70)	LTeRk = 64.5	(78)
GrpRk = 110.2	(97)	VolRk = 80.5	(86)	ERG = 88.5	(96)
Price = 23.1	(80)	AnaRk = 51.0	(35)	FunRk = N/A	( )
LGrRk = 50.5	(62)	InsRk = 31.0	(7)	EPSRk = 93.0	(88)
GrRat = 1.6	(75)				

Exhibit 5.4   (continued)

21> RUS   – RUSS BERRIE & CO INC COM   .RME
    ValRk = 76.0   (96)   STeRk = 56.0   (61)   LTeRk = 51.0   (49)
    GrpRk = 106.6   (93)   VolRk = 68.5   (67)   ERG   = 82.8   (91)
    Price = 16.3   (66)   AnaRk = 64.5   (60)   FunRk = N/A   ( )
    LGrRk = 42.5   (47)   InsRk = 88.0   (86)   EPSRk = 76.0   (72)
    GrRat = 1.2   (55)

22> BBI   – BARNETT BANKS INC COM   .BAN
    ValRk = 49.5   (58)   STeRk = 83.0   (97)   LTeRk = 70.5   (88)
    GrpRk = 105.3   (83)   VolRk = 84.0   (90)   ERG   = 76.5   (84)
    Price = 62.9   (96)   AnaRk = 43.5   (23)   FunRk = N/A   ( )
    LGrRk = 44.5   (51)   InsRk = 89.5   (89)   EPSRk = 76.0   (71)
    GrRat = 1.0   (41)

23> AB   – ALEX BROWN INC COM   .SEC
    ValRk = 59.5   (76)   STeRk = 69.0   (84)   LTeRk = 35.5   (26)
    GrpRk = 106.3   (92)   VolRk = 78.5   (83)   ERG   = 70.6   (75)
    Price = 49.6   (94)   AnaRk = 76.5   (86)   FunRk = N/A   ( )
    LGrRk = 45.0   (52)   InsRk = 34.5   (9)   EPSRk = 97.0   (95)
    GrRat = 1.4   (66)

24> PPD   – PRE PAID LEGAL SVCS INC COM   .SER
    ValRk = 58.0   (74)   STeRk = 68.0   (82)   LTeRk = 39.5   (31)
    GrpRk = 105.2   (78)   VolRk = 75.5   (79)   ERG   = 90.0   (97)
    Price = 13.9   (57)   AnaRk = 78.5   (92)   FunRk = N/A   ( )
    LGrRk = N/A   ( )   InsRk = 27.5   (6)   EPSRk = 97.0   (95)
    GrRat = N/A   ( )

25> PLX   – PLAINS RESOURCES INC COM   .OCP
    ValRk = 49.0   (56)   STeRk = 83.5   (97)   LTeRk = 90.5   (98)
    GrpRk = 104.1   (72)   VolRk = 88.5   (94)   ERG   = 77.1   (85)
    Price = 13.5   (55)   AnaRk = 54.0   (40)   FunRk = 42.5   (7)
    LGrRk = N/A   ( )   InsRk = 94.5   (97)   EPSRk = 67.0   (61)
    GrRat = 0.8   (26)

This report is based on mathematical calculations and, as such, no investment decision should be based solely on its conclusions.

Source: ProSearch 5.0, courtesy of Telescan, Inc.

Exhibit 5.5   On a maximum-term graph, Countrywide Credit is well below its LSQ line.

Open: 23.25   Hi: 23.50   Lo: 23.00   Last: 23.00   Change: -.25   Vol: 1768

Instead, for the next few pages, we will become advocates of momentum investing, one of today's more popular investing concepts.

Momentum investors are more technically oriented than value investors. They are concerned primarily with a stock's price pattern, rather than its earnings, P/E ratios, or insider trading. Specifically, they look for price patterns that indicate upward momentum. If they find a fast-moving stock, they will hop on and ride it until it shows signs of slowing or until they see one moving faster.

In a momentum search, we're looking for stocks that have the greatest possible price momentum, the greatest possible industry group momentum, and the greatest possible earnings momentum. We will create a momentum search just as we created the previous searches. We will use certain indicators to eliminate stocks, other indicators to score and rank the remaining stocks, and still others to list relevant information.

Exhibit 5.6   Countrywide Credit has been trading between $20 and $25 over the past year.

8/5/96   COUNTRYWIDE CREDIT INDS COM (CCR)   23.00

Open: 23.25   Hi: 23.50   Lo: 23.00   Last: 23.00   Change: -.25   Vol: 1768

No Tortoises Allowed

In a search for high momentum stocks, the first thing we'll do is eliminate all the dullards: those steadily plodding stocks that may be acceptable to long-term investors but are undesirable to momentum investors. With our momentum hats on, we want the quick burst of energy from fast-moving stocks. We want momentum and we want it now. And frequently, we must pay more for high-momentum stocks than value investors would find palatable.

To find such stocks, ProSearch offers several indicators that rank stocks according to their momentum in price, earnings, and industry group. We will use three to separate the hares from the tortoises—*price rank, EPS rank,* and *group rank*—and we'll tell the computer to eliminate all stocks ranked below 80 percent in each area. This will give us a search universe limited to high momentum stocks: whose prices are increasing faster than 80 percent of all stocks, whose earnings are growing faster than 80 percent of all stocks, and whose industry groups are moving faster than 80 percent of all industry groups.

Maximize the Momentum

As a result of the preceding restrictions, every stock found by this search will be in the top 20 percent of all stocks with regard to price, earnings, and industry group momentum. It is possible, however, that a stock could be in the top 20 percent and be moving down rather than up. To make sure a stock's momentum is increasing and not decreasing, we need to coax to the top of the list those stocks with the largest recent increases in price rank, earnings rank, and industry group rank. In effect, we want to maximize the momentum of the stocks at the top of the list.

To accomplish this, we'll use several indicators in the ProSearch toolkit that measure the *change* in price, earnings, and industry group rank and ask for the highest scores.

- To ensure the greatest possible price momentum, we'll use three indicators that measure the *1-week, 3-week, and 6-week change in price rank.*

- To ensure the greatest possible earnings momentum, we'll use three indicators that measure the *change in EPS rank* over the past three quarters (13 weeks, 26 weeks, and 39 weeks).

- To ensure industry group momentum, we'll use the *3-week group rank change indicator.*

Follow the Money

There is one more factor to consider in a momentum search: the direction of money flow in a stock. This can be determined by measuring the volume on up days and down days. If, over a specified period of time, volume is higher on days when the stock price is rising (up days) than on days when the stock price is falling (down days), money is said to be flowing into the stock. This could indicate simply a preponderance of buyers over sellers, or it could mean that institutional investors (who more heavily influence the market) are moving into the stock. Either way, a stock whose volume is higher on up days than on down days is said to be under accumulation, which could be interpreted as a movement of institutional investors into the stock. The reverse signals that the stock is under distribution. If volume is heavier on down days than on up days, money is flowing out of the stock, which could mean that institutions are selling.

Accumulation would obviously enhance a stock's momentum and should drive up the P/E ratio. If we want to follow the money—and we do if we are momentum investors—we will pay attention to this money flow.

ProSearch offers an *accumulation/distribution indicator* for this purpose. This indicator is scored a little differently from the others. Stocks under accumulation are scored from 60 to 99; the higher the score, the more steadily money is flowing into the stock. Stocks under distribution arc scored from 40 to zero; the lower the score, the more steadily money is flowing out of the stock. Scores between 40 and 60 are essentially neutral.

To make sure money is flowing into the stock, we'll use the accumulation/distribution indicator twice: once to eliminate all stocks with scores below 60, and then to rank the remaining stocks by the highest scores.

Info Check

True momentum advocates would dismiss P/E ratios, but our fundamental bias won't let us completely ignore them. We want at least to see the relationship between the current P/E and relative P/E ratios. (Relative P/E tells you where the current P/E is in relation to the stock's history.) So we'll use *P/E ratio* and *relative P/E ratio* as list-only indicators, which will not affect the actual search. We will also list the *stock price,* as we do in cvcry search.

Search Results: Stocks on the Fast Track

Our momentum search request now includes 15 indicators, as shown in Exhibit 5.7. Four are used to eliminate stocks and narrow the universe of the search, eight are for scoring and ranking stocks, and three are for listing information.

The results of the momentum search are shown in Exhlblt 5.8. These are the 15 highest momentum stocks out of 9,000 on the day of the search; the higher they are on the list, the greater the combined momentum of price, earnings, and industry group. The question now is how to select the best of the best.

With high-momentum stocks, we want those that have not yet peaked. That is where a comparison of P/E ratio and relative P/E ratio comes in. A relative P/E of 80 or higher would give us pause. (Recall that relative P/E means the ratio of the stock's current P/E to its all-time P/E range.) We would also take a hard look at the accumulation/distribution ranking; the higher ranking would get our attention.

At first glance, the two best candidates from this search appear to be Aztec Manufacturing (4) and Coachmen Industries (15). Aztec's current P/E of 13 is 29 percent of its all-time high whereas Coachmen's 14 P/E is only 15 percent of its all-time high. Accumulation/distribution scores for both are among the highest on this list. We would be wary of the number-one ranked stock, Wet Seal, because of its high P/E (53.5), although high P/Es are not unusual for momentum stocks.

Exhibit 5.7   Search request 3: Momentum stocks.

Indicators (Abbreviation on Report)	Action: Narrow the Universe
Price rank ($Rank)	Eliminate stocks below 70% ranking
EPS rank (EPSRk)	Eliminate stocks below 70% ranking
Group rank (GrpRk)	Eliminate stocks in industry groups below 70% ranking
Accumulation/distribution (AcDst)	Eliminate stocks below 60% ranking

Indicators	Action: Score and Rank Stocks/Weight
1-Week Price-rank change (c$-1)	Rank stocks by highest scores/100%
3-Week Price-rank change (c$-3)	Rank stocks by highest scores/80%
6-Week Price-rank change (c$-6)	Rank stocks by highest scores/40%
13-Week EPS-rank change (cEA13)	Rank stocks by highest scores/100%
26-Week EPS-rank change (cEA26)	Rank stocks by highest scores/80%
39-Week EPS-rank change (cEA39)	Ranks stocks by highest scores/40%
3-Week Group-rank change (cGRP3)	Rank stocks by highest scores/60%
Accumulation/distribution (AcDst)	Rank stocks by highest scores/20%

Indicators	Action: List Information
P/E ratio (P/E)	List only
Relative P/E ratio (RelPE)	List only
Stock price (Price)	List only

Note: The abbreviation shown in parentheses after the indicator name identifies the indicator on the search report.

Exhibit 5.8   Results of search 3: The top 25 stocks with greatest momentum on May 30, 1996.

Criteria	Criteria Values		
GROUP RANK	80	999998	r
EPS RANK	80	999998	r
PRICE RANK	80	999998	r
GROUP RANK CHG 3-WK	High	60%	
EPS RANK CHG 13-WK	High	100%	
PRICE RANK CHG 1-WK	High	100%	
ACCUMULATION DIST.	High	20%	
EPS RANK CHG 26-WK	High	80%	
PRICE RANK CHG 3-WK	High	80%	
EPS RANK CHG 39-WK	High	40%	
PRICE RANK CHG 6-WK	High	40%	
ACCUMULATION DIST.	60	999998	r
P/E RATIO	List Only		
RELATIVE P/E RATIO	List Only		
STOCK PRICE	List Only		

Prosearch Top Stock Report
All Stocks
5/30/96

```
1> WTSLA  – WET SEAL INC CL A                        .RAP
     GrpRk = 118.9   (95)    EPSRk = 93.0   (87)    $Rank = 191.3   (99)
     cGRP3 – 2.0     (72)    cEA13 = 28.0   (93)    c$-1  = 15.2    (98)
     AcDst = 81.0    (91)    cEA26 = 61.0   (98)    c$-3  = 47.8    (99)
     cEA39 = 48.0    (92)    c$-6  = 43.8   (99)    AcDst = 81.0    (91)
     P/E   = 53.5    (88)    RelPE = 58.0   (70)    Price = 24.6    (79)
2> SBIO    – SYNBIOTICS CORP COM                      .MLR
     GrpRk = 114.6   (92)    EPSRk = 90.0   (82)    $Rank = 135.5   (95)
     cGRP3 = 4.6     (92)    cEA13 = 48.0   (99)    c$-1  = 13.0    (98)
     AcDst = 79.0    (90)    cEA26 = 42.0   (93)    c$-3  = 12.5    (95)
     cEA39 = 7.0     (60)    c$-6  = 42.8   (98)    AcDst = 79.0    (90)
     P/E   = 18.7    (53)    RelPE = N/A    ( )     Price = 4.5     (11)
3> STLY    – STANLEY FURNITURE INC COM                .HFU
     GrpRk = 111.6   (85)    EPSRk = 94.0   (89)    $Rank – 119.7   (88)
     cGRP3 = 7.7     (98)    cEA13 = 17.0   (85)    c$-1  = 3.5     (92)
     AcDst = 92.0    (96)    cEA26 = 54.0   (97)    c$-3  = 3.5     (83)
     cEA39 = 84.0    (99)    c$-6  = 2.9    (79)    AcDst = 92.0    (96)
     P/E   = 12.3    (24)    RelPE = N/A    ( )     Price = 12.1    (45)
4> AZTC    – AZTEC MANUFACTURING CO COM               .MIU
     GrpRk = 111.4   (83)    EPSRk = 89.0   (80)    $Rank = 120.1   (88)
     cGRP3 = 1.5     (67)    cEA13 = 36.0   (96)    c$-1  = 5.3     (95)
     AcDst = 79.0    (90)    cEA26 = 61.0   (98)    c$-3  = 3.1     (82)
     cEA39 = 64.0    (97)    c$-6  = 11.9   (92)    AcDst – 79.0    (90)
     P/E   = 13.3    (30)    RelPE = 29.0   (44)    Price = 6.1     (15)
```

(continued)

Exhibit 5.8 (continued)

5> JOL	– JOULE INC COM			.SER		
GrpRk = 113.4	(89)	EPSRk = 89.0	(80)	$Rank = 133.0	(94)	
cGRP3 = 2.3	(77)	cEA13 = 25.0	(91)	c$-1 = 6.2	(96)	
AcDst = 72.0	(77)	cEA26 = 18.0	(77)	c$-3 = 12.8	(95)	
cEA39 = 53.0	(94)	c$-6 = 16.2	(94)	AcDst = 72.0	(77)	
P/E = 18.9	(53)	RelPE = 29.1	(44)	Price = 6.6	(16)	
6> BSH	– BUSH INDUSTRIES INC CL A			.HFU		
GrpRk = 111.6	(85)	EPSRk = 97.0	(95)	$Rank = 138.4	(95)	
cGRP3 = 7.7	(98)	cEA13 = 6.0	(70)	c$-1 = 4.5	(94)	
AcDst = 78.0	(89)	cEA26 = 45.0	(94)	c$-3 = 8.1	(92)	
cEA39 = 51.0	(93)	c$-6 = 6.3	(87)	AcDst = 78.0	(89)	
P/E = 21.0	(59)	RelPE = 76.8	(83)	Price = 34.8	(88)	
7> NTSC	– NATIONAL TECH SYSTEMS INC COM			.SER		
GrpRk = 113.4	(89)	EPSRk = 95.0	(92)	$Rank = 145.6	(96)	
cGRP3 = 2.3	(77)	cEA13 = 5.0	(68)	c$-1 = 9.8	(97)	
AcDst = 76.0	(85)	cEA26 = 48.0	(95)	c$-3 = 36.7	(99)	
cEA39 = 79.0	(99)	c$-6 = 36.4	(98)	AcDst = 76.0	(85)	
P/E = 27.8	(71)	RelPE = 34.1	(50)	Price = 3.6	(8)	
8> TBUD	– TEAM RENTAL GROUP INC COM			.ARS		
GrpRk = 112.0	(85)	EPSRk = 98.0	(98)	$Rank = 128.5	(93)	
cGRP3 = 2.9	(82)	cEA13 = 9.0	(75)	c$-1 = 1.0	(84)	
AcDst = 71.0	(75)	cEA26 = 50.0	(95)	c$-3 = 15.8	(96)	
cEA39 = 27.0	(80)	c$-6 = 15.6	(94)	AcDst = 71.0	(75)	
P/E = 22.1	(62)	RelPE = N/A	( )	Price = 15.5	(60)	
9> DGTL	– DIGITAL SYSTEMS INTL INC COM			.TES		
GrpRk = 110.8	(81)	EPSRk = 96.0	(93)	$Rank = 136.1	(95)	
cGRP3 = 2.6	(81)	cEA13 = 6.0	(70)	c$-1 = 1.7	(87)	
AcDst = 79.0	(90)	cEA26 = 52.0	(96)	c$-3 = 3.0	(81)	
cEA39 = 69.0	(97)	c$-6 = 6.6	(87)	AcDst = 79.0	(90)	
P/E = 26.1	(69)	RelPE = 35.7	(52)	Price = 23.0	(77)	
10> KEQU	– KEWAUNEE SCIENTIFIC CORP COM			.MIU		
GrpRk = 111.4	(83)	EPSRk = 91.0	(83)	$Rank = 113.2	(82)	
cGRP3 = 1.5	(67)	cEA13 = 14.0	(82)	c$-1 = 0.5	(79)	
AcDst = 97.0	(98)	cEA26 = 40.0	(92)	c$-3 = 7.9	(92)	
cEA39 = 35.0	(86)	c$-6 = 3.9	(82)	AcDst = 97.0	(98)	
P/E = 23.0	(64)	RelPE = N/A	( )	Price = 4.4	(10)	
11> WHT	– WHITEHALL CORP COM			.ASV		
GrpRk = 127.6	(99)	EPSRk = 97.0	(95)	$Rank = 114.1	(83)	
cGRP3 = 14.6	(99)	cEA13 = 6.0	(70)	c$-1 = 3.5	(92)	
AcDst = 81.0	(91)	cEA26 = 26.0	(84)	c$-3 = 3.4	(83)	
cEA39 = 21.0	(75)	c$-6 = 2.7	(78)	AcDst = 81.0	(91)	
P/E = 33.4	(78)	RelPE = 22.1	(36)	Price = 40.8	(91)	
12> LAN	– LANCER CORP TEXAS COM			.BEV		
GrpRk = 113.9	(91)	EPSRk = 97.0	(96)	$Rank = 121.2	(89)	
cGRP3 = 4.1	(89)	cEA13 = 12.0	(79)	c$-1 = 0.8	(82)	
AcDst = 67.0	(68)	cEA26 = 35.0	(90)	c$-3 = 4.4	(86)	
cEA39 = 8.0	(61)	c$-6 = 6.7	(87)	AcDst = 67.0	(68)	
P/E = 20.7	(58)	RelPE = 73.9	(81)	Price = 23.0	(77)	

Exhibit 5.8   (continued)

13> URBN	– URBAN OUTFITTERS INC COM				.RAP		
GrpRk = 118.9	(95)	EPSRk = 90.0	(82)		$Rank = 132.7	(94)
cGRP3 = 2.0	(72)	cEA13 = 24.0	(91)		c$-1 = 0.5	(79)
AcDst = 73.0	(79)	cEA26 = 24.0	(82)		c$-3 = 9.8	(93)
cEA39 = 5.0	(58)	c$-6 = 18.8	(95)		AcDst = 73.0	(79)
P/E = 29.8	(74)	RelPE = N/A	( )		Price = 41.8	(91)
14> YORK	– YORK RESEARCH CORP COM				.MSG		
GrpRk = 119.9	(96)	EPSRk = 97.0	(95)		$Rank = 123.5	(90)
cGRP3 = 1.4	(66)	cEA13 = 5.0	(68)		c$-1 = 5.5	(95)
AcDst = 77.0	(87)	cEA26 = 24.0	(82)		c$-3 = 8.9	(93)
cEA39 = 31.0	(83)	c$-6 = 17.5	(95)		AcDst = 77.0	(87)
P/E = 27.1	(71)	RelPE = 13.5	(24)		Price = 9.5	(27)
15> COA	– COACHMEN INDUSTRIES INC COM				.AMH		
GrpRk = 111.5	(84)	EPSRk = 92.0	(85)		$Rank = 127.7	(92)
cGRP3 = 4.7	(93)	cEA13 = 1.0	(56)		c$-1 = 1.6	(87)
AcDst = 81.0	(91)	cEA26 = 19.0	(78)		c$-3 = 13.3	(95)
cEA39 = 28.0	(81)	c$-6 = 10.6	(91)		AcDst = 81.0	(91)
P/E = 14.4	(36)	RelPE = 15.9	(28)		Price = 35.5	(89)
16> CRLBF	– CORE LABORATORIES N V COM				.OWD		
GrpRk = 119.5	(96)	EPSRk = 95.0	(92)		$Rank = 135.3	(95)
cGRP3 = 1.0	(54)	cEA13 = 2.0	(60)		c$-1 = 4.8	(94)
AcDst = 95.0	(97)	cEA26 = 28.0	(86)		c$-3 = 17.0	(96)
cEA39 = 51.0	(93)	c$-6 = 32.0	(98)		AcDst = 95.0	(97)
P/E = 24.2	(66)	RelPE = N/A	( )		Price = 15.3	(59)
17> RFP	– R F POWER INC COM				.BRA		
GrpRk = 125.5	(98)	EPSRk = 98.0	(98)		$Rank = 144.6	(96)
cGRP3 = 6.8	(97)	cEA13 = 0.0	(51)		c$-1 = 0.6	(80)
AcDst = 76.0	(85)	cEA26 = 22.0	(80)		c$-3 = 14.8	(96)
cEA39 = 28.0	(81)	c$-6 = 31.4	(98)		AcDst = 76.0	(85)
P/E = 45.6	(85)	RelPE = N/A	( )		Price = 7.3	(18)
18> RGIS	– REGIS CORP COM				.RSP		
GrpRk = 113.9	(91)	EPSRk = 89.0	(80)		$Rank = 128.6	(93)
cGRP3 = 4.8	(95)	cEA13 = 10.0	(77)		c$-1 = –0.1	(65)
AcDst = 78.0	(89)	cEA26 = 20.0	(79)		c$-3 = 5.3	(88)
cEA39 = 30.0	(82)	c$-6 = 0.7	(67)		AcDst = 78.0	(89)
P/E = 27.2	(71)	RelPE = 48.4	(63)		Price = 41.8	(91)
19> GLS	– SCHULLER CORP COM				.BRW		
GrpRk = 119.1	(95)	EPSRk = 93.0	(88)		$Rank = 125.0	(91)
cGRP3 = 9.1	(98)	cEA13 = 0.0	(51)		c$-1 = 2.0	(89)
AcDst = 75.0	(83)	cEA26 = 17.0	(75)		c$-3 = 7.6	(91)
cEA39 = 22.0	(76)	c$-6 = 16.0	(94)		AcDst = 75.0	(83)
P/E = 11.0	(17)	RelPE = 85.5	(89)		Price = 11.6	(42)
20> KHLR	– KAHLER REALTY CORP COM				.HOT		
GrpRk = 115.4	(92)	EPSRk = 90.0	(81)		$Rank = 123.8	(91)
cGRP3 = 0.4	(35)	cEA13 = 21.0	(88)		c$-1 = 2.6	(90)
AcDst = 86.0	(93)	cEA26 = 26.0	(84)		c$-3 = 2.1	(76)
cEA39 = 36.0	(87)	c$-6 = 5.8	(86)		AcDst = 86.0	(93)
P/E = 20.9	(59)	RelPE = 7.5	(14)		Price = 16.4	(63)

(continued)

Exhibit 5.8   (continued)

21> DLTR   – DOLLAR TREE STORES INC COM   .RDI

GrpRk = 115.5	(93)	EPSRk = 98.0	(97)	$Rank = 139.7	(96)
cGRP3 = 6.6	(97)	cEA13 = 4.0	(65)	c$-1 = 3.5	(92)
AcDst = 68.0	(70)	cEA26 = 2.0	(55)	c$-3 = 15.0	(96)
cEA39 = 5.0	(58)	c$-6 = 13.2	(93)	AcDst = 68.0	(70)
P/E = 51.6	(87)	RelPE = N/A	( )	Price = 40.3	(91)

22> MIR   – MIRAGE RESORTS INC COM   .LCG

GrpRk = 122.8	(97)	EPSRk = 93.0	(87)	$Rank = 119.5	(88)
cGRP3 = 3.2	(86)	cEA13 = 2.0	(60)	c$-1 = 1.7	(87)
AcDst = 65.0	(64)	cEA26 = 30.0	(87)	c$-3 = 3.0	(81)
cEA39 = 14.0	(68)	c$-6 = 0.6	(66)	AcDst = 65.0	(64)
P/E = 28.8	(73)	RelPE = 34.2	(50)	Price = 54.5	(94)

23> THRX   – THERAGENICS CORP COM   .MLR

GrpRk = 114.6	(92)	EPSRk = 98.0	(98)	$Rank = 143.2	(96)
cGRP3 = 4.6	(92)	cEA13 = 1.0	(56)	c$-1 = 5.0	(95)
AcDst = 95.0	(97)	cEA26 = 3.0	(57)	c$-3 = 25.5	(98)
cEA39 = 6.0	(59)	c$-6 = 20.2	(96)	AcDst = 95.0	(97)
P/E = 78.2	(92)	RelPE = N/A	( )	Price = 14.9	(58)

24> REGL   – REGAL CINEMAS INC COM   .FTH

GrpRk = 120.2	(96)	EPSRk = 95.0	(92)	$Rank = 128.5	(93)
cGRP3 = 4.2	(89)	cEA13 = 16.0	(84)	c$-1 = 4.5	(94)
AcDst = 63.0	(60)	cEA26 = 25.0	(83)	c$-3 = 4.5	(86)
cEA39 = 5.0	(58)	c$-6 = –2.2	(20)	AcDst = 63.0	(60)
P/E = 42.5	(84)	RelPE = 84.5	(88)	Price = 45.5	(93)

25> SLOT   – ANCHOR GAMING COM   .LCG

GrpRk = 122.8	(97)	EPSRk = 95.0	(92)	$Rank = 153.9	(97)
cGRP3 = 3.2	(86)	cEA13 = 1.0	(56)	c$-1 = 12.1	(98)
AcDst = 79.0	(90)	cEA26 = 1.0	(53)	c$-3 = 8.6	(92)
cEA39 = 16.0	(70)	c$-6 = 20.4	(96)	AcDst = 79.0	(90)
P/E = 32.6	(77)	RelPE = N/A	( )	Price = 55.5	(95)

This report is based on mathematical calculations and, as such, no investment decision should be based solely on its conclusions.

Source: ProSearch 5.0, courtesy of Telescan, Inc.

We particularly recommend that stocks from a momentum search be evaluated for intrinsic value, because of the relative risk associated with momentum stocks. This perhaps could best be done with the LSQ trading channel, described earlier. Momentum stocks have a tendency to reach or exceed the top of these channels, which implies extra risk. Viewing stocks through the LSQ lens will help you assess the potential risk/reward.

Two stocks from our momentum search graphically illustrate the difference in relative risk. Aztec Manufacturing (Exhibit 5.9) is right at

Exhibit 5.9   At the end of May, 1996, Aztec Manufacturing was selling slightly below its long-term price trend.

9/4/96   AZTEC MANUFACTURING CO COM (AZTC)   7.87

May 1996

Open: 7.87 Hi: 8.12 Lo: 7.75 Last: 7.87 Change: .00 Vol: 323

the LSQ line on the date of the search; it is at the midpoint of its long-term price action. On the other hand, Coachmen Industries (Exhibit 5.10) is near the top of its LSQ trading channel. Considering the fact that Aztec has even greater momentum than Coachmen (it is ranked 5th to Coachmen's 15th), there is no question in our minds that Aztec is more likely to be the better buy.

This is not to say, of course, that stocks do not occasionally break through the top of their trading channels. They do. But common sense tells us there is more risk involved.

COMBINING SEARCHES

Can you combine the undervalued growth search with the momentum search; the momentum search with the ranking search; or any of these with the insider trading search from Chapter 4? Certainly. But be careful how you do it.

Exhibit 5.10   At the end of May, 1996, Coachmen Industries was selling near the top of its long-term LSQ channel.

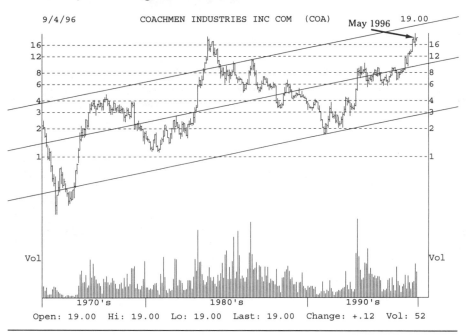

On most searches, we list insider trading and use it as an analysis tool. We often do the same with momentum indicators and several of the ranking indicators. But to combine two different searches in their entirety is a lot trickier. For instance, if you combined the undervalued growth search with the momentum search, stocks would get high scores for being low-priced, for having high growth, *and* for having high momentum. That is trying to do too many things in one search. In our experience, the results tend to be a bit of a hodgepodge.

There is a better way to reap the benefits of two searches as different as undervalued growth and momentum. Run them separately. You will end up with two lists, one with high momentum stocks, the other with the best undervalued growth stocks. When a stock turns up on both lists, you may have a winner. In fact, this is the strategy of the retired dentist we mentioned in Chapter 1. A stock does not appear on both lists very often—undervalued stocks rarely display high momentum—but it has happened often enough in the dentist's experience to generate an annual return of over 40 percent!

All you can do is try it and see what happens. If a stock does appear on both lists, we strongly suggest you still put it through its paces, as we will describe in Chapters 7 and 8.

YOU MUST REMEMBER THIS . . .

A computerized search can undoubtedly increase the odds for success. A well-designed search can find stocks with a greater-than-average potential for price increase or—if you wish to short stocks—a greater-than-average potential for price decrease. Keep these thoughts in mind when creating a search:

- Use your most important goals as score-and-rank indicators to bring the most desirable stocks into your search report.
- Use your minimum requirements to eliminate unacceptable stocks from the search universe.
- Supplement your major goals with score-and-rank indicators to help move the best stocks to the top of the list. (Use lower weighting for these.)
- An indicator can be used to eliminate stocks *and* to score and rank stocks in the same search.
- Before buying any stocks found by a search, evaluate them as described in Chapters 7 and 8. Use list-only indicators to retrieve information needed for the evaluation.
- Many different kinds of searches can be created with computerized search programs. Experiment with the indicators to find those that best match your investment goals.
- The undervalued growth search and the momentum search are on the Telescan diskette. See the Quick Start Guide at the end of the book for instructions on using them.

In the next chapter, we'll show you how to go back in time and test a search in different kinds of markets. You will be able to see for yourself how stocks from a search would have performed over time. This is the best way we know to find a search that will produce good results in the future. After that, we'll move on to analyze the stocks from our undervalued growth stock search.

6

THE TIME MACHINE

How would you like to see the actual performance of stocks found by your search? In this computerized age, you can do just that. In effect, you can travel back in time, run a search, and see how the stocks from that search performed over time. This is called backtesting, and it is one of the most valuable features of any search product because it gives you a chance to develop confidence in your searches before you place your bets.

Backtesting follows Confucius's advice: "Study the past if you would divine the future." It is based on the assumption that if a search strategy worked consistently well in the past, it should generate comparable results in the future. It is like having a time machine at your fingertips.

DIVINING THE FUTURE

The backtesting procedure is simple. After you create a search, simply select the backtesting option, specify the date you wish to start the test, enter a time period for the test, and then run the search.[1] For a valid backtest, you need to see at least 25 to 50 stocks from a search.

---

[1] There are two restrictions for backtesting in ProSearch: The maximum number of backtesting months is 36; backtests always start on the first day of the month. Other programs allow you to backtest technical trading theories based on the data you've accumulated on your own computer.

A backtested search evaluates the stocks on the basis of their indicator values at the time of the search, as opposed to their current values. This is what gives backtesting its power and validity.

Incidentally, you will occasionally find a blank return for a stock on a backtested search. When this happens, it is because the stock wasn't priced at the time the new search was run, most likely because the company had been bought out. Such stocks are not counted in the Average Total Return at the bottom of the search report (although those with 0.0% return are). It is a good idea to check out these stocks, as they often have some of the best results, which could improve the overall return of your search.

SEARCHES THAT BEAT THE MARKET: THREE FOR THREE

For illustration, we backtested three searches that we created in this book: the insider trading search (expanded) from Chapter 4, and the undervalued growth and momentum searches from Chapter 5. We used 6/1/95 as the date of the backtest (one year prior to the time of writing). For the undervalued growth search and insider trading search, we asked the computer to test the results over the 200 days (40 trading weeks) following the date of the test. These kinds of searches require a relatively long period to judge performance, because undervaluation doesn't correct overnight, and because insiders usually act well in advance of events that may affect their company. We tested the performance of the momentum search over just 45 days (nine trading weeks) because we would expect momentum stocks to achieve results more quickly than stocks based on undervaluation. The results are shown in Exhibits 6.1, 6.2, and 6.3.

HOW GOOD IS GOOD?

Each of our searches beat the market during the period of the backtest, as you can see by looking at the comparisons at the bottom of the search reports. The average total return of all 25 stocks from each search was more than any of the market averages. This is a good sign!

- The insider trading search (Exhibit 6.1) returned an average of 35.1 percent over 200 days versus a Nasdaq return of 26.2 percent

Exhibit 6.1   The insider trading backtest: The top 25 stocks for the 200-day period from 6/1/95 through 3/6/96.

ProSearch Backtesting Report
6/01/95–3/06/96

	Symbol	Stock Name	Industry Group	Return
1>	AETC	APPLIED EXTRUSION TECH	.PLA	−14.3%
2>	SHLO	SHILOH INDUSTRIES	.SSP	47.8%
3>	GGG	GRACO INC	.MSP	13.3%
4>	CAS	CASTLE (A.M.)	.MET	91.7%
5>	EBCP	EASTERN BANCORP INC		33.9%
6>	TKR	TIMKEN CO	.MBE	8.9%
7>	KMT	KENNAMETAL, INC	.MOF	6.1%
8>	AR	ASARCO INC	.MCP	8.6%
9>	STFC	STATE AUTO FINANCIAL	.IPC	25.5%
10>	APPB	APPLEBEE'S INTL	.FRS	−16.4%
11>	JLGI	JLG INDUS	.MCM	197.0%
12>	TDY	TELEDYNE INC .CON		19.4%
13>	RXL	REXEL INC		44.7%
14>	CMZ	CINCINNATI MILACRON	.MMT	4.1%
15>	IOMG	IOMEGA CORP	.DPE	277.0%
16>	LOC	LOCTITE CORP	.CHE	7.2%
17>	UCC	UNION CAMP	.PAP	−8.2%
18>	HUM	HUMANA INC	.HHC	17.1%
19>	DKAI	DAKA INT'L	.FOS	36.3%
20>	LMT	LOCKHEED MARTIN MARIETTA	.AMC	30.6%
21>	SIAL	SIGMA-ALDRICH	.CHE	30.6%
22>	DG	DOLLAR GENERAL	.RDI	4.4%
23>	CHV	CHEVRON CORP	.OIN	13.9%
24>	MAGI	MAGNA GROUP, INC	.BAN	12.7%
25>	EXC	EXCEL INDUSTRIES	.APT	−12.8%

Average total return	= 35.1%
Dow Jones Industrials total return	= 26.0%
New York Stock Exchange total return	= 22.0%
S&P 500 total return	= 22.2%
NASDAQ total return	= 26.2%
American Stock Exchange total return	= 15.7%

Source: ProSearch 5.0, courtesy of Telescan, Inc. Indicator scores have been omitted to save space; headings have been added for clarity.

Exhibit 6.2   The undervalued growth backtest: The top 25 stocks for the 200-day period from 6/1/95 through 3/6/96.

ProSearch Backtesting Report
6/01/95–3/06/96

	Symbol	Stock Name	Industry Group	Return
1>	NX	QUANEX CORP	.SOS	−14.7%
2>	NATR	NATURE'S SUNSHINE PROD	.RME	117.7%
3>	ECILF	ECI TELECOM LTD	.TES	41.4%
4>	SGC	SUPERIOR SURGICAL	.MED	−18.4%
5>	CEFT	CONCORD EFS	.DSE	109.6%
6>	LUC	LUKENS INC	.SOS	−18.2%
7>	PENW	PENWEST LTD	.CHE	−15.0%
8>	MO	PHILIP MORRIS COS	.TCI	42.1%
9>	POWL	POWELL INDUS	.ECC	62.0%
10>	IR	INGERSOLL-RAND	.MID	10.0%
11>	ABX	AMER BARRICK RES	.MGO	15.8%
12>	TMC	TIMES MIRROR	.PNE	54.8%
13>	HUB.B	HUBBELL INC CL'B'	.ECC	18.0%
14>	FITB	FIFTH THIRD BANCORP	.BAN	58.6%
15>	MKG	MALLINCKRODT GROUP	.MED	6.1%
16>	RLM	REYNOLDS METALS	.ALU	9.6%
17>	MOCO	MODERN CONTROLS	.SPE	42.6%
18>	SJM.A	SMUCKER (J.M.) CL'A'	.FOO	−10.0%
19>	CKR	CKE RESTAURANTS	.FFF	106.4%
20>	STK	STORAGE TECHNOLOGY	.DPE	32.1%
21>	PRE	PREMIER INDUSTRIAL	.ESE	29.8%
22>	STH	STANHOME INC	.RME	0.0%
23>	PHI	PHILIPPINE LONG D TEL	.TFO	−16.7%
24>	MRK	MERCK & CO	.DET	40.9%
25>	NTRS	NORTHERN TRUST	.BAN	42.5%

Average total return	= 29.8%
Dow Jones Industrials total return	= 26.0%
New York Stock Exchange total return	= 22.0%
S&P 500 total return	= 22.2%
NASDAQ total return	= 26.2%
American Stock Exchange total return	= 15.7%

Source: ProSearch 5.0, courtesy of Telescan, Inc. Indicator scores have been omitted to save space; headings have been added for clarity.

Exhibit 6.3   The momentum backtest: The top 25 stocks for the 45-day period from 6/1/95 through 8/02/95.

ProSearch Backtesting Report
6/01/95–8/02/95

	Symbol	Stock Name	Industry Group	Return
1>	LNCT	LANCIT MEDIA PRODUCTIONS	.BPE	4.8%
2>	BTUI	BTU INTERNATIONAL	.EEE	42.8%
3>	GECM	GENICOM CORP	.DPE	25.7%
4>	JMAR	JMAR INDUSTRIES	.MED	44.4%
5>	GGG	GRACO INC	.MSP	10.3%
6>	AINN	APPLIED INNOVATION	.TES	25.1%
7>	CCSC	COHERENT COMMUNIC SYS	.TES	46.5%
8>	WLV	WOLVERINE TUBE	.MPF	12.7%
9>	MLI	MUELLER INDUSTRIES	.MOF	13.1%
10>	HSBK	HIBERNIA SAVINGS BK	.BSB	12.4%
11>	MOND	ROBERT MONDAVI 'A'	.BWL	20.7%
12>	CGNX	COGNEX CORP	.MSP	51.1%
13>	NBSC	NEW BRUNSWICK SCIENT	.SPE	−17.2%
14>	IKOS	IKOS SYSTEMS	.DCO	15.9%
15>	MCDY	MICRODYNE CORP	.TES	15.4%
16>	THM	THERMWOOD CORP	.MMT	−20.0%
17>	GEN	GENRAD, INC	.EEE	0.0%
18>	KMT	KENNAMETAL, INC	.MOF	12.6%
19>	BSTN	BOSTON TECHNOLOGY	.TES	14.1%
20>	MO	PHILIP MORRIS COS	.TCI	0.3%
21>	BJS	BJ SERVICES	.OWD	−3.5%
22>	NDC	NATL DATA	.DAT	24.6%
23>	TTRR	TRACOR INC NEW COM NEW	.EDE	15.0%
24>	XICO	XICOR INC	.ESE	18.6%
25>	ASEC	ASECO CORP	.EEE	26.2%

Average total return	=	16.5%
Dow Jones Industrials total return	=	5.0%
New York Stock Exchange total return	=	4.7%
S&P 500 total return	=	4.7%
NASDAQ total return	=	13.7%
American Stock Exchange total return	=	6.3%

Source: ProSearch 5.0, courtesy of Telescan, Inc. Indicator scores have been omitted to save space; heading have been added for clarity.

and a 22 percent return for the New York Stock Exchange index and the S&P 500.

- The undervalued growth search (Exhibit 6.2) generated an average return of 29.8 percent over the same period.
- The momentum search (Exhibit 6.3) returned an average of 16.5 percent in only 45 days. On an annualized basis, that's over 100 percent per year! During that 45-day period, the Dow was up only 5 percent, and the only market index that even approached our return was the Nasdaq at 13.7 percent.

Keep in mind, all 25 stocks were used in the calculations for each search. In real life, we would evaluate the search and select only those stocks that appear to have the best chances for growth, which should improve these returns. Nevertheless, all we can ask of any search is that the stocks it finds outperform the market.

There are other ways to determine how good a backtested search is before you try it out in real life. Look at the individual percentage gain or loss figures for each stock. If the search is valid, the stocks should move from highest gain to lowest gain (more or less) as you go down the list. (This assumes a list of 25 or more stocks.) In other words, the better-performing stocks should be collected near the top of the list, allowing, of course, for considerable variation among individual stocks. If there doesn't seem to be any pattern at all, the search could possibly be improved, especially if your report contained at least 50 stocks.

Two of our backtests look very good in this regard. The top five stocks from the undervalued growth search (Exhibit 6.2) had an average return of 47 percent whereas the top five from the momentum search (Exhibit 6.3) averaged 25.6 percent over just 9 weeks! The stocks from the insider buying search are less than ideally ranked. The top five stocks have an average gain of almost 35 percent, which is equal to the average of the group as a whole, but there are three outstanding performers, with returns of 44 to 277 percent ranked 11th or lower. This would prompt us to take a careful look at their scores to see which indicators seem to be holding them down. Then we would refine the search to try to move these stocks closer to the top of the list (which we'll do later this chapter). If we can accomplish this over other market periods, we will have more confidence in the search.

Keep in mind that these three searches were backtested on only one market period. To prove any kind of true validity, a search should be tested over several different markets, as we discuss below. The insider buying search, incidentally, was tested by others against many market periods, and despite its relative simplicity, it outperformed the market in all eight time periods tested.[2]

Another way to evaluate a backtested search is to compare the number of losses to the number of gains. This reveals the volatility of the search. Certain kinds of searches tend to produce a list of stocks with a considerable variance in the returns: a large number of big gainers but a larger number of big losers. If such a search produces a good overall result, it is probably a valid search, but you may not like its volatility. You would need considerable confidence in your ability to pick the winners from the losers. You might prefer to look for searches that produce more consistent results.

Here is a comparison of gains to losses for our three searches:

Backtested Search	Stocks with Over 30% Return	Losses out of 25 Stocks
Insider search	9	4
Undervalued growth search	12	6
Momentum search	9*	3

*Because the momentum search was tested over a 45-day period rather than 200 days, we used 20% as the basis of comparison; it returned 9 stocks with over 20% return.

All three searches show very acceptable volatility in that the number of stocks with large positive returns was at least double the number of losses. The number of losses from the undervalued growth search is a little excessive for our tastes, but on the other hand, this search produced some of the largest returns.

REFINING A SEARCH

When evaluating a search report, it is only natural to pay more attention to the higher ranked stocks at the top of the list. Therefore, we can place more confidence in a search if, in the backtest, the best performing stocks are ranked near the top of the list. If they are not, we should refine the

[2] Mark Draud and Paul Alvim, *ProSearch Strategy Handbook, Volume II* (Houston: Telescan, 1994).

search to move them closer to the top of the list and then test it over several periods.

Look at the insider trading backtest in Exhibit 6.1. Several stocks that performed very well over the backtested period are ranked near the middle of the list: JLG Industries, with a return of 197 percent, is ranked 11th; Rexel, Inc., with 44.7 percent, is ranked 13th; Iomega Corporation, with 277 percent, is ranked 15th. Either these high performers have lower scores on criteria for which you wanted high scores *or* they have higher scores on criteria for which you wanted low scores, or both.

To correct the situation, we need to determine which criteria are holding down these top performers; then we may have to change the weighting of those criteria, and rerun the search. For example, we could try increasing or decreasing the weighting percentage on a score-and-rank indicator that appears to be at fault. Then rerun the search to see if the high-return stocks move up the list. If that doesn't do the job, we could eliminate the indicator or eliminate its effect on the search by changing it to list only.

Closer inspection of the stocks in Exhibit 6.1 reveals one possible culprit: the relative P/E ratio. All three of the high performers have relative P/E ratios that are somewhat higher than stocks near the top of the list. In the search strategy, we used the relative P/E indicator to score and rank the stocks, asking for low scores and weighting it 20 percent. Somehow we need to decrease the importance of this indicator. We cannot decrease the weight any further without removing it altogether. That is what we'll do. We will change the indicator to list only, thereby removing it as a factor in the ranking but still allowing us to use it in our final evaluation.

Exhibit 6.4 shows the results of this refinement of the insider trading search. Iomega Corporation (277% gain) moved to the top of the list; Rexel (44.7%) moved from number 13 to number 12; but JLG Industries (197% gain) did not even appear in the top 25 stocks! So, should we have more confidence in this search or not? Let's look at the search report as a whole. Compare the refined search with the original backtest on the following points:

- Average gain of all the stocks
- Number of stocks with losses
- Average performance of the top five stocks
- Number of stocks with gains over 40 percent

Exhibit 6.4   The "refined" insider trading backtest: The top 25 stocks for the 200-day period from 6/1/95 through 3/6/96.

ProSearch Backtesting Report
6/01/95–3/06/96

	Symbol	Stock Name	Industry Group	Return
1>	IOMG	IOMEGA CORP	.DPE	277.0%
2>	MSEA	METROPOLITAN BANCORP WASH COM		31.7%
3>	STFC	STATE AUTO FINANCIAL	.IPC	25.5%
4>	CELS	COMMNET CELLULAR	.TMC	7.9%
5>	INMT	INTERMET CORP	.APT	47.0%
6>	TKN	THERMOTREX CORP	.MED	99.4%
7>	DUAL	DUAL DRILLING	.OWD	48.1%
8>	BSX	BOSTON SCIENTIFIC	.MED	63.4%
9>	ESE	ESCO ELECTRONICS	.EHA	41.7%
10>	AETC	APPLIED EXTRUSION TECH	.PLA	−14.3%
11>	SHLO	SHILOH INDUSTRIES	.SSP	47.8%
12>	RXL	REXEL INC		44.7%
13>	GGG	GRACO INC	.MSP	13.3%
14>	UMC	UNITED MERIDIAN	.OCP	25.4%
15>	EBCP	EASTERN BANCORP INC		33.9%
16>	CTI	CHART INDUSTRIES	.MSP	83.7%
17>	CAS	CASTLE (A.M.)	.MET	91.7%
18>	EFTC	ELECTRONIC FAB TECHNOLOGY	.ELE	−29.7%
19>	DGP	USX-DELHI GROUP	.UPG	−13.2%
20>	TKR	TIMKEN CO	.MBE	8.9%
21>	CPU	COMPUSA INC	.RSP	56.1%
22>	AR	ASARCO INC	.MCP	8.6%
23>	AMT	ACME-CLEVELAND	.MMT	−14.5%
24>	KMT	KENNAMETAL, INC	.MOF	6.1%
25>	FLFC	FIRST LIBERTY FINL CORPN GA		37.0%

Average total return	=	41.1%
Dow Jones Industrials total return	=	26.6%
New York Stock Exchange total return	=	22.0%
S&P 500 total return	=	22.2%
NASDAQ total return	=	26.2%
American Stock Exchange total return	=	15.7%

Source: ProSearch 5.0, courtesy of Telescan, Inc. Indicator scores have been omitted to save space; heading have been added for clarity.

On all these points, the results of refined insider search showed an improvement over the original backtest. The average gain of all 25 stocks improved by 6 percent, and, although the number of losses remained the same, the number of stocks with gains over 40 percent more than doubled. The most spectacular improvement was in the average performance of the top five stocks, which went from 35 percent on the original backtest to 77.8 percent on the refined search. Thus, the refinement more than doubled the effectiveness of the original report and the performance of the top five stocks.

All this would increase our confidence in the refined search strategy. We would feel more able to pick a winning stock from this insider search than from the original strategy.

In the above refinement, we changed a score-and-rank indicator to a list-only indicator (because the weight was too low to merely decrease the weight). But don't ignore the indicators used to eliminate stocks. One of them may not be restrictive enough. You might try narrowing the range to eliminate some of the less desirable stocks and allow the better stocks to move up the list. However, don't change an elimination indicator to a score-and-rank indicator or a list-only indicator, because that will widen the universe of stocks, which might defeat your purposes. Unless, of course, that is your intention.

Be sure to rerun the backtest after each change so you can assess cause and effect. Also, once you're happy with the refinement, test it on several different time periods. Otherwise, you could be artificially forcing stocks to the top of the list in one time period when that adjustment might produce poor results over other time periods.

Refining a search is mostly a matter of trial and error. Make a few changes, and rerun the search after each change to see if the better stocks have moved up. Then test the refined search over different time periods. The better a search works on historical markets, the more confidence you will have when you use it in real life.

No Pain, No Gain?

Refining a search may also mean weeding out highly volatile stocks. Look at the stock graph for Storage Technology Corporation (Exhibit 6.5) from our undervalued growth backtest. It returned 32 percent in 200 days, but you would have had a fairly bumpy ride from June 1995 through March 1996. Could you—would you—have held on for the whole ride? If the

Exhibit 6.5 Storage Technology Corporation, from the undervalued growth backtest, shows considerable volatility in the middle of the test period (June 1995 to March 1996).

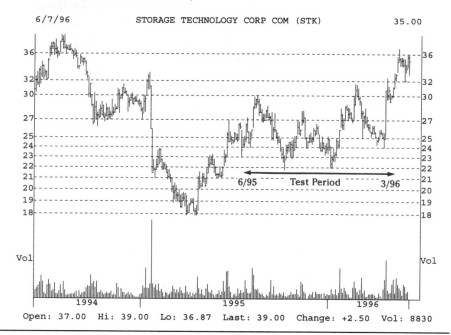

answer is no, it might be a good idea to check for volatility by looking at graphs of the highest performing stocks on your backtest.

To check for volatility, backdate the graphs to six months or a year after your theoretical purchase. You can see at a glance how much volatility you would have had to endure. If you decide you can handle the volatility, the stock graphs will give you some idea of how much leeway to give a stock when it starts to drop. If a search produces good results but delivers highly volatile stocks, you may want to put a volatility indicator in your search and specify the lowest scores.

TEST, TEST, AND TEST AGAIN

The most important test of validity is how well a search performs over *many* historical periods. If you have a search that backtested well, be sure to test it on past bearish markets and sideways markets and see what happens. You might have inadvertently backtested a roaring bull market (like the one that began in late 1994) when most stocks did well. A search that does well in a bull market might stumble in a sideways market and fall flat on its face in front of the bears.

We recommend using at least six periods for most backtests:

- A long and a short bullish market
- A long and a short bearish market
- Two flat markets

Searches designed to find quick, short-term profits, such as a momentum search, should be tested only on short periods.

HOW DO YOU TELL A BULL FROM A BEAR?

A bullish market is one in which there is persistent upward trend over a period of months, despite minor corrections. There are higher highs and higher lows as the market moves inexorably higher. A bearish market is exactly the opposite, with lower highs and lower lows as the market moves downward. A sideways or flat market is virtually trendless, when viewed over a period of months, with no significant net movement in either direction.

In real life, it is sometimes hard to know whether you are in a bull market, a bear market, or a sideways market. A 20-point drop might be a correction in a bull market, a dip in a sideways market, or the first growl of the approaching bears. The past, however, gives us 20-20 vision. To find past bull and bear markets, all you have to do is look at a graph of one of the market indexes, which can be done with any stock analysis program.

If you like smaller cap stocks, print a graph of the Nasdaq index (Exhibit 6.6) over the past two or three years (or the period of time available for backtesting). If you're interested in large cap stocks, use the New York Stock Exchange Index (Exhibit 6.7) or the S&P 500 index. (The Dow, with only 30 blue chip stocks, is too narrow an index for market analysis.) Use a pen to mark the down periods, the up periods, and the sideways periods. Then backtest your search over the various periods.

Exhibit 6.6   The Nasdaq index over three years: Note the bullish, bearish and flat or sideways market periods.

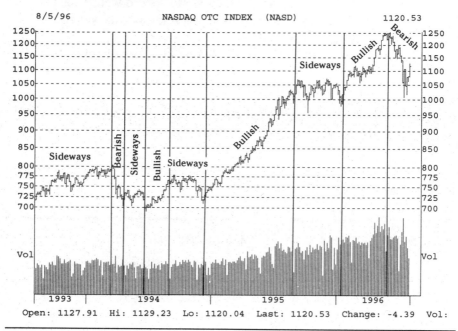

You may want to consider developing a "bull market search" (one that does well in bull markets) and a "bear market search" (one that does well in bear markets). This can be a problem because it is often difficult, except in retrospect, to distinguish a bearish period within a bull market from a true bear market (which is why we prefer a search that works well over various markets). Nevertheless, if you wish to try, you would test the bull market search only against bullish periods and the bear market search only against bearish periods. Keep in mind that almost any search will appear to do well in a bull market. The question becomes one of degree. Because most profits usually come during bull markets, a bull market search should outperform the market; an *outstanding* bull market search should outperform the market by a large degree. A bear market search is a different story. When the market is retreating, you're basically just trying to hold on to your capital. A bear market search that simply breaks even should serve you well.

Exhibit 6.7   The New York Stock Exchange index over three years: Note the bullish, bearish and flat or sideways market periods.

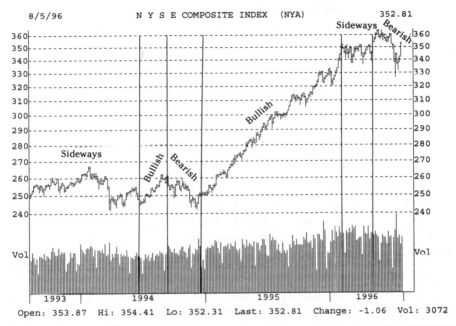

8/5/96   N Y S E COMPOSITE INDEX   (NYA)   352.81

Open: 353.87 Hi: 354.41 Lo: 352.31 Last: 352.81 Change: -1.06 Vol: 3072

YOU MUST REMEMBER THIS . . .

Here are some hints for successful backtesting:

- Start with a simple search using your favorite indicator. Then add one indicator at a time to see how it changes the results.

- In general, technical indicators are more predictive over shorter periods than fundamental indicators. So judge them accordingly when you backtest a search. (Technical indicators measure price movement and price patterns; fundamental indicators measure the basic health and viability of a company.) For example, if you're using a technical indicator that generates buy and sell signals every two weeks, test the performance over 15 days or so. For searches based on fundamental indicators, such as the insider buying or undervalued growth searches, test the results over six months or a year.

- Tailor the backtest to your own goals. If you are particularly averse to risk, test your searches against a number of bear markets.

- Notice whether a search produces widely varying results—big losers as well as big gainers. Such fluctuations may or may not suit your taste.

- If the higher performing stocks are clustered near the bottom of the list, refine your search strategy to coax them toward the top.

- Test a search against six or more market periods, being sure to include bearish markets and sideways markets.

- If you're technically inclined, have a backtesting contest among the various technical indicators (testing one indicator at a time). You will quickly see which ones have done well in the past.

- Discard a search that doesn't backtest well over several periods. No matter how much you like it, if it didn't pick winners in the past, it probably won't pick winners in the future when your money is riding on it.

- A good search is one that outperforms the market. You can match the market, remember, by throwing darts or buying broad-based mutual funds. So all you are looking for in a backtest is a search that beats the market.

Backtesting results assume the purchase of every stock on the list. In the next chapter, we will discuss various tools that can be used to eliminate the marginal companies on a search report and thereby improve your chances for higher returns. If you can design a search that tests better than the market, it should do even better when you qualify the stocks on the list.

7
STAGE-ONE
EVALUATION

A search report is like a list of job candidates who represent the top one-half of one percent of all those who are applying for a certain position. Each has the education, skills, and experience to do a good job. Each embodies the personal qualities needed for success. They all appear to be equal in most respects. But there is only one job. Obviously, the candidates must be evaluated further to find the one who has an edge over the others. It is the same with the stocks on a search report. We are going to show you several computerized tools to help you evaluate the stocks to find the ones with the winning edge.

We have divided the evaluation process into two stages. In this chapter, which describes stage one, we will use information retrieved during the search to compare various characteristics of each stock. The dozen or so stocks that make the first cut will become candidates for the hands-on evaluation of stage two, described in Chapter 8. There, we'll introduce several research and analysis tools to help further narrow the list to half a dozen or so finalists. In Chapter 9, we'll show you how to decide which of the finalists to buy.

GATHERING THE DATA

Recall that we added several list-only indicators to our original undervalued growth search to retrieve information for the stage-one evaluation.
Now let's compare these indicator scores for all the stocks on the list.
Stocks with the most negative scores will be eliminated; stocks with the
most positive scores will become candidates for the stage-two evaluation.

In our original undervalued growth search, we used 13 indicators to
eliminate undesirable stocks and to score and rank the remaining stocks.
Those indicators, which represented our most important objectives, gave
us a working list of 25 top stocks that match our goals. (Although we limited the list to 25 for this book, it is better to look at 50 or even 100 stocks
from each search.) For the stage-one evaluation, we added a group of list-
only indicators that we consider important but secondary in their ability
to meet our goals. They will help us determine which of the stocks are
the better candidates for our purposes.

Please note we did not do two searches. The list-only indicators were
selected at the same time as the primary indicators that control the
search, and only one search was run. We are explaining them separately
for clarity.

The indicators we chose to list information for the stage-one evaluation are:

Debt-to-equity ratio

5-year earnings growth rate

5-year cash flow growth rate

One-month change in projected EPS growth rate

P/E ratio

Relative P/E ratio

Company growth ratio

Insider trading

Number of analysts following the company

Price rank

EPS rank

5-day to 30-day average volume ratio

Accumulation/distribution

The selection of these indicators, like the other indicators in our strategy, is based on our own investment philosophy. (We will explain each one as we go through the evaluation.) If you are technically inclined, you might wish to include several technical indicators, or you may prefer different ones altogether. Feel free to add your favorites.

The entire search strategy appears in Exhibit 7.1. It contains the 13 indicators from the previous chapter, plus stock price, and the 13 indicators shown above. The report from this search (shown at the end of this chapter) is identical to the undervalued growth search in Chapter 5, except it lists all 27 indicators. The list-only indicators described below did not affect the results of the search.

Low-Tech Tools in a High-Tech World

The stage-one evaluation is very low tech. Let's set aside our computerized tools for the moment and pick up a pen. We will circle good scores on our working list of stocks and draw an × over bad scores. You may wish to use a different method for this evaluation: checkmarks, pluses and minuses, pink and yellow highlight pens, whatever. The point is to be able to easily distinguish good scores from bad scores. If your search returned 50 or 100 stocks (as we recommend), you will need a method that makes it easy to spot the best stocks.

A Few Pointers Before We Continue

Before we go on, we would like to point out several things about this evaluation:

- Don't concentrate only on the top several stocks on the list. All of the stocks are relatively good. All scored well on the standards imposed by the search, so there may be only a very fuzzy line between the merits of, say, number 4 and number 14. As we go through the evaluation, that fuzzy difference should come into sharper focus. The point is, these stocks are the top 25 stocks out of 9,000—the top quarter of one percent of the available stocks—so there are relatively small differences between the number-1 stock and the number-25 stock.

- During the stage-one evaluation, consider only the scores for list-only indicators. The other indicators have already done their jobs by eliminating or ranking the stocks.

Exhibit 7.1   The complete search request for undervalued growth stocks, including the list-only indicators.

Indicators (Abbreviation on Report)	Action: The Basic Search/Weight
10-Year LSQ deviation (10LDv)	Eliminate stocks that aren't at least 10% below their LSQ line
10-Year LSQ deviation (10LDv)	Rank stocks by lowest scores/100%
10-Year price growth rate (10$Gr)	Rank stocks by highest scores/80%
5-Year projected EPS growth rate (5yPEG)	Rank stocks by highest scores/100%

Indicators	Action: Narrow the Universe
8/17/9 weekly MACD (Mc8wC)	Eliminate stocks that aren't technically positive
3-week relative performance (3-Wk)	Eliminate stocks that have not had a positive move within the past 3 weeks
Group rank (GrpRk)	Eliminate stocks below 50% ranking

Indicators	Action: Seasoning/Weight
3-Year LSQ deviation (3LDv)	Rank stocks by lowest scores/60%
Quarter-over-quarter earnings— Most recent quarter (%cELt)	Rank stocks by highest scores/80%
Quarter-over-quarter earnings— Second most recent quarter (%cE-2)	Rank stocks by highest scores/60%
3-Week price rank change (c$-3)	Rank stocks by highest scores/80%
6-Week price rank change (c$-6)	Rank stocks by highest scores/40%
3-Week group rank change (cGRP3)	Rank stocks by highest scores/20%

Indicators	Action: List Information
Debt-to-equity ratio (%D/Eq)	List only
5-Year earnings growth rate (5YrEg)	List only
5-Year cash flow growth rate (5YrCf)	List only
One-month change in earnings estimates (1mEGC)	List only
P/E ratio (P/E)	List only
Relative P/E ratio (RelPE)	List only
Company growth ratio (GrRat)	List only
Insider buying (Insdr)	List only
Number of analysts following company (#AnCF)	List only
Price rank ($Rank)	List only
EPS rank (EPSRk)	List only
5-to-30-day average volume (5–30)	List only
Accumulation/distribution (Ac/Dst)	List only
Stock price (Price)	List only

- Look only for extremes in the scores. In our rating system, very good scores merit a circle; very bad scores, an ×. Many scores will not fit either extreme, so we may end up with a number of stocks without circles or ×s. We will probably ignore those, because in selecting the top 10 or 12 candidates—the semifinalists, so to speak—we will be looking for stocks that have a preponderance of extremely good scores (lots of circles).

- The ProSearch report lists two scores for each indicator: the raw score, such as the actual P/E ratio, and the percentile rank, which is always shown in parentheses. In the following evaluation, we will tell you whether we judged the raw score or the percentile rank and give you what we consider to be an acceptable score or rank.

- The percentile rank shows where the stock is ranked, compared with all other stocks, on that indicator; possible rankings are 0 to 99. If higher is better, 99 would be the best score; if lower is better, zero would be the best score.

- Because of space limitations, we'll use just two stocks from the search to illustrate the low-tech analysis: Quanex Corporation (NX) ranked number 1 on the report, and ECI Telecom Ltd. (ECILF) ranked number 10. The complete stage-one evaluation of these two stocks is shown in Exhibit 7.2.

A list of 25 undervalued growth stocks is now in front of us. We have a pen ready. Let's begin.

TOOLS TO CONFIRM FUNDAMENTAL STRENGTH

We will start with the nine indicators used to extract more information about the fundamental strength of a company: debt-to-equity ratio, 5-year-earnings growth rate, 5-year cash-flow growth rate, one-month change in projected EPS growth rate, P/E ratio, relative P/E ratio, company growth ratio, insider trading, and the number of analysts following the company.

Low Debt

If you have two equally good stocks, why buy the one with the extra risk of high debt? ProSearch states debt-to-equity ratio as a percentage: A

Exhibit 7.2   Two stocks from the undervalued growth search reflecting the low-tech stage-one evaluation

	Absolute Value	Ranking Value
1> QUANEX CORPORATION		
Debt/equity (%D/Eq)	81	(85)
5-Year earnings growth (5YrEg)	19.5	(58)
5-Year cash flow growth (YrCf)	10.6	(65)
Revision in earnings est. (1mEGC)	>1.4	(15)
P/E ratio (P/E)	9.9	(13)
Relative P/E (RelPE)	27.9	(44)
Company growth ratio (GrRat)	3.3	(98)
Insider buying (Insdr)	0.0	(91)
Number of analysts (#AnCF)	5.0	(67)
Price rank (Price)	102.5	(46)
EPS rank (EPSRk)	96	(93)
5-to-30-day average volume (5/30)	238.6	(94)
Accumulation/distribution (AcDst)	61	(56)
Stock price (Price)	22.6	(77)
3> ECI TELECOM		
Debt/equity (%D/Eq)	1.8	(60)
5-Year Earnings growth (5YrEg)	31.7	(71)
5-Year cash flow growth (5YrCf)	71.4	(97)
Revision in earnings est. (1mEGC)	0.0	(78)
P/E ratio (P/E)	22.3	(64)
Relative P/E (RelPE)	58.2	(72)
Company growth ratio (GrRat)	1.5	(76)
Insider buying (Insdr)	0.0	(91)
Number of analysts (#AnCF)	7.0	(76)
Price rank ($Rank)	108.7	(76)
EPS rank (EPSRk)	77.0	(73)
5-to-30-day average volume (5/30)	108.5	(62)
Accumulation/distribution (AcDst)	29.0	(25)
Stock price (Price)	25.3	(80)

score of 100 means that the company's debt is 100 percent of its equity, or 1 to 1; a score above 100 means the debt-to-equity ratio is more than 1 to 1; a score below 100, less than 1 to 1. We consider more than a 1 to 1 ratio as high, so we'll put an × over any score above 100 percent; we'll circle scores of 20 percent or lower.

On our list, Quanex with 81 percent falls between the extremes and doesn't get a mark; ECI gets a circle with a low 1.8 percent. (*Note:* If you aren't sure what a good score is or is not, use the percentiles. If you want high scores, a percentile of 80+ rates a circle whereas 20 or lower deserves an ×.)

Good Earnings Trend

Good growth stocks generally have a history of good earnings, which is revealed by the 5-year-earnings growth indicator. Circle any scores above 20 percent; draw an × through any scores below 10 percent. Ignore scores of N/A, which means that 5-year earnings weren't available. If such a stock should make it to the next stage because of other high scores, we suggest that you take a look at its earnings over the past year or two.

Quanex barely misses a circle, with 19.5 percent. If push came to shove, we would consider it circled. ECI is well over our minimum with 31.7 percent and gets a circle.

Cash Counts

The bottom line in business is to generate cash. Therefore, we like to compare a company's cash flow growth rate with its earnings growth rate. If the growth of cash flow is substantially higher than the growth of earnings—for example, cash flow at 25 percent and earnings at 15 percent—that's good. If cash flow is significantly lower—say, 5 percent cash to 20 percent earnings—we consider that bad. This is simply a judgment call.

Quanex's cash flow growth rate is about half its earnings growth rate for five years (10.6 to 19.5) whereas ECI's is more than double (71.4 to 31.7). ECI gets a circle; Quanex, nothing.

Up with Estimates

In the insider trading search in Chapter 4, we talked about the importance of revisions of earnings estimates by Wall Street analysts. An upward revision may cause the stock price to go up; a downward revision may take the stock price down. It makes sense, then, to take a hard look at this score. Circle any positive number; draw an × through any negative number. (Many stocks will have zeros for this indicator because there were no revisions of the estimates.)

Quanex is branded × for its negative revision; ECI has no revision at all.

P/E Again

The importance of P/E ratio was established in Chapter 2, along with the danger of extremely high or extremely low P/Es. For this evaluation, we will consider P/E ratios under 5 and over 35 to be undesirable; give them an ×. Circle any P/E from 7 to 14, which, in general, would be below the market multiple and have a better than average chance of moving up. (Historically, the average market P/E has ranged from 5 to 20 or so; as of this writing, it is about 18.)

Quanex gets a circle for a low P/E of 9.9; ECI falls in the no-action category at 22.

. . . and Again

To confirm a company's undervaluation, we have used an indicator called *relative P/E ratio,* which tells us how the current P/E ratio measures up against its own history. Possible scores are 0 to 100 percent. Zero means the stock is currently selling at its all-time low P/E; 100 means it is selling at its all-time high. Obviously, the lower the score for relative P/E, the more room the current P/E has to grow, which points to undervaluation. We will circle relative P/Es of 30 or below and draw an × through scores of 70 or above.

Quanex looks relatively undervalued with a relative P/E of 27.9; give it a circle. We can ignore ECI's score of 58.2 percent: too high for a circle, too low for an ×.

. . . and Again

How much bang do you get for your buck? The company growth ratio will tell you. Basically, it is the price you pay for growth. It is calculated by dividing the 5-year projected-earnings growth rate by the projected P/E ratio. (Projected P/E is the P/E ratio that will exist at the end of the next fiscal year if the company meets its earnings projections.) A projected EPS growth rate of 10 over a projected P/E ratio of 10 would give a company growth ratio of 1; a projected EPS growth rate of 20 over a projected P/E of 10 would give a company growth ratio of 2. The higher growth ratio is better. Most stocks fall in the 0.6 to 2.0 range, so in our evaluation, we'll circle any score above 1.2 and cross out anything below 0.8.

Both Quanex and ECI are above average with 3.3 and 1.5, respectively. Both get circles.

The Inside Touch

In Chapter 4 we extolled the merits of insider buying. That is why we want to know what insiders think of these undervalued stocks.

Recall that ProSearch's insider trading indicator subtracts insider sales from insider purchases to give the *net* insider purchases for a company. Thus, a positive figure indicates more insider buying than selling; a negative figure, more insider selling than buying. We will circle any positive figure and draw an × through any negative figure.

Don't be too quick, however, to throw out a stock that has insider selling but is otherwise excellent. People often sell stocks just because they need the money, so insider selling should only be considered a red flag to check out the conditions. Find out who is selling and how much. (If you're using Telescan, look up the insider text report.) If the president, chairman, and directors are unloading half their shares, that's cause for alarm. If a couple of insiders are selling a small percent of their holdings, it's probably not significant.

Neither Quanex nor ECI has insiders buying their stock; neither get a mark.

How Many Elves Does It Take to . . .

A strong upward revision in earnings estimates can occur if several analysts raise their estimates or if one analyst raises his or her estimate by a large percentage. All things considered, it is probably better to have several analysts raising their estimates 5 or 6 percent than to have an optimistic Lone Ranger upping his 20 percent. Hence, it is a good idea to find out how many analysts follow the company, which is the purpose of the indicator called *number of analysts projecting earnings for current fiscal year.* If there are several and if the upward revision is substantial, we have greater confidence in their projections.

The number of analysts you require for comfort—and how you distribute your circles and ×s—depends on how conservative you are. Some investors might feel better with eight or ten analysts; we would be happy with five. Therefore, we'll circle scores of 5 or higher and draw an ×through scores of zero or N/A. (Incidentally, some savvy investors prefer companies followed by two or fewer analysts, believing that such under-followed companies have better chances for substantial appreciation, as they become discovered.)

Both Quanex and ECI are well represented by analysts, with 5 and 7, respectively. Both get circles.

TOOLS TO CONFIRM PERFORMANCE

Next we'll look at a couple of performance indicators—price rank and EPS rank—to see if the stock is indeed on its way up.

The Price Is Right

Price rank, as you may recall from Chapter 5, measures a stock's quarterly price performance over a year, with a bias to the most recent three months, and compares its momentum with all other stocks. If the price rank is in the top 25 percent, the stock is a performance leader; if the price rank is in the bottom 25 percent, the stock has lost steam. With that in mind, we will circle percentile ranks (the number in parentheses) of 75 and above, and draw an × through ranks of 25 or below.

Quanex has a price rank of 46, which rates no mark; ECI is in the 70th percentile, just high enough for a circle.

. . . So Are Earnings

Just as the price rank indicator measures price momentum, the EPS rank indicator measures a company's earnings momentum against all other companies. It uses the weighted sum of quarterly EPS growth rates over the past five years, biased for the most recent quarter. Look at the percentile rank figure: 75 or above gets a circle; 25 or below gets an ×.

Quanex has excellent earnings momentum, in the 93rd percentile of all stocks. Give it a circle. With a percentile ranking of 73, ECI is just two points below the top 25 percent of all stocks. It will not receive a notation, but in a "photo finish," this ranking would carry some weight.

TOOLS TO DETECT INSTITUTIONAL INTEREST

Finally, we'll look at two tools that point to an increasing level of interest (perhaps by institutional investors): the 5-to-30-day average volume indicator and the accumulation/distribution indicator. High scores on these indicators are often precursors to rising P/Es and stock prices, which is the ultimate goal of our search.

High Volume Rising

Increasing volume is obviously a sign of increasing interest in a stock, be it institutional or otherwise. The 5-to-30-day average volume indicator compares the average volume over the last five days with the average volume over 30 days. Any number over 150 percent would signify increasing interest and would get a circle. A number under 50 percent says the stock isn't attracting much attention, right now at least, and would get an ×.

Quanex gets a circle for its high volume of 238.6 percent; ECI falls in the neutral range, at 108.5.

The Money Flow

The accumulation/distribution indicator, which we used in the momentum search in Chapter 5, tells us whether money is flowing into or out of a stock, as compared with all other stocks. Generally speaking, if the highest volume occurs on up days, money is flowing into the stock. We interpret this to mean institutions are accumulating the stock. On the other hand, if the highest volume occurs on down days, money is flowing out of the stock (institutions are selling, we assume). Scores of 60 or above get a circle; 40 or below, an ×.

Quanex deserves a circle for its score of 61; ECI is clearly under distribution with a score of 29, which earns it an ×.

THE SHORT LIST

We now have a search report filled with circles and ×s, like our two examples in Exhibit 7.2. To select candidates for the next stage of the evaluation, we will:

- Eliminate stocks that have a preponderance of ×s.
- Select stocks with the most circles and fewest ×s as candidates for the next stage of the evaluation.

Only nine of the 25 stocks on our list made the cut:

		No. of Circles	No. of ×s
No. 1	Quanex Corp. (NX)	7	1
No. 2	OEA Inc., (OEA)	7	1
No. 7	Max & Erma's Restaurants (MAXE)	6	1
No. 10	ECI Telecom, Ltd., (ECILF)	6	1
No. 15	Valero Energy Corp. (VLO)	6	2
No. 18	Myers Industries, Inc. (MYE)	6	2
No. 19	Hon Industries, inc. (HONI)	5	1
No. 22	King World Productions, Inc. (KWP)	7	1
No. 23	Holly Corporation (HOC)	6	1

Both of the stocks used to illustrate this process made the short list. Quanex had a fairly important negative—a downward revision in earnings estimates. Normally, this would signal a possible drop in stock price. If five experts say they don't think the company's earnings are going to increase as much as they previously thought, as in the case of Quanex, that's bad news for the stock. Nevertheless, the other scores for Quanex were so good that it bears further evaluation. (We were specifically impressed by its almost 20 percent growth over the past five years and its 5-year projected earnings growth rate of 28.3.)

We did eliminate two otherwise qualified stocks for downward revisions in earnings: Quantum Corporation and Novell, Inc. (You can see their scores in Exhibit 7.3.) Both had negative 5-year earnings on top of the downward revisions.

A mixture of good and bad scores in the evaluation process is common. Even the best stocks often have one or two bad scores, and in fact, all of our nine finalists had one or more ×s. In actuality, we might take a closer look at such stocks as Hooper Holmes, Inc. (No. 6), which had 5 circles and 3 ×s; it has a negative 5-year-earnings growth, but an upward revision in earnings estimates. In addition, we normally would look at 50 or more stocks because candidates just as attractive as our finalists may be lingering in the lower ranked stocks, held down by one of the indicators.

Exhibit 7.3   The top 25 stocks from the undervalued growth search. This is the same as the search report in Exhibit 5.2, except it shows the list-only indicators.

ProSearch Top Stock Report
5/08/96

```
1> NX       – QUANEX CORP COM                          .SOS
   %cELt = 30.4   (70)    10LDv  = –24.6  ( 8)    10LDv  = –24.6  ( 8)
   %cE-2 = 60.0   (83)    3LDv   = –3.5   (18)    Mc8wC  = 24.0   (84)
   c$-3  = 2.7    (83)    5yPEG  = 28.3   (85)    3-Wk   = 107.1  (81)
   c$-6  = –0.1   (64)    10$Gr  = 15.6   (84)    GrpRk  = 108.0  (72)
   cGRP3 = 1.0    (85)    %D/Eq  = 81.0   (85)    5YrEg  = 19.5   (58)
   5YrCf = 10.6   (65)    1mEGC  = –1.4   (15)    P/E    = 9.9    (13)
   RelPE = 27.9   (44)    GrRat  = 3.3    (98)    Insdr  = 0.0    (91)
   #AnCF = 5.0    (67)    $Rank  = 102.5  (46)    EPSRk  = 96.0   (93)
   5/30  = 238.6  (94)    AcDst  = 61.0   (56)    Price  = 22.6   (77)
2> OEA      – O E A INC COM                            .APT
   %cELt = 20.0   (62)    10LDv  = –16.3  (13)    10LDv  = –16.3  (13)
   %cE-2 = 172.7  (95)    3LDv   = 30.0   (88)    Mc8wC  = 46.0   (91)
   c$-3  = 1.8    (80)    5yPEG  = 26.1   (82)    3-Wk   = 103.2  (71)
   c$-6  = 1.8    (75)    10$Gr  = 31.9   (97)    GrpRk  = 106.2  (62)
   cGRP3 = 0.0    (78)    %D/Eq  = 0.0    (57)    5YrEg  = 14.6   (52)
   5YrCf = 21.5   (83)    1mEGC  = 1.5    (88)    P/E    = 30.9   (77)
   RelPE = 58.2   (72)    GrRat  = 1.2    (60)    Insdr  = –4.0   ( 3)
   #AnCF = 3.0    (50)    $Rank  = 115.6  (87)    EPSRk  = 94.0   (89)
   5/30  = 76.0   (36)    AcDst  = 65.0   (64)    Price  = 39.6   (91)
3> RADIF    – RADA ELECTRONICS INDS LTD COM            .EDE
   %cELt = 23.3   (65)    10LDv  = –36.3  ( 3)    10LDv  = –36.3  ( 3)
   %cE-2 = 4100.0 (99)    3LDv   = 26.4   (86)    Mc8wC  = 12.0   (75)
   c$-3  = 14.4   (96)    5yPEG  = 40.0   (96)    3-Wk   = 121.6  (94)
   c$-6  = 8.9    (90)    10$Gr  = 5.8    (45)    GrpRk  = 105.2  (57)
   cGRP3 = –4.3   (15)    %D/Eq  = 57.5   (80)    5YrEg  = N/A    ( )
   5YrCf = N/A    ( )     1mEGC  = –5.3   ( 8)    P/E    = 7.0    ( 4)
   RelPE = 0.9    ( 1)    GrRat  = 6.9    (99)    Insdr  = 0.0    (91)
   #AnCF = 1.0    (22)    $Rank  = 109.7  (79)    EPSRk  = 94.0   (89)
   5/30  = 122.1  (70)    AcDst  = 25.0   (20)    Price  = 3.9    (10)
4> SPAR     – SPARTAN MOTORS INC COM                   .APT
   %cELt = 66.6   (85)    10LDv  = –66.4  ( 0)    10LDv  = –66.4  ( 0)
   %cE-2 = –78.3  ( 4)    3LDv   = –3.1   (18)    Mc8wC  = 1.0    (52)
   c$-3  = 3.3    (85)    5yPEG  = 19.0   (62)    3-Wk   = 105.1  (77)
   c$-6  = 1.4    (73)    10$Gr  = 34.6   (98)    GrpRk  = 106.2  (62)
   cGRP3 = 0.0    (78)    %D/Eq  = 10.5   (65)    5YrEg  = –1.1   (26)
   5YrCf = N/A    ( )     1mEGC  = 0.0    (78)    P/E    = 28.7   (75)
   RelPE = 20.9   (35)    GrRat  = 1.9    (88)    Insdr  = 0.0    (91)
   #AnCF = 3.0    (50)    $Rank  = 91.0   ( 4)    EPSRk  = 43.0   (35)
   5/30  = 83.9   (42)    AcDst  = 28.0   (23)    Price  = 7.8    (21)
```

(continued)

Exhibit 7.3   (continued)

5> NOVL   – NOVELL INC COM   .DSO

%cELt = –22.8	(24)	10LDv = –62.1	(0)	10LDv = –62.1	(0)
%cE-2 = 166.6	(94)	3LDv = –0.5	(26)	Mc8wC = 41.0	(90)
c$-3 = 4.1	(87)	5yPEG = 17.6	(57)	3-Wk = 109.9	(85)
c$-6 = 5.3	(85)	10$Gr = 34.6	(98)	GrpRk = 107.1	(68)
cGRP3 = –2.9	(26)	%D/Eq = 0.0	(57)	5YrEg = –0.3	(27)
5YrCf = 12.7	(70)	1mEGC = –1.7	(14)	P/E = 16.7	(47)
RelPE = 4.1	(7)	GrRat = 1.2	(60)	Insdr = 1.0	(96)
#AnCF = 26.0	(98)	$Rank = 94.4	(7)	EPSRk = 65.0	(58)
5/30 = 100.1	(56)	AcDst = 72.0	(77)	Price = 14.4	(57)

6> HH   – HOOPER HOLMES INC COM   .HHC

%cELt = 100.0	(91)	10LDv = –17.5	(12)	10LDv = –17.5	(12)
%cE-2 = 100.0	(91)	3LDv = 44.8	(92)	Mc8wC = 26.0	(85)
c$-3 = 9.1	(93)	5yPEG = 15.8	(50)	3-Wk = 125.9	(95)
c$-6 = 11.0	(92)	10$Gr = 9.9	(64)	GrpRk = 105.2	(57)
cGRP3 = –7.0	(5)	%D/Eq = 105.8	(89)	5YrEg = –26.6	(10)
5YrCf = 4.2	(47)	1mEGC = 1.7	(89)	P/E = 42.4	(85)
RelPE = 56.0	(70)	GrRat = 1.1	(53)	Insdr = 0.0	(91)
#AnCF = 6.0	(72)	$Rank = 108.9	(77)	EPSRk = 90.0	(82)
5/30 = 155.0	(82)	AcDst = 50.0	(45)	Price = 10.6	(38)

7> MAXE   – MAX & ERMAS RSTRS INC COM   .FRS

%cELt = –28.6	(21)	10LDv = –26.2	(7)	10LDv = –26.2	(7)
%cE-2 = –8.4	(29)	3LDv = –0.2	(28)	Mc8wC = 22.0	(83)
c$-3 = 6.8	(91)	5yPEG = 20.0	(68)	3-Wk = 117.9	(92)
c$-6 = 7.6	(89)	10$Gr = 21.8	(92)	GrpRk = 113.3	(91)
cGRP3 = –0.9	(55)	%D/Eq = 178.6	(94)	5YrEg = 40.5	(77)
5YrCf = 55.1	(95)	1mEGC = 0.0	(78)	P/E = 16.0	(44)
RelPE = 29.4	(46)	GrRat = 1.9	(88)	Insdr = 0.0	(91)
#AnCF = 6.0	(72)	$Rank = 104.1	(58)	EPSRk = 43.0	(35)
5/30 = 18.5	(5)	AcDst = 83.0	(92)	Price = 7.4	(19)

8> QNTM   – QUANTUM CORP COM   .DPE

%cELt = 42.7	(77)	10LDv = –10.8	(17)	10LDv = –10.8	(17)
%cE-2 = –62.2	(7)	3LDv = 3.8	(51)	Mc8wC = 72.0	(94)
c$-3 = 4.3	(87)	5yPEG = 16.4	(52)	3-Wk = 117.9	(92)
c$-6 = 0.3	(67)	10$Gr = 23.1	(93)	GrpRk = 114.9	(93)
cGRP3 = 0.1	(79)	%D/Eq = 82.5	(85)	5YrEg = –24.1	(11)
5YrCf = 0.8	(35)	1mEGC = –2.2	(13)	P/E = 21.0	(61)
RelPE = 3.8	(6)	GrRat = 2.2	(92)	Insdr = 2.0	(97)
#AnCF = 12.0	(88)	$Rank = 108.6	(76)	EPSRk = 33.0	(26)
5/30 = 221.8	(92)	AcDst = 62.0	(58)	Price = 22.6	(77)

9> CMFB   – CHEMFAB CORP COM   .MIU

%cELt = 41.1	(77)	10LDv = –16.6	(12)	10LDv = –16.6	(12)
%cE-2 = 46.6	(78)	3LDv = –3.6	(17)	Mc8wC = 4.0	(62)
c$-3 = –1.3	(37)	5yPEG = 20.0	(68)	3-Wk = 107.4	(82)
c$-6 = –5.1	(13)	10$Gr = 14.4	(82)	GrpRk = 110.5	(85)
cGRP3 = –2.4	(31)	%D/Eq = 10.5	(65)	5YrEg = –2.3	(24)
5YrCf = –11.5	(11)	1mEGC = 0.0	(78)	P/E = 14.3	(37)
RelPE = 5.6	(11)	GrRat = 1.8	(85)	Insdr = –5.0	(2)
#AnCF = 1.0	(22)	$Rank = 99.7	(23)	EPSRk = 94.0	(90)
5/30 = 117.8	(67)	AcDst = 29.0	(25)	Price = 12.6	(49)

Exhibit 7.3 (continued)

10> ECILF   – ECI TELECOM LTD COM   .TES

%cELt = 15.3	(57)	10LDv = –53.7	(1)	10LDv = –53.7	(1)	
%cE-2 = 16.0	(57)	3LDv = 32.9	(89)	Mc8wC = 17.0	(80)	
c$-3 = –0.1	(67)	5yPEG = 21.8	(72)	3-Wk = 116.7	(92)	
c$-6 = –2.6	(25)	10$Gr = 70.0	(99)	GrpRk = 108.2	(74)	
cGRP3 = 0.0	(78)	%D/Eq = 1.8	(60)	5YrEg = 31.7	(71)	
5YrCf = 71.4	(97)	1mEGC = 0.0	(78)	P/E = 22.3	(64)	
RelPE = 58.2	(72)	GrRat = 1.5	(76)	Insdr = 0.0	(91)	
#AnCF = 7.0	(76)	$Rank = 108.7	(76)	EPSRk = 77.0	(73)	
5/30 = 108.5	(62)	AcDst = 29.0	(25)	Price = 25.3	(80)	

11> DNAP   – DNA PLANT TECH CORP COM   .MLR

%cELt = 9.6	(50)	10LDv = –63.5	(0)	10LDv = –63.5	(0)	
%cE-2 = 16.0	(57)	3LDv = –10.8	(9)	Mc8wC = 4.0	(62)	
c$-3 = 7.9	(92)	5yPEG = 50.0	(99)	3-Wk = 115.3	(91)	
c$-6 = 4.0	(82)	10$Gr = –15.2	(3)	GrpRk = 109.0	(76)	
cGRP3 = 2.3	(91)	%D/Eq = 18.1	(68)	5YrEg = N/A	( )	
5YrCf = N/A	( )	1mEGC = 0.0	(78)	P/E = N/A	( )	
RelPE = N/A	( )	GrRat = N/A	( )	Insdr = 0.0	(91)	
#AnCF = 1.0	(22)	$Rank = 83.6	(2)	EPSRk = 57.0	(49)	
5/30 = 113.0	(64)	AcDst = 33.0	(30)	Price = 0.8	(1)	

12> NWL   – NEWELL CO COM   .HSW

%cELt = –8.7	(32)	10LDv = –22.5	(9)	10LDv = –22.5	(9)	
%cE 2 = 7.6	(48)	3LDv = 1.6	(40)	Mc8wC = 12.0	(75)	
c$-3 = 3.0	(84)	5yPEG = 14.1	(40)	3-Wk = 107.6	(82)	
c$-6 = 1.8	(75)	10$Gr = 24.3	(94)	GrpRk = 104.0	(52)	
cGRP3 = 1.0	(85)	%D/Eq = 71.1	(83)	5YrEg = 11.4	(46)	
5YrCf = 8.5	(59)	1mEGC = 0.0	(78)	P/E = 20.3	(59)	
RelPE = 49.5	(65)	GrRat = 0.9	(38)	Insdr = –1.0	(12)	
#AnCF = 17.0	(94)	$Rank = 104.2	(59)	EPSRk = 53.0	(45)	
5/30 = 168.5	(85)	AcDst = 40.0	(38)	Price = 28.3	(84)	

13> ELT   – ELSCINT LTD ORD SHS NEW   .SPE

%cELt = 100.0	(91)	10LDv = –28.5	(6)	10LDv = –28.5	(6)	
%cE-2 = 25.0	(66)	3LDv = 61.1	(95)	Mc8wC = 32.0	(87)	
c$-3 = 0.6	(73)	5yPEG = 15.0	(48)	3-Wk = 110.1	(86)	
c$-6 = 2.9	(79)	10$Gr = 9.8	(63)	GrpRk = 110.0	(82)	
cGRP3 = –2.8	(29)	%D/Eq = 2.6	(61)	5YrEg = –11.1	(17)	
5YrCf = –8.3	(15)	1mEGC = 0.0	(78)	P/E = 16.6	(47)	
RelPE = 79.2	(85)	GrRat = N/A	( )	Insdr = 0.0	(91)	
#AnCF = 1.0	(22)	$Rank = 116.2	(87)	EPSRk = 78.0	(74)	
5/30 = 205.2	(91)	AcDst = 88.0	(94)	Price = 15.0	(60)	

14> IV   – MARK IV INDUSTRIES INC COM   .APT

%cELt = 10.0	(51)	10LDv = –10.6	(17)	10LDv = –10.6	(17)	
%cE-2 = 12.5	(53)	3LDv = 4.6	(54)	Mc8wC = 6.0	(65)	
c$-3 = –0.2	(65)	5yPEG = 16.0	(51)	3-Wk = 101.2	(61)	
c$-6 = –1.7	(36)	10$Gr = 22.9	(93)	GrpRk = 106.2	(62)	
cGRP3 = 0.0	(78)	%D/Eq = 101.1	(88)	5YrEg = 14.3	(51)	
5YrCf = 3.8	(45)	1mEGC = –0.6	(20)	P/E = 14.3	(37)	
RelPE = 66.6	(77)	GrRat = N/A	( )	Insdr = 0.0	(91)	
#AnCF = 3.0	(50)	$Rank = 104.6	(62)	EPSRk = 70.0	(64)	
5/30 = 72.2	(33)	AcDst = 24.0	(18)	Price = 21.0	(75)	

(continued)

Exhibit 7.3 (continued)

15> VLO   – VALERO ENERGY CORP COM   .ORF
    %cELt = 1850.0   (99)   10LDv = –11.4   (17)   10LDv = –11.4   (17)
    %cE-2 = 1050.0   (99)   3LDv   = 22.0   (84)   Mc8wC = 38.0   (89)
    c$-3 = –3.1   (16)   5yPEG = 17.7   (58)   3-Wk   = 106.3   (80)
    c$-6 = –0.4   (61)   10$Gr = 13.7   (80)   GrpRk = 111.8   (89)
    cGRP3 = 2.0   (89)   %D/Eq = 107.4   (89)   5YrEg = –36.0   (7)
    5YrCf = 4.1   (46)   1mEGC = 4.2   (94)   P/E   = 18.5   (53)
    RelPE = 3.7   (6)   GrRat = 1.3   (67)   Insdr = 0.0   (91)
    #AnCF = 14.0   (91) $Rank = 107.3   (73)   EPSRk = 92.0   (86)
    5/30 = 72.6   (33)   AcDst = 71.0   (75)   Price = 27.3   (83)

16> WMT   – WALMART STORES INC COM   .RDI
    %cELt = –8.9   (32)   10LDv = –37.2   (3)   10LDv = –37.2   (3)
    %cE-2 = 3.8   (43)   3LDv   = 3.1   (47)   Mc8wC = 23.0   (83)
    c$-3 = 3.3   (85)   5yPEG = 13.9   (39)   3-Wk   = 103.8   (73)
    c$-6 = 1.5   (73)   10$Gr = 19.5   (90)   GrpRk = 108.2   (74)
    cGRP3 = 2.7   (94)   %D/Eq = 90.8   (87)   5YrEg = 17.2   (55)
    5YrCf = 17.5   (79)   1mEGC = 0.0   (78)   P/E   = 19.5   (57)
    RelPE = 23.8   (39)   GrRat = 0.9   (38)   Insdr = –4.0   (3)
    #AnCF = 38.0   (99) $Rank = 101.3   (39)   EPSRk = 52.0   (44)
    5/30 = 124.3   (71)   AcDst = 62.0   (58)   Price = 23.5   (78)

17> RPOW   – RPM INC COM   .COA
    %cELt = 10.0   (51)   10LDv = –13.5   (15)   10LDv = –13.5   (15)
    %cE-2 = –4.8   (32)   3LDv   = –3.1   (18)   Mc8wC = 13.0   (76)
    c$-3 = 2.5   (82)   5yPEG = 11.8   (27)   3-Wk   = 104.1   (74)
    c$-6 = 3.5   (81)   10$Gr = 11.3   (71)   GrpRk = 108.7   (75)
    cGRP3 = 2.3   (91)   %D/Eq = 106.4   (89)   5YrEg = 13.2   (49)
    5YrCf = 5.4   (50)   1mEGC = 0.0   (78)   P/E   = 18.1   (52)
    RelPE = 56.6   (70)   GrRat = 0.8   (29)   Insdr = 1.0   (96)
    #AnCF = 14.0   (91) $Rank = 100.1   (29)   EPSRk = 56.0   (48)
    5/30 = 86.3   (44)   AcDst = 42.0   (39)   Price = 15.6   (62)

18> MYE   – MYERS INDUSTRIES INC COM   .APT
    %cELt = 34.7   (73)   10LDv = –12.1   (16)   10LDv = –12.1   (16)
    %cE-2 = –15.7   (25)   3LDv   = 31.5   (88)   Mc8wC = 33.0   (88)
    c$-3 = 7.7   (92)   5yPEG = 12.5   (32)   3-Wk   = 120.7   (94)
    c$-6 = 6.3   (87)   10$Gr = 22.0   (92)   GrpRk = 106.2   (62)
    cGRP3 = 0.0   (78)   %D/Eq = 9.9   (65)   5YrEg = 9.5   (42)
    5YrCf = 7.5   (56)   1mEGC = 1.5   (88)   P/E   = 18.8   (54)
    RelPE = 95.8   (94)   GrRat = 1.0   (46)   Insdr = 0.0   (91)
    #AnCF = 5.0   (67) $Rank = 110.5   (80)   EPSRk = 65.0   (58)
    5/30 = 192.9   (89)   AcDst = 64.0   (62)   Price = 19.6   (72)

19> HONI   – HON INDUSTRIES INC COM   .OFU
    %cELt = 34.1   (73)   10LDv = –16.5   (12)   10LDv = –16.5   (12)
    %cE-2 = –51.8   (10)   3LDv   = 11.6   (73)   Mc8wC = 102.0   (96)
    c$-3 = 13.6   (96)   5yPEG = 12.5   (32)   3-Wk   = 115.3   (91)
    c$-6 = 20.3   (97)   10$Gr = 14.7   (82)   GrpRk = 108.9   (75)
    cGRP3 = 11.3   (99)   %D/Eq = 27.7   (72)   5YrEg = 11.8   (47)
    5YrCf = 4.0   (46)   1mEGC = 4.7   (94)   P/E   = 18.9   (55)
    RelPE = 72.1   (81)   GrRat = 0.9   (38)   Insdr = 5.0   (99)
    #AnCF = 3.0   (50) $Rank = 114.4   (85)   EPSRk = 55.0   (47)
    5/30 = 160.7   (83)   AcDst = 78.0   (89)   Price = 28.3   (84)

Exhibit 7.3   (continued)

20> SCOR	– SYNCOR INTL CORP DEL COM				.DDW		
%cELt = 60.0	(84)	10LDv = –36.7	(3)		10LDv = –36.7	(3)
%cE-2 = 33.4	(72)	3LDv = 61.1	(95)		Mc8wC = 48.0	(91)
c$-3 = 4.4	(87)	5yPEG = 11.5	(25)		3-Wk = 113.1	(89)
c$-6 = 13.0	(94)	10$Gr = 9.7	(63)		GrpRk = 104.8	(54)
cGRP3 = –2.7	(30)	%D/Eq = 9.5	(65)		5YrEg = –37.3	(6)
5YrCf = N/A	( )	1mEGC = N/A	( )		P/E = 19.1	(56)
RelPE = 5.4	(10)	GrRat = N/A	( )		Insdr = 0.0	(91)
#AnCF = N/A	( )	$Rank = 112.2	(83)		EPSRk = 71.0	(65)
5/30 = 38.7	(12)	AcDst = 63.0	(60)		Price = 9.8	(31)

21> KNAP	– KNAPE & VOGT MFG CO COM				.HFU		
%cELt = 0.0	(41)	10LDv = –20.9	(10)		10LDv = –20.9	(10)
%cE-2 = –28.0	(19)	3LDv = –11.3	(9)		Mc8wC = 12.0	(75)
c$-3 = 4.3	(87)	5yPEG = 15.0	(48)		3-Wk = 104.5	(75)
c$-6 = 2.7	(78)	10$Gr = 7.0	(51)		GrpRk = 103.9	(51)
cGRP3 = 0.5	(81)	%D/Eq = 47.6	(77)		5YrEg = 6.8	(38)
5YrCf = N/A	( )	1mEGC = –6.1	(7)		P/E = 12.1	(24)
RelPE = 48.4	(64)	GrRat = 1.5	(76)		Insdr = 1.0	(96)
#AnCF = 1.0	(22)	$Rank = 97.0	(11)		EPSRk = 38.0	(30)
5/30 = 88.0	(46)	AcDst = 54.0	(48)		Price = 14.1	(56)

22> KWP	– KING WORLD PRODS INC COM				.FDI		
%cELt = 16.2	(58)	10LDv = –11.5	(16)		10LDv = –11.5	(16)
%cE-2 = 56.0	(82)	3LDv = 7.2	(64)		Mc8wC = 2.0	(54)
c$-3 = –2.4	(22)	5yPEG = 16.3	(52)		3-Wk = 103.6	(72)
c$-6 = –0.5	(60)	10$Gr = 15.0	(83)		GrpRk = 106.6	(64)
cGRP3 = –1.3	(41)	%D/Eq = 0.0	(57)		5YrEg = 5.5	(36)
5YrCf = 6.2	(52)	1mEGC = 1.4	(88)		P/E = 11.6	(21)
RelPE = 17.0	(30)	GrRat = 1.4	(72)		Insdr = 0.0	(91)
#AnCF = 11.0	(87)	$Rank = 101.5	(40)		EPSRk = 78.0	(74)
5/30 = 158.3	(83)	AcDst = 24.0	(18)		Price = 43.0	(92)

23> HOC	– HOLLY CORP COM				.ORF		
%cELt = 41.6	(77)	10LDv = –25.8	(7)		10LDv = –25.8	(7)
%cE-2 = –16.0	(25)	3LDv = 20.1	(82)		Mc8wC = 42.0	(90)
c$-3 = 0.6	(73)	5yPEG = 12.5	(32)		3-Wk = 104.3	(75)
c$-6 = 3.0	(79)	10$Gr = 12.6	(76)		GrpRk = 111.8	(89)
cGRP3 = 2.0	(89)	%D/Eq = 125.0	(91)		5YrEg = 52.7	(83)
5YrCf = 18.0	(80)	1mEGC = 1.4	(88)		P/E = 19.1	(56)
RelPE = 28.7	(45)	GrRat = 1.2	(60)		Insdr = 0.0	(91)
#AnCF = 6.0	(72)	$Rank = 103.8	(56)		EPSRk = 51.0	(43)
5/30 = 101.3	(57)	AcDst = 70.0	(73)		Price = 27.0	(82)

24> PSCX	– PSC INC COM				.EIC		
%cELt = –81.9	(4)	10LDv = –19.1	(11)		10LDv = –19.1	(11)
%cE-2 = 60.8	(83)	3LDv = –19.9	(4)		Mc8wC = 36.0	(89)
c$-3 = –1.9	(28)	5yPEG = 24.3	(76)		3-Wk = 113.1	(89)
c$-6 = 4.1	(82)	10$Gr = 16.6	(86)		GrpRk = 108.4	(75)
cGRP3 = –1.2	(43)	%D/Eq = 1.2	(59)		5YrEg = –11.1	(17)
5YrCf = 36.3	(91)	1mEGC = 0.0	(78)		P/E = 25.6	(70)
RelPE = 10.3	(19)	GrRat = 1.9	(88)		Insdr = 0.0	(91)
#AnCF = 2.0	(38)	$Rank = 96.3	(9)		EPSRk = 23.0	(17)
5/30 = 177.5	(87)	AcDst = 55.0	(49)		Price = 9.8	(31)

(continued)

115

Exhibit 7.3   (continued)

25> TAC	– TANDYCRAFTS INC COM				.RSP		
%cELt = 10.8	(52)	10LDv = –43.6	(2)	10LDv = –43.6	(2)		
%cE-2 = –126.3	(0)	3LDv = 5.9	(59)	Mc8wC = 14.0	(77)		
c$-3 = 5.8	(90)	5yPEG = 15.2	(49)	3-Wk = 110.3	(86)		
c$-6 = 6.2	(87)	10$Gr = 14.3	(81)	GrpRk = 110.2	(84)		
cGRP3 = –1.9	(37)	%D/Eq = 75.2	(84)	5YrEg = 0.6	(28)		
5YrCf = 13.2	(71)	1mEGC = 0.0	(78)	P/E = N/A	( )		
RelPE = N/A	( )	GrRat = 2.1	(90)	Insdr = 2.0	(97)		
#AnCF = 4.0	(59)	$Rank = 93.9	(7)	EPSRk = 19.0	(13)		
5/30 = 83.3	(42)	AcDst = 64.0	(62)	Price = 6.6	(17)		

Note: Scores of N/A mean the data was not available or pieces of the data that make up the calculation, such as negative numbers, would cause the score to be invalid. The most likely reason for a P/E ratio of N/A is that, at the time of the search, the company had no earnings or negative earnings.

Source: ProSearch 5.0, courtesy of Telescan, Inc.

In the end, you have to weigh the importance of the bad scores against the preponderance of the good. If a relatively unimportant score gets thumbs down, you can safely ignore it. But take heed if it is a factor you consider important. After all, you might buy a car without air bags, but you wouldn't buy one without brakes.

YOU MUST REMEMBER THIS . . .

Never take a search at face value. Computerized search products are valuable and powerful tools, but they simply compare or calculate raw data. Any list of stocks found by a search should be evaluated further, whether you use our method or one of your own. Here are a few points to keep in mind.

- The selection of tools we used to evaluate the stocks in this chapter reflects *our* philosophical bent.

- Use as many list-only indicators as you have room for in a search. (For space considerations, we had to limit ourselves in this chapter.) If you use 10 or 12 indicators to eliminate and rank stocks, you could conceivably use as many as 28 to 30 to list information for evaluation.

- In the stage-one evaluation, concentrate only on extreme scores. The objective is to eliminate the very worst stocks on the list and carry the very best ones on to the next evaluation.

- Be sure you're judging the right score. In some cases, you'll want to look at the raw score; in other cases, at the percentile rank.[1] If in doubt, use the percentiles.

- In most cases, an N/A score means that the data was not available, or there were pieces of data (such as negative numbers) that make up a calculation that caused the score to be invalid.

- Use common sense in evaluating the list-only scores. There are no right answers, except in retrospect.

- As you gain experience, you should get a feel for which secondary indicators are the most important to you. At some point, you might consider using some of the more important ones to eliminate or score the stocks on your list, rather than just to list information.

Let's go on to the analysis tools we use to judge the stocks that make our short list. Our goal, remember, is to end up with the *creme de la creme*— the three or four stocks that we think will give us the best returns.

---

[1] A range of desirable scores for many ProSearch indicators is available from Telescan.

8

STAGE-TWO EVALUATION

We are now half-way through our evaluation. Let's take time out to review how we got to this point.

Up to now, everything has been done with a stock search tool. We created a search strategy that narrowed the search universe to meet our minimum standards; we scored and ranked the stocks based on our most important objectives; then, we "seasoned the search" to coax stocks with specific qualities to the top of the list. Finally, we listed information on the search report that we used in Chapter 7 to evaluate the stocks found by the search. Nine stocks made it through the first stage of the evaluation process. Now we are ready to put these semifinalists through stage two.

This time we will look at price-and-volume graphs and qualitative information on the company itself. The stock graphs will show us the long-term and short-term price trend and the volatility of the stock. We'll use the long-term stock graph to demonstrate an important tool that can help you determine whether the stock has sufficient room to grow, based on its historical trading range. The qualitative information includes news, earnings-estimates reports, and company profiles. These allow us to assess the importance of any recent event and its possible effect on the stock's growth potential. Stocks that make it through this evaluation are the ones we will consider buying, given the appropriate technical buy signal.

Our method for the stage-two evaluation is to use computerized tools to retrieve the information and then grade each stock for each item evaluated. We will use letter grades (A through F, as in school); you may wish to use ratings of 1 to 5 or 1 to 10. At the end of this chapter, we will tally up the grades and pick our winners.

IN LIEU OF A THOUSAND WORDS . . .

A stock graph, like a picture, is worth a thousand words. It shows you at a glance a stock's price and volume history over one month, one year, 10 years, or 20. We like to look at a one-year graph for each of our candidates because, in most charting programs, each day's trading is represented by a single bar. This clearly displays the day-to-day activity. We will also look at a long-term graph that shows price and volume over a much longer period. (By the way, we will use these stock graphs in the next chapter to evaluate several technical indicators.)

Price Pattern and Volatility

We look for two things on the one-year graph: price pattern and volatility. If the stock has been falling more or less steadily for several months or a year and has shown no sign of turning up, we would give it an F. This is not the time to jump in if the most recent action is all downhill. Most of our searches are structured so as to preclude this situation, but yours may not be.

Two examples from our candidates may be instructive. (Note that this analysis was done on the date that appears on the stock graph, May 8, 1996). Beginning about March 1, Valero Energy Corp. (Exhibit 8.1) turned sharply upward, then dropped back somewhat in early May; more important is the general uptrend that began last July, which underlays the more recent upturn. We gave Valero a B+ for this short-term price pattern.

King World Productions (Exhibit 8.2) has been zigzagging upwardly since October 1995, but because it was in a downward trend before that, we gave it a C+ for price pattern.

A stock's volatility is measured by the range of the price swing as the stock moves. A highly volatile stock may have a history of success but with steep drops followed by sharp rises. In judging volatility, you have to decide just how many ups and downs your tummy can take. Will you be comfortable on a roller-coaster ride? Or will you be inclined to panic and

Exhibit 8.1   Valero Energy Corp. shows a generally positive short-term price pattern and moderate volatility.

5/8/96   VALERO ENERGY CORP COM (VLO)   26.62

Open: 27.12   Hi: 27.12   Lo: 26.37   Last: 26.62   Change: -.63   Vol: 927

jump off at the first downward dip? We suggest you check the volatility on both long-term and short-term graphs.

Seven of our candidates had more or less average volatility, with only ECI Telecom and Holly Corp. getting good grades in this area. Valero, shown in Exhibit 8.1, earned a C because it dropped 10 percent three different times in just over eight months. King World (Exhibit 8.2), with three smaller drops since its upturn in October 1995, received a C+.

The Long-Term Price Trend

A one-year graph does not give a true representation of a company's history. For a longer perspective, we look at a graph that shows a much longer history of the company, up to 25 years.

If you'll recall, we used the 10-year LSQ deviation indicator in the search to eliminate all stocks that weren't at least 10 percent below the LSQ line. Generally speaking, we're satisfied with this to narrow our search universe. But a stock can be below its 10-year LSQ line and *not* be as attractive on a longer-term graph. (Valero, in Exhibit 8.4, is a good

Exhibit 8.2   King World Productions has an overall flat price pattern, short term, with a recent positive trend and moderate volatility.

5/8/96   KING WORLD PRODS INC COM (KWP)   41.87

Open: 42.75   Hi: 42.75   Lo: 40.87   Last: 41.87   Change: -1.13   Vol: 1010

example.) That's why we like to look at the trading history on a maximum-term graph, (20 years or more).

An LSQ line reveals how the current stock price relates to its historical price trend. An LSQ trading channel carries this one step further and shows how much room the stock has to rise (or fall) within its historical trading range. We've found the LSQ trading channel to be valuable in assessing the upward or downward potential of a stock, based on history.

To plot the LSQ trading channels, we'll download a stock graph for the maximum available time span for each of our candidates. You should use the longest period offered by your stock analysis program. Next, we'll draw an LSQ line on the graph to find out the current position of the stock with respect to its long-term trend. Finally, we'll draw parallel lines on either side of the LSQ line to form a trading channel.[1]

---

[1] To draw the LSQ trading channel, first draw the LSQ line by selecting the appropriate command. Then mark a representative top and press the parallel line key; then mark a representative bottom and press the parallel line key again. The parallel lines need not be

Exhibit 8.3   On a maximum-term graph, Myers Industries was right at its long-term LSQ line in May 1996 (although it was below the 10-year LSQ line).

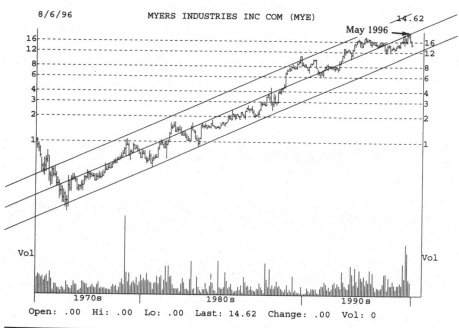

We prefer those stocks that are the farthest below their long-term LSQ lines because, based on their long-term trend, they have more room to grow. Although all nine of our semi-finalists received an A for their *10-year* LSQ deviation (as a result of the search), their *long-term* graphs tell a slightly different story. Only four of the nine stocks were below their maximum-term LSQ lines (Max & Irma's, Hon Industries, Holly Corp., and King World). Three were right at the LSQ line (Quanex, OEA, and Myers), and two were in the upper channel (ECI and Valero).

Myers and Valero are particularly instructive in this regard. Myers (Exhibit 8.3) has had a long, relatively smooth upward climb. We'd give it a B+ for long-term LSQ deviation because it is sitting at the midpoint of

---

equidistant from the LSQ line. There should be as many touches and as few significant penetrations as possible. The idea is to build a historical channel. Some stocks do not provide a very neat channel, but most do.

its price history (on May 8). Valero, on the other hand, would get a D, because (on May 8) it is well up in the top of the channel (Exhibit 8.4).

Being at the top of a long-term LSQ trading channel doesn't necessarily signal potential disaster. Companies *do* break out of long-term trends. But if we find a stock that is nudging the top channel, we'd disqualify it. After all, if the stock hasn't broken out of its long-term trend in 20 years or longer, why bet on its breaking out now? The risk is high and the potential reward, small.

Occasionally, however, you'll find a stock that has pushed through the top band. It is possible that it will keep right on going. However, were it to show up on a search, we would disqualify it as a possible candidate, based on this one indicator. It simply carries too much risk. There are many other candidates with equally good prospects and less potential risk. Now that we have the computerized tools to assess such things, we prefer not to take that risk.

Exhibit 8.4   On a maximum-term graph, Valero Energy Corp. was well up in the LSQ trading channel on May 8 (although it was below the 10-year LSQ line). Notice the volatility.

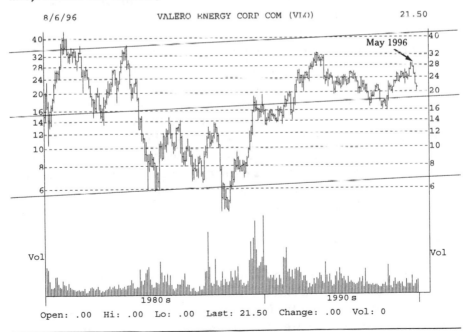

8/6/96   VALERO ENERGY CORP COM (VLO)   21.50

Open: .00 Hi: .00 Lo: .00 Last: 21.50 Change: .00 Vol: 0

RESEARCHING THE COMPANY

There are a number of company information tools that provide a variety of information about public companies. They range from filings with the Securities and Exchange Commission to research reports from Wall Street analysts to quantitative data on earnings estimates to the latest stories from the newswires. The three tools we consider indispensable are news, analysts' earnings estimates, and company profiles published by independent services.

All the News That's Worth a Byte

Jumping into a stock without looking at the news is like boarding a plane without looking at a flight schedule: You may end up in a place you really don't want to be. With cyber-investing, you can check the news electronically, which means you often may learn about an event before you see it in the regular media.

Most online services offer electronic news from various newswires, such as Reuters. Usually, a list of headlines appears first; you may then select the article you wish to read. The headlines themselves will do for starters. At this point, we're simply looking for late breaking news that might be important to our decision.

Exhibit 8.5 shows headlines for OEA, Inc. on the date of our analysis (early May, 1996). Most look very good, especially the "Research Alert" on 3/19. The article behind the headline (Exhibit 8.6) tells us that the analyst not only raised the target stock price less than six weeks earlier, but also the earnings estimates for 1998 and 1999. This wins OEA an A for news. On the other hand, headlines for ECI (not shown) included the resignation of the CFO and two institutional shareholders selling off several million shares. Closer inspection revealed that the news wasn't as bad as the headlines implied, but the articles earned ECI a C– in our rating system.

There are no rigid guidelines for judging the news. Common sense should tell you which event might affect a stock positively or negatively.

A Consensus of Analysts

Among the most valuable computerized tools are reports that summarize earning estimates from Wall Street analysts. They provide a consensus of Wall Street's opinion about the future earnings prospects for a particular stock (which is why they are called *consensus* earnings estimates). The

Exhibit 8.5   News Headlines for OEA, Inc. on May 8, 1996. The full article may be viewed by selecting the corresponding number key. The full article for the first OEA headline appears in Exhibit 8.6.

REUTERS NEWS—5/08/96

Number of reports found = 15

01>	3/19/96	RESEARCH ALERT-OEA (OEA.N) stock target raised
02>	2/28/96	OEA Inc (OEA.N) Q2 Jan 31 net rises
03>	2/28/96	OEA INC (OEA.N) Q2 SHR $0.30 VS $0.25
04>	12/11/95	CONSENSUS: U.S. corporate earnings surprise data
05>	12/11/95	OEA Inc (OEA.N) Q1 Oct 31 net advances
06>	11/07/95	OEA Inc (OEA.N) boosts annual div to $0.25/shr
07>	10/18/95	OEA (OEA.N) wins big GM (GM.N) order for inflators
08>	10/04/95	CONSENSUS: U.S. corporate earnings surprise data
09>	6/07/95	CONSENSUS: U.S. corporate earnings surprise data
10>	6/07/95	OEA Inc (OEA.N) Q3 April 30 shr rises
11>	3/08/95	OEA Inc (OEA.N) Q2 Jan 31 net rises
12>	12/15/94	OEA Inc (OEA.N) Q1 Oct 31 oper net rises
13>	12/13/94	OEA (OEA.N) fined for breaking environmental laws
14>	12/07/94	OEA (OEA.N) to make inflators for airbags
15>	12/06/94	OEA(OEA.N)to make automobile side-impact inflators

Source: Courtesy of Reuters, Inc.

major online suppliers for these reports are Zacks Investment Research, I.B.E.S., and First Call. These companies collect the earnings estimates from research reports published by Wall Street analysts and tabulate the information in various ways. As part of your Cyber-Investing Kit, you may obtain free Zacks reports through Telescan for 30 days.

A Zacks report contains an abundance of information, as shown for Quanex in Exhibit 8.7.[2] For our stage-two evaluation, we will concentrate on the following:

- *Earnings projections:* The Zacks report tabulates earnings projections for the next two quarters and next two years. An

---

[2] Zacks follows more than 5,000 companies. The reports are available from Zacks Investment Research either directly or via the Internet, and through Telescan. (See listing in the Source List at the end of the book.)

Exhibit 8.6   A news article behind one of the OEA headlines dated March 19, 1996.

3/19/96—RESEARCH ALERT-OEA (OEA.N) stock target raised

Dean Witter analyst Ronald Glantz said he raised his target price on OEA Inc stock to $45 from $40, based on earnings growth through the end of the decade.

Glantz, who maintains his buy recommendation on the stock, said he also raised his fiscal 1998 and 1999 earnings per share estimates to $2.45 from $2.20 and to $3.05 from $2.75, respectively.   `)`

Glantz maintained his fiscal 1996 and 1997 eps estimates of $1.40 and $1.85, respectively.

    —OEA shares were up 1-7/8 at 37 at midday.

    —Chicago newsroom (312) 408-8787.

REUTER Rtr 13:55 03-19-96
End of Report

Source: Courtesy of Reuters, Inc.

---

annualized earnings growth rate for the next five years is given, if available. Be sure to look at the quarterly earnings, as well as the longer term; if the short term is not good, you may have to wait several years for your profits. Unless you're willing to do that, you should probably discard that stock. Also, pay attention to the 5-year-earnings growth rate, especially if it wasn't used as an indicator in your search. Quanex shows positive earnings forecasts for the next two years, plus a 28 percent growth rate over the next 5 years.

- *Revisions:* Each Zacks report includes a column that shows the average revision, upward or downward, in each estimate over the past 30 days. Quanex has downward revisions for the third quarter and for fiscal 1996 and 1997. Even though they are small, negative revisions are generally undesirable.

- *Number of Analysts:* If you don't use the number of analysts as a search tool, you can get it from the Zacks report. Quanex has 5 for current year projections, which is adequate.

- *P/E Comparisons:* Zacks compares a company's current P/E ratio and projected P/E ratio with the industry average and S&P 500

Exhibit 8.7   Zacks Earning Estimates: Selected information for Quanex Corporation from the May 8, 1996 report.

WALL STREET ESTIMATES

	Mean	High	Low	Number Est	Mean Chg Last Mnth ($)
FISC YR END 9610	2.14	2.25	2.01	5	−0.03
FISC YR END 9710	2.59	2.70	2.47	4	−0.04
QUARTER END 9604	0.54	0.55	0.52	4	0.00
QUARTER END 9607	0.60	0.66	0.52	4	−0.02
NEXT 5 YR GRTH (%)	28.33	40.00	15.00	3	0.00

COMPANY VS INDUSTRY

	EPS Growth Rates				
	(Cur FY = 9612; FOR NX, CUR = 9610)				P/E on
	Last 5 Yrs Actual (%)	Cur/Last (%)	Nxt/Cur (%)	Nxt 5 Yrs (%)	Cur Yr EPS
COMPANY	7.0	−2.7	20.9	28.3	10.3
IND. STEEL-PIPE&TUB (T = 275)	21.0	−5.4	35.8	15.8	15.7
S & P 500	11.2	1.3	5.5	6.8	16.2
COMPANY/INDUSTRY	N/M	N/M	0.6	1.8	0.7
COMPANY/S&P	0.7	−2.0	3.8	4.2	0.6

QUARTERLY EARNINGS SURPRISES

	Last	Previous Four Qtrs			
	Qtr0	Qtr1	Qtr2	Qtr3	Qtr4
Month FQ End	Apr 96	Jan 96	Oct 95	Jul 95	Apr 95
Mean Estimate	N/A	0.30	0.67	0.56	0.44
Actual EPS	N/A	0.30	0.72	0.63	0.63

	Qtr0	Qtr1	Qtr2	FY1	FY2
30-Day Median	N/A	0.44	0.75	2.29	2.57

Primary Shares Outstanding as of Jun 96 : 13,595,000

Recent Reported EPS —Last Report Qtr Date: Jan 96

Last Qtr	Prev Qtr	Last 12 Mth	Last Rprtd FY
0.30	0.72	2.27	2.20

CURRENT RATINGS:

Strong Buy (1)	0
Moderate Buy (2)	2
Hold (3)	3
Moderate Sell (4)	0
Strong Sell (5)	0
Mean Rating (1 to 5 scale) =	2.6

Source: Courtesy of Zacks Investment Research.

companies. (Projected P/E is the P/E earned if estimates are met.) At 10.3, Quanex's projected P/E ratio is below both the industry average of 15.7 and the S&P 500 average of 16.2, which means it has room to increase. More important, the ratio of P/E to growth rate is excellent. Quanex's forecasted 5-year growth rate of 28.3 is higher than its industry (15.8) and more than 4 times that of the S&P 500 (6.8). Yet, Quanex's P/E of 10.3 is only about two-thirds of the industry group P/E (15.7) and the S&P 500 (16.2). All this is extremely favorable.

- *Earnings Surprises.* An *earnings surprise* occurs when the company's actual earnings exceed (a positive surprise) or fail to meet (a negative surprise) the analysts' estimates. The Zacks report lists both for the past five quarters. If we see a steady stream of negative earnings surprises, we'll avoid the stock. On the other hand, a company like Quanex, which had positive earnings surprises in three of the past four quarters, would find a warm spot in our hearts.

- *Buy, Hold, and Sell Recommendations:* Zacks also tabulates the number of buy, hold, and sell recommendations by analysts. If a Zacks report lists a dozen sell recommendations and no buys or holds, we probably would not want to swim against the tide. Quanex has two moderate buys and three holds, an average recommendation that's neither positive nor negative.

The positives outweigh the slightly negative revisions and neutral buy recommendations, so we gave Quanex a B for its Zacks report.

The Company Profile

It is important to look at a company profile to get a feel for what the company does and how well it is doing it. A number of services offer profiles, including Standard & Poor's (S&P), Market Guide, and Value Line. Value Line has an extensive hard copy service and is available online to a limited degree, but the basic service covers less than 2,000 companies. Market Guide™, available through Telescan and other online services, offers comprehensive financial data (plus a three-page synopsis) and extensive ratio analysis; it does not provide qualitative recommendations.

The MarketScope® report from Standard & Poor's, also available on Telescan, includes a brief synopsis of a company's business, commentary (usually) on the expected earnings trend and cash flow, and summary financial information. It also features a "stock appreciation ranking system"—a sort of corporate report card that it calls STARS. Five STARS is S&P's highest rating. The STARS ratings go all the way down to one, which is given to stocks that S&P recommends avoiding.

Exhibit 8.8 shows the S&P MarketScope for ECI Telecom. It has 5 STARS; its earnings have grown steadily over the past three years; its P/E ratio is 17.7, which is below the past three years and well below its 1993 high of 39.5. Moreover, eight analysts recommend ECI as a buy. We gave it an A for its overall MarketScope evaluation.

Six of our stocks did not have a STARS rating at all. This is not necessarily bad, because S&P doesn't rate all stocks with its STARS system. If one of your stocks doesn't have a STARS rating, read the report to see if it contains anything negative or particularly positive and act accordingly. We gave all six stocks a C because there was nothing particularly exciting or alarming in their S&P reports. Despite its lack of an S&P STAR, Valero Energy turned out to be one of our five finalists.

None of our ten stocks had a 1-STAR rating, but we would probably disqualify one that did, regardless of its other merits. With all the other good stocks, why bother with one that S&P says to avoid? Maybe they know something we don't.

It may occur to you to consider just stocks with 5-STAR S&P ratings and forget about all this searching and analysis. This is not necessarily a good idea. At any given time, there are several hundred 5-STAR stocks. Second, the ratings are not good for early signals because they tend to lag the market significantly (at least in our experience). We prefer to consider the S&P STARS ratings in context with the rest of our evaluation.

Evaluating a company profile, as you can see, is somewhat subjective, but it can reveal important information about a stock. It can also give you a chance to act on any bias you might have. This is the stage at which you may wish to boycott a company just because you found out it manufacturers widgets that go against your political sympathies!

Et Cetera

There are other company information tools you might wish to consider. Various forms filed by public companies with the SEC (including the full text of annual reports) are available through Dow Jones (Disclosure™), Telescan (SEC Online™), EDGAR™ on the Internet, and others. If you don't mind reading lengthy documents, you may wish to look at these reports.

Exhibit 8.8   S&P MarketScope® Report: ECI Telecom on May 8, 1996.

ECI TELECOM LTD. *****,RECOMMENDATION

Israeli co. . . Makes telecomm systems using digital speech processing, switching technologies, ISDN compatible technologies. . . 12/7/95 Receives orders from Deutsche Telekom of about $44.5M at current exchange rates for ASLMX access multiplexers, PCM-11 pair gain products. . . '95 EPS up 15% on 17% rise in revenues. . . includes $0.02/share restructuring charge. . . 1Q '96 EPS up 19% on 23% sales rise.

*****Outlook: '97 EPS estimated $1.80, '96's seen $1.43 vs. '95's $1.16. . . Annual Dividend $0.13.

Sales	'94	'93
Europe	24%	46%
North America	53%	32%
Asia/Pacific	13%	12%
Other	10%	10%

Tel.#212-838-3777

5/6/96 1:05 pm. . . STILL BUY ECI TELECOM LTD. (ECILF 25*****). . . Posts Q1 EPS of $0.32 vs. $0.27, in line with expectations. . Solid top line growth was led by 57% rise in sales of Access Network products (pair gain and HDSL systems), 77% increase in synchronous digital hierarchy sales. . . But gross margins narrowed on less favorable product mix, weakness in unit U.S. Telematics. . . Telematics should begin to turn around in 2nd half '96. . . Orders rose 52% in Q1. . . Still see '96 EPS $1.43, could trend higher in coming months. . . should see acceleration in growth rate in '97. . . Target price in low $30s by end of '96. /R.Gross

-0- ECILF $ (0837) 05-07-96 01:35 PM EST

ECI TELECOM LTD. ***** 06-MAY-96 — STATS

Share Earnings		Market Action		NMS
3 Mo Mar	.32/.27:96 Rng	27.87	20.75:S&P Rank NR	
Last 12 Mos	1.21:Avg Vol		617700:	
P/E	17.7:Beta		1.5:	
5-Yr Growth %	+ 23:Inst Holdings		38%:	

Dividends		Balance Sheet		BV/SH	
Rt&Yd	.10	0.3%	:Cur Ratio	3.86	:95	N/A
Last Div		.050	:LT Dt(M)	1	:94	4.25
Ex-Date		02/13	:Shs(M)	75.71	:93	3.34
PayDate		03/14/96	:Rpt.of 12/31/94		:92	2.43

CBOE:Cycle 2. 2-for-1,'91,'92,'93.

Exhibit 8.8   (continued)

Yr	High	Low	P/E Range		Div	EPS	Rev(M)	Net(M)
95	24.25	11.25	20.9	9.7	.10	1.16	451.4	87.8
94	28.50	11.50	28.2	11.4	.16	1.01	384.6	76.6
93	26.87	15.00	39.5	22.1	.09	.68	295.7	51.3

-0- ECILF $ (0838) 05-07-96 01:35 PM EST

Earnings Estimates   05/05/96

	New	Old	High	Low	Ests
Current Quarter (Q2-96) Consensus Estimate	0.34	N/A	0.35	0.33	4
Current Year 1996 (DEC) Consensus Estimate	1.43	N/A	1.50	1.37	9
Next Year 1997 (DEC) Consensus Estimate	1.76	N/A	1.82	1.70	5

Next EPS Report Date: 05/09/96

Street Guidance:	Buy	Buy/Hold	Hold	Hold/Sell	Sell
	8	0	0	0	0

End of Report

Source: Reprinted by permission of Standard & Poor's, a division of McGraw-Hill, Inc.

Research reports from analysts who follow the company are available on the Internet through Investex™ and Multex™, both full text and summaries (see Chapter 16).[3] These are the same reports used by Zacks for its earnings estimates (which contain the raw numbers but no text). Although the full research reports are more expensive than the Zacks reports, we predict that, in the tradition of online information, their costs will come down and will eventually be practical for most investors. The prices aren't yet quite low enough that we can strongly recommend them. Still, if cost is no objection, research reports can be a valuable supplement to your evaluation.

---

[3] Investex reports are also available through Dow Jones News/Retrieval®; Multex reports are available through Telescan.

WHAT TO DO WITH A HOT STOCK TIP

It's inevitable. One day you'll get a stock tip from your brother-in-law or your dentist or a well-meaning friend. "You gotta get in on this thing," they'll tell you in an admirable gesture to share the wealth. Before you do, however, put the stock through a little computerized evaluation.

- Read the news headlines and check out any recent story. If your "scoop" is in the news, the market has already discounted it. Even if it is not in the news, there's a good chance that those in the know already know.
- Look at the LSQ trading channels on a long-term and short-term stock graph. Note where the stock is in relation to the LSQ line.
- Assess the technical condition of the stock. (We'll show you how in the next chapter.)
- Note the current volume level and compare it with the past 15 to 30 days. If the stock is moving up on increasing volume, that's good.
- Look at the analysts' earnings estimates and check all the items discussed in this chapter, including P/E ratio and P/E comparisons.
- Check out the insiders. Are they buying or selling?
- Read a company profile. Note any buy and sell recommendations, as well as any comments about future earnings.
- Look at the industry-group graph. (The industry group symbol will vary, depending on whose service you use.) Is it trending upward or downward? To compare its rank with other industry groups, run the industry group search described in Chapter 14.
- If you use Telescan, download the valuation report (called the ProSearch Criteria Report in ProSearch 5.0) which lists the values for the various indicators used by ProSearch. Check out the relative P/E ratio and other fundamentals.

Once you have done all this, you can make a decision based on information, not on emotion. The same goes for a stock that you learn about in the media. Obviously, the news is already out, so evaluate the stock thoroughly to make sure you're not the last one on the bandwagon.

The Envelope, Please!

Five stocks from our nine top candidates made the final cut: Quanex, OEA, Inc., ECI Telecom, Valero Energy Corp., and King World Productions. Their report card from the stage-two evaluation is shown in Exhibit 8.9. In the next chapter we will view these five stocks through other technical lenses. We'll be looking for technical buy signals that will help us enter the market at the most favorable time.

YOU MUST REMEMBER THIS . . .

The stage-two evaluation is just as important as the evaluation in stage one. To review:

- Look at the long-term LSQ trading channels to make sure the stock has room to grow; look at the short-term trend to make sure it is going in the right direction.

Exhibit 8.9   A typical "report card" from the stage-two evaluation. From these ratings, we will select the finalists in our search for the best undervalued growth stocks.

We used the following rating system:

A = Excellent
B = Good
C = Average
D = Below Average
F = Unacceptable

Stock Symbol	LSQ Deviation Maximum Term	Price Pattern	Volatility	News	S&P MarketScope	Zacks Report	Final Score
NX	B	C	C	A-	A(5-Star)	B	B+
OEA	B	B	C	A	B+(4-Star)	B-	B
MAXE	A	C+	D	C	B	C	C
ECILF	C	B-	B+	C-	A(5-Star)	B	B
VLO	D	B+	C	B	C-	B+	B-
MYE	B+	B+	C	B-	C	C	C+
HONI	A	B	C-	B-	C+	C-	C+
KWP	A	C+	C+	B-	B-(4-Star)	B+	B-
HOC	A	B+	B	C+	D+	C	C+

- Consider the stock's volatility in light of your investing personality.
- Make sure there is no late-breaking news that might adversely affect the stock.
- Carefully analyze the earnings estimates report.
- Review a company profile from an independent source. Beware of any sell recommendations.
- If you get a stock tip—whatever the source—check it out thoroughly. It may be as cold as last night's pizza.

So far we have introduced you to about 10 percent of the 300+ search tools available in ProSearch. But no matter how powerful search tools are, they can't do the job by themselves. You need analysis and information tools to complete the evaluation process, some of which we've described in this chapter. The important thing, however, is not which tools you use but that you use them.

In the next chapter, we'll talk about timing your entry to maximize your returns.

9

TO BUY OR
NOT TO BUY

If you have followed the five-step investing process thus far, you have a
short list of excellent stocks. They are, based on the goals defined by the
search strategy and the two-stage evaluation, the cream from a crop of
more than 9,000 stocks. Chances are, you could buy any or all of them at
this point and do just fine, assuming you hold them long enough. But you
can improve your risk/reward potential by identifying trend reversals or
price support levels. Based on our experience and backtesting, this can
add as much as three percentage points to annualized returns. If you recall from Chapter 1 how much three points can mean in dollars and cents,
you'll agree it's worthwhile to wait for a good technical "buy" signal.

This chapter, then, deals not with which of the stocks to buy, but
when to buy it.

WHAT'S IT ALL ABOUT?

In theory, when a stock starts moving up or down and gains momentum,
it doesn't easily reverse direction. In part, such uptrends and downtrends
are caused by the activity of institutional investors (who represent about

135

70 percent of all trading). Eventually, however, a reversal will occur. At some point in an uptrend, buyers will dry up, which will result in an overbought condition making the stock susceptible to a downward correction (a good time to sell). Likewise, at some point in a downward trend, sellers will diminish, resulting in an oversold condition with the stock susceptible to a reversal. Obviously, the best time to buy stocks is when the selling has dried up and a trend reversal is apparent. This is the point technical analysis seeks to discover and label as a buy signal.

Cyber-investing offers dozens of technical analysis tools that can help identify the likelihood of a trend reversal. We can't go into all of them here—there are entire books devoted to technical analysis and to the individual tools themselves—but we will touch on a few.

First, we'll talk briefly about some of the most common technical tools: support and resistance lines and trendlines. Then we'll discuss basing period breakouts, which typically signal the beginning of a new trend. Finally, we'll show you three of our favorite tools for determining technical buy signals: the moving average convergence/divergence (MACD) indicator, the stochastics index, and trading bands.

We will briefly describe the underlying technical concept of each indicator and then show you how to interpret it on a few stock graphs. At the end of the chapter, we will show you how we applied these tools to the top five stocks from our stage-two evaluation.

FLOORS AND CEILINGS

Support and resistance lines are among the most basic of technical analysis tools, and they can be helpful in assessing entry and exit points in a stock. A support line is a horizontal line drawn through stock bottoms; it represents a "floor" or price level that supports the stock at that price. A resistance line is a horizontal line drawn through stock tops; it represents a "ceiling" or price barrier that the stock has difficulty penetrating. Pushing through a resistance line is a positive signal; a breakdown of a support line is negative.

Both support and resistance are created, for the most part, by institutional investors. A support level represents the price that one or more institutions have targeted as an entry point for the stock. Because they are long-term investors, it may take months for an institution to accumulate a position in a stock at its targeted price. With patience carved out of necessity, the institution waits until the stock falls to the desired price; then it steps in with its considerable purchasing power and the stock rebounds. As a result, support forms under the stock at that price level. (See Exhibits 9.1, 9.2, and 9.3.) Over time, this floor becomes more solid as the stock falls again and again to that point and then rebounds. The more frequently this happens, the more credence investors give to that support level and the more willingly they will enter at that point. It becomes, in effect, a self-fulfilling prophecy.

A mirror image of this takes place with resistance levels. A ceiling is formed at a price that represents for many investors a target level for that stock. (See Exhibits 9.4 and 9.5.) When the stock reaches an important resistance level, selling accelerates. This sends the stock into a reversal and strengthens the resistance to that particular price level. Selling must dry up before the stock is likely to break through that particular ceiling of resistance. This isn't likely to occur until earnings prospects, P/E ratios, or the market in general improves.

Exhibit 9.1   Merck & Co. has a 7-month support level at about $56.

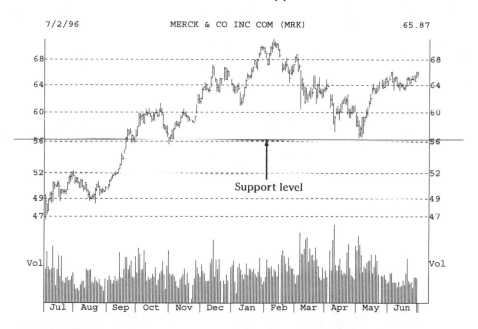

Exhibit 9.2   AT&T has support at about $60.

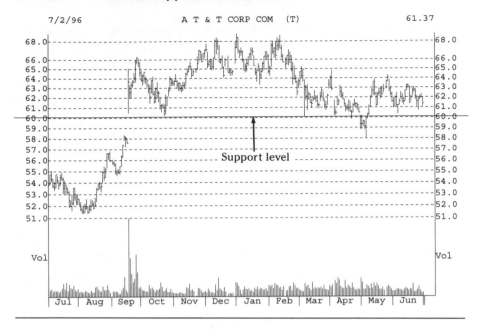

Exhibit 9.3   Mobil Corp. has strong support at $112 and secondary support at $108.

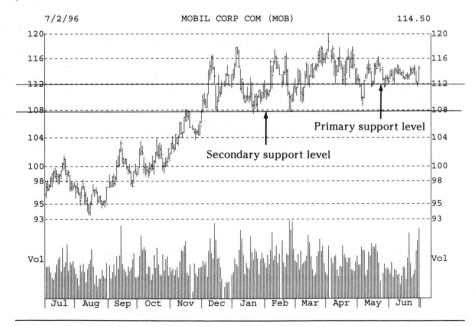

Exhibit 9.4   In May 1996 Procter & Gamble broke through a fairly strong re-sistance, then dropped back to that level (which became support) in July.

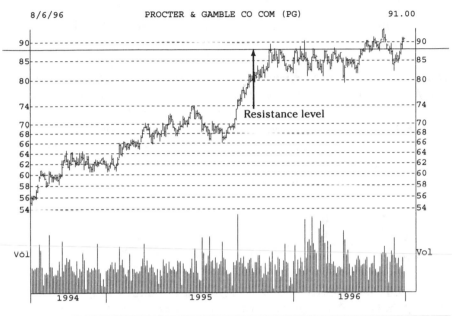

When analyzing support and resistance levels, keep these points in mind:

- Support lines are drawn through stock bottoms; resistance lines, through stock tops.

- The importance of a support or resistance level can be judged by the number of times the stock has tested it and failed. The more approaches and failures, the more important the resistance or support.

- A strong breakthrough of a resistance level is an excellent entry point, especially if the stock is in a long-term uptrend and if the breakthrough was on high volume.

- A support line can be a good point of entry under two conditions: *if* support has held and the stock has reversed direction and *if* there are positive signals from other indicators.

- A good time to consider selling is when the stock fails at an important resistance level or when it falls through a strong support level.
- Support and resistance lines can also be applied to the market as a whole.

One final point before we leave the subject of support and resistance levels. A resistance level frequently becomes an area of support *after* the stock breaks through it. You can see this clearly in the Proctor and Gamble graph in Exhibit 9.4. When resistance and support come fairly close together and are well defined, a stock may trade between the two lines for a period of time. This then becomes known as a basing period, which we will talk about later in this chapter.

Exhibit 9.5   Mobil Corp. had heavy resistance at about $85, which it broke through in late 1994. It is now meeting fairly difficult resistance at about $118.

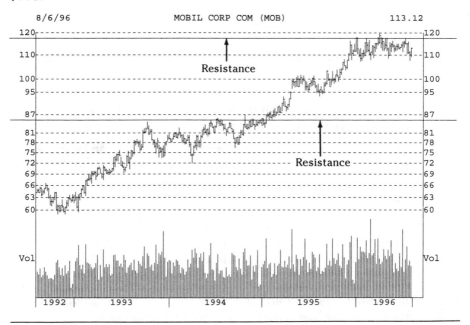

THE TRENDSETTERS

Among the most widely used technical tools are trendlines. Volumes have been written about the subject, but we have not found much value in complicated patterns such as "head and shoulders," "double tops," "cup and handles," and the like. Simple trendline analysis, however, is very helpful. Trendlines are part of every technical analysis package and are easy to use. In this section we'll talk about how to use rising and falling trendlines to time entry and exit points in a stock.

The foundation of trendline analysis rests on the simple rising trendline and falling trendline. A rising trendline is drawn diagonally through stock bottoms and represents an important support zone on a stock's upward climb. A falling trendline is drawn diagonally through stock tops and represents an area of resistance. The more times the stock touches

Exhibit 9.6 Mobil Corp. has had a general upward trend for most of the past 10 years. An even sharper uptrend began in September 1994, but it was broken in July 1996.

the trendline, the stronger the support or resistance and the more valid the trend.

The rising trendlines shown in Exhibits 9.6, 9.7, and 9.8 are fairly well defined. Mobil Corporation's long-term upward trend (Exhibit 9.6) has lasted for ten years, and in late 1994 it began an even sharper uptrend. American International (Exhibit 9.7) repeatedly found support over four years as it reached its trendline. Exxon (Exhibit 9.8) shows a well-defined upward trend over ten months on its 20-point rise. Rising trendlines are generally fueled by the same factors we have discussed previously: expectations of increased earnings and/or rising P/E ratios.

A good time to buy during a rising trend is when the stock hits support (i.e., touches the rising trendline) and reverses direction to continue its upward climb. At every test of the rising trendline, however, there is a chance that the trend will fail. It is a good idea to wait for the stock to rebound from the trendline, as well as to consider other signals. When a

Exhibit 9.7 Within a 5-year upward trend, American International Group has had a couple of short but sharper uptrends, although it is now hitting resistance at about $100.

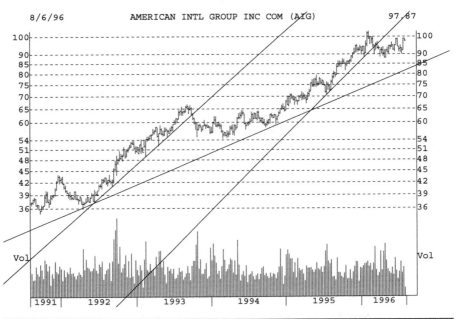

Exhibit 9.8   Over the past year, Exxon has trended upward from $68 to $88 where it appears to be meeting resistance. Notice the number of times it approached or touched the trendline from February through June 1996.

stock drops below the rising trendline, it is a negative sign and a reason to consider selling.

Falling trendlines track the decline of a stock. When that trend reverses and the stock breaks through the trendline upward—as shown in Exhibits 9.9, 9.10, and 9.11—it is generally considered a good opportunity to buy, particularly if the trend break is confirmed by other technical signals.

Here are some points to keep in mind when drawing rising and falling trendlines:

- Trends can be long-term as well as short-term; you might wish to look at both when looking for confirmation of entry or exit points.

- Rising trendlines should be drawn through stock bottoms; falling trendlines, through stock tops.

Exhibit 9.9 AT&T broke a 2-year downtrend in mid-1995 for a 16 point rise, then fell back to a strong support level at around $51.

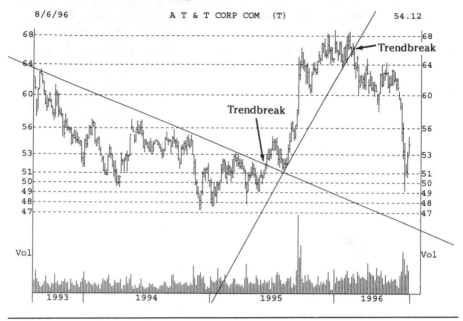

Exhibit 9.10 Bristol Myers slid from $88 to $50 over 3 years and in mid-1994 began 2-year climb back to $88.

Exhibit 9.11   Westinghouse broke through a 4-year downtrend in late 1994 but appears to be meeting fairly strong resistance at about $20 on its upward push.

- The more tops or bottoms a trendline touches, the more valid the trend.

- A trend break (upward or downward) that occurs on large volume is a more important signal than one that occurs on low volume.

- A trend break (upward) accompanied by buy signals from other technical indicators is particularly significant.

- In a long uptrend, the ideal time to enter a new position would be when the stock successfully tests the trendline—that is, when it approaches the trendline and reverses direction. As a confirmation, check to see that the MACD remains positive (more about this later). A bad time to enter a long uptrend would be when the stock is farthest from the rising trendline.

- In a long downtrend, the best time to enter a new position would be when the stock breaks through the falling trendline to a significant degree. This should also be confirmed by other indicators.

BASING, BASING, BASING . . .

When support and resistance lines come together, as mentioned earlier, the stock goes into a basing period. It trades within a narrow price range for several days or weeks, as Telescan did from August through November 1995 (Exhibit 9.12). During a basing period, supply and demand are more or less equally matched. There is an overhead supply every time new buyers move in. Enough sellers are satisfied with the market price and are willing to sell and move on to something else, which prevents the stock from moving higher. In the same way, each time the stock reaches a support level, enough buyers recognize a buying opportunity and move in. As a result, the stock just sort of treads water, basing within a narrow trading range, often on low volume.

Basing periods themselves can be boring, as the stock virtually goes nowhere. Eventually, the stock will break out of its basing pattern

Exhibit 9.12   From September through mid-November Telescan was basing between about $6 and $7, and then it had a one-point breakout on very strong volume.

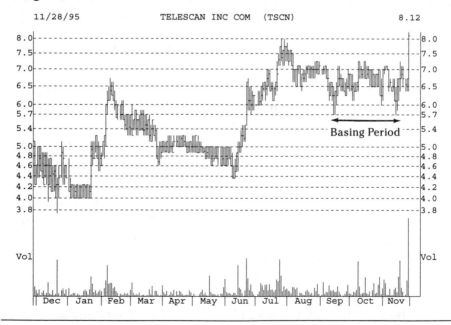

in one direction or the other, and the basing period breakout can be a powerful buy signal, particularly for short-term trading. A positive (upward) breakout, like the one in Exhibit 9.12, means the selling has been sharply curtailed or more buying has started to come in. A negative (downward) breakout means the opposite: Buying has dried up and selling has accelerated.

The Quality of the Breakout

The quality of a basing period breakout can be judged on three points: (a) the pattern of the basing period, (b) the magnitude of the breakout, and (c) the volume on the day of the breakout.

The basing pattern consists of the length of the basing period and the percentage of the price range in which the stock trades during that period. In other words: How long did the stock base? Between which price levels? Investors have varying ideas about what constitutes a superior basing pattern breakout, although a breakout from a tight pattern is usually considered good. For example, a stock that trades between, say, $20 and $22 for six months is in a 10 percent, 26-week basing period, which is considered a very tight pattern.

The longer the stock has stayed in a tight basing pattern (so technicians generally say), the more powerful a move it will make when it breaks out. It seems obvious to us that a stock that trades in a short price range over a long period—say, a 10-percent range for 13 weeks—and then breaks out is far more impressive than a stock that breaks out of a 20-percent, 3-week basing pattern. We're not aware of any academic studies that correlate the tightness of the basing pattern with the subsequent move, but our observations support that tendency.

The magnitude of the breakout is also important. A quarter of a point, for example, is not particularly exciting. Take a stock that has been basing from $20 to $22. A sudden move to $22¼ would be considered a breakout, but the reaction would probably be: So what? If the same stock broke out to $22½ or $22¾, it would be more impressive, especially if it did so on large volume.

Volume is very important in judging the quality of a basing pattern breakout. If a stock breaks out on weak volume, it may drift right back into the basing pattern the next day. Stocks that break out of tight basing patterns on high volume have tended to move significantly higher. The rationale for this is that the high volume associated with the breakout dries up the sellers and sets up a condition for rapid price increase.

Searching for Basing Pattern Breakouts

Not all basing patterns are as easy to recognize as the one in Exhibit 9.12. Those with broader bases and wider ranges are harder to distinguish on a stock graph. The solution to this problem is to use a search tool to find basing pattern breakouts and then view them on the stock graph to discern their quality.[1] You could also run a basing pattern search and an undervalued growth search (like the one in Chapter 5), and wait for a stock to appear on both lists. That would assure you of the basic merit of the stock, although it should then be evaluated as described in Chapters 7 and 8. Remember to take a close look at the volume and the magnitude of the breakout.

THE ANCESTOR OF TECHNICAL ANALYSIS

We are now ready to approach the more complex technical indicators included in this book: trading bands, the MACD indicator, and the stochastics index. But first, we need to refresh our understanding of the simple moving average, upon which so many technical indicators are based.

A moving average smooths out the fluctuations in stock prices to show a smooth directional trend. It can be plotted for any time period, but the simplest is the 30-day moving average, the grandaddy of technical analysis.

To calculate a simple 30-day moving average, total the closing prices of a stock over 30 days and divide the sum by 30. That's the average. To make it "move," add the most recent closing price to the 30-day total and subtract the oldest closing price and divide the remainder by 30. These points can then be plotted on a stock graph and connected with a line. In the old days, investors or analysts had to do this by hand, laboriously plotting the stock price on a graph and then calculating and plotting the moving average. Personal computers now do it all instantaneously.

The 30-day moving-average indicator is based on the idea that when a stock breaks through its 30-day moving average headed upward, it is likely to continue to move up. Vice versa: When a stock breaks through the moving average headed downward, it is likely to continue to fall. This

---

[1] ProSearch provides basing-period breakout indicators with a variety of ranges (10 percent, 20 percent, and 30 percent) and periods (3, 6, 13, and 26 weeks).

Exhibit 9.13   This graph shows the 30-day moving average for General Motors. Notice the positive breakout on strong volume in November 1995, followed by a sharp climb and then a long series of "whipsaws."

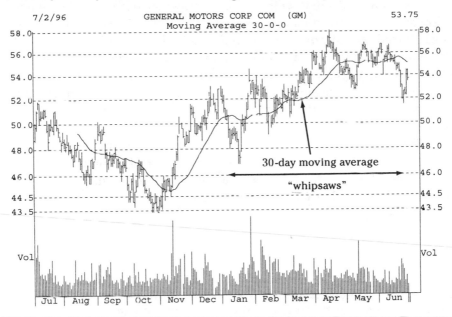

is based on market psychology. When a stock is above its 30-day moving average, it is higher than the price at which most people have recently bought. Thus, they feel reassured about their investment. As long as it stays above its 30-day moving average, there is a more positive tone to the stock. However, when the stock falls below its 30-day moving average, there are an increasing number of people who bought at prices higher than the current price. So fear sets in, which is likely to drive the price down further or at least act as a brake as the stock attempts to move higher.

There is nothing magic about the 30-day moving average, except that it is the most widely followed of all the averages and, therefore, the most likely to create psychological impairment when the stock falls below that line. The problem with using it for buy and sell signals is that it tends to give a lot of false breakouts (referred to as "chatter" or "whipsaws"), in which the stock jumps back and forth across the moving average. (This is likely caused by the competing interest of short-term traders

and longer-term investors.) Whipsaws and chatter are graphically illus-
trated in Exhibit 9.13 for General Motors and in Exhibit 9.14 for Mobil
Corporation.

One way to combat whipsaws is to consider both a 30-day moving
average and a 200-day moving average. (Exhibit 9.15 shows both averages plotted on a Microsoft graph.) If the stock is *already* above its 200-
day moving average when it moves above its 30-day moving average (as
Microsoft was in early August), it is even more likely to continue moving
upward. The positive longer trend is said to help buoy the shorter trend.
Penetration of the shorter moving average should be minor. The reverse
is also true.

The problem of whipsaws has been attacked by many brilliant minds
over the years. They have come up with a number of technical tools that
reduce the whipsaw effect and generate more reliable signals. One is the
use of trading bands that create a channel on either side of the 30-day
moving average.

**Exhibit 9.14   Notice the chatter from January through July, as Mobil Corp.
moves back and forth across its 30-day moving average.**

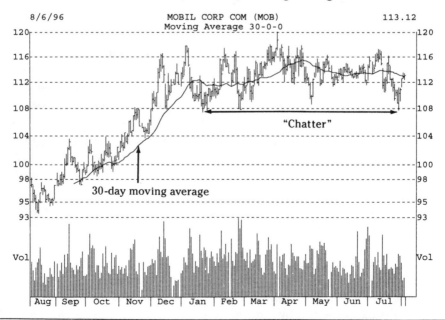

Exhibit 9.15   This graph shows a 30-day and a 200-day moving average for Microsoft.

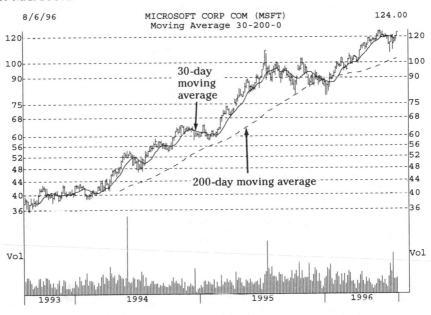

TRADING WITH TRADING BANDS

The trading band concept is based on the tendency of a stock to trade within a predictable range around its moving average. If we draw an "envelope" around the moving average to encompass the trading range of the stock (Exhibit 9.16), we can predict with some confidence which way the stock will go next and how far it might go. (Trading bands can be drawn automatically with almost any technical analysis program.)[2]

Interpreting trading bands is more of an art than a science. Like all technical indicators, this one is based on market psychology. As the stock approaches the top of the band, a tug of war tends to set up between short-term and long-term traders. Short-term traders begin to take their

---

[2] A special kind of trading band, called Bollinger Bands, was developed by John Bollinger, the popular technical analyst who appears on CNBC. Bollinger Bands are drawn a certain number of standard deviations away from the moving average.

Exhibit 9.16   Trading bands are shown on a one-year graph for Merck & Co. Notice the negative failure swing in February 1996 when it approached the top band and fell back, and the positive swing in early May when it bounced off the bottom band.

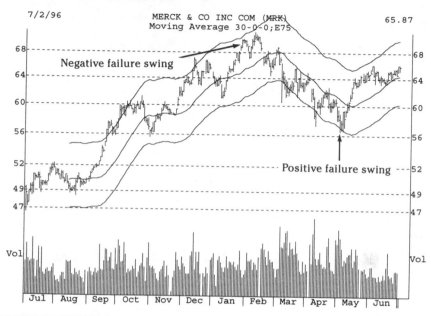

profits, which slows down the stock's momentum. If nothing happens to offset this, there will be a failure swing at the top band (the stock will reverse without touching the band). If, however, the stock makes it all the way to the top band, short-term sellers may be shaken out whereas long-term investors continue to add to their positions. When this happens with sufficient strength, the stock may break loose from the pull of the short-term traders and penetrate the top of the band. A significant penetration of the top band indicates gathering momentum and a likely continuation of the trend. This is often a good entry point.

Generally speaking, the stock will then "climb the band," that is, it will ride along the top of the band as the band itself moves up with the stock price. Finally, a point will be reached when even long-term traders start selling, either to take their profits or in fear of the inevitable reversal. At this point, the stock will start to fall. If it finds support at the 30-day moving average (which it normally does in strong stocks as short-term traders re-enter their positions), it may renew its charge toward the top, which is a good buy confirmation.

If it does not find support at the 30-day moving average, what happened at the top band will be mirrored at the bottom band. If the stock penetrates the bottom band significantly, it is likely to continue its downward trend. On the other hand, a failure swing at the bottom—where the stock reverses without touching the bottom band—is a sign of strength. If the stock continues upward, it may meet resistance at the 30-day moving average, but if it pushes on through, that is a sign of continuing strength.

We generally use trading bands to confirm an MACD buy signal (which we'll talk about next). The three best confirmations of a buy signal are, as previously discussed (a) a failure swing at the bottom band; (b) bouncing off the 30-day moving average *after* a penetration of the top band, and (c) a fresh penetration of the top band.

It may take a while to become confident with your interpretation of trading bands. The more charts you study, the better you will be able to read the signals.

BREAKING OUT WITH MACD

Our personal favorite among technical indicators—because it backtested the best—is the moving average convergence/divergence indicator, or the MACD, as it is commonly known.

The MACD trading method was developed and popularized by Gerald Appel, publisher of *Systems & Forecasts,* a market letter that has one of the best long-term records for market timing. The MACD is said to measure the intensity and direction of the market's mood and to confirm a trend reversal. The MACD uses three exponential moving averages:[3] a short one, a long one, and a third that plots the moving average of the difference between the other two and forms a signal line on an MACD graph. (The MACD may also be shown as a histogram, which plots the difference between the signal line and the MACD line. We prefer histograms because they show breakouts more clearly.)

Trend reversals are signaled by the convergence and divergence of these moving averages, thus the name: moving average convergence/

---

[3] An exponential moving average is similar to a simple moving average except it gives more weight to the most recent closing prices.

Exhibit 9.17 This graph shows the <u>daily</u> 8/17/9 MACD for SmithKline Beecham. The whipsaws that you see in the daily MACD would have been overridden by the weekly MACD (Exhibit 9.18) which was mostly positive during the last half of 1995 and negative through the first 5 months of 1996.

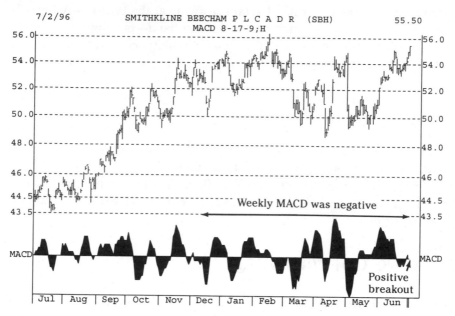

divergence. Exhibit 9.17 shows positive and negative breakouts on a daily MACD histogram for SmithKline Beecham. A positive breakout occurs when the histogram crosses the zero line upward (a buy signal); a negative breakout occurs when the histogram crosses the zero line downward (a sell signal).

To avoid the whipsaws that appear with the daily MACD, many short-term traders follow Appel's trading theory, which uses the weekly MACD as the primary indicator. Specifically, the weekly MACD must be positive (that is, above the zero line) before they act on a daily MACD breakout. The weekly MACD offers a longer perspective on the price movement of the stock and prevents acting on false signals.

Compare, for example, the daily and weekly MACDs for SmithKline Beecham. In Exhibit 9.17, the daily MACD gave numerous buy signals during the first six months of 1996, but the weekly MACD (Exhibit 9.18) was negative from January through late May 1996. Requiring the weekly MACD

MORE ABOUT MACD

One of the most popular MACDs is the 8/17/9 MACD. These numbers refer to the length of the three moving averages. On a daily 8/17/9 MACD, the short moving average would be 8 days; the long one, 17 days; and the signal line, 9 days. On a weekly 8/17/9 MACD, the periods would be 8, 17, and 9 weeks. The daily MACD is a short-term signal and generates many more signals than the weekly MACD, which is considered a longer-term signal.

Gerald Appel, who developed the MACD indicator, has a system for defining the quality of the MACD breakout, although this is more of a pure technical trader's "game." If you wish to pursue this, ProSearch offers a number of MACD indicators that can help find and rank stocks in order of the quality of their MACD breakouts.

---

to be positive would have avoided the false daily signals during the first half of the year. The daily and weekly signals were in sync for the sharp rise from $50 to $56 that began in late May.

No indicator is perfect, of course, but requiring the weekly MACD to be positive before acting on a daily MACD breakout helps avoid the chatter or false signals.

STALKING THE STOCHASTICS

The stochastics index, developed by George C. Lane of Investment Educators, is an overbought/oversold oscillator based on moving averages and relative strength techniques. It is definitely a child of the personal computer age because, as William F. Eng says, "It is hard to imagine someone even having the idea for something like Lane's Stochastics without a PC at hand."[4] With a PC, the stochastics index is a valuable and easy-to-use tool.

In simple terms, the stochastics index is expressed as a percentage of the difference between the low and the high during the period of the stochastics. A 14-day stochastics means that you are going to consider the low point in price versus the high point in price for the past 14 days. On the day it is calculated, the stochastics is the percentage that the

---

[4] William F. Eng, *The Technical Analysis of Stocks, Options and Futures: Advanced Trading Systems and Techniques* (Chicago: Probus Publishing, 1988). p. 95

Exhibit 9.18   This graph shows the weekly 8/17/9 MACD for SmithKline Beecham. Compare it with the daily MACD in Exhibit 9.17.

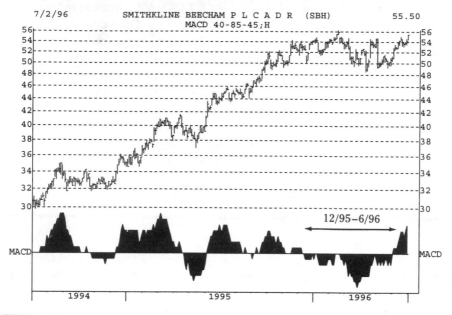

price represents of the difference between the low and high. In other words, if the stock has traded between $10 and $15 in a 14-day period, at a price today of $10 the stochastics reading is zero. (It is at the very bottom of the range.) At $15, the stochastics reading is 100, the very top of the range. At $12½ the stochastics would be 50; at $13, it would be 60. It is simply the percentage of the difference between the low and high.

In actual usage, the stochastics index takes a slightly more complex but more useful form. It uses a moving average of the simple stochastics to plot the indicator. For example, the popular 14-5 stochastics shown in Exhibit 9.19 is calculated over a 14-day period with the final plot of the index based on a 5-day moving average of the simple stochastics. The 75 percent line and the 25 percent line measure oversold and overbought conditions as follows:

- *Oversold:* When the stochastics falls below the 25 percent line, it generally indicates an oversold condition; then, when the index

Exhibit 9.19   The popular 14/5 stochastics for Allstate Corp. is in over-bought territory and likely to develop a sell signal shortly.

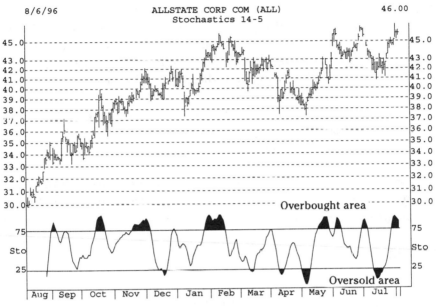

crosses the 25 percent line upward (a positive breakout), a new uptrend is anticipated.

- *Overbought:* An overbought condition is generally indicated when the stochastics goes above the 75 percent line; then, when it crosses the 75 percent line downward (a negative breakout), a new downtrend is signaled.

We prefer to use the MACD for actual buy signals and the stochastics to confirm an oversold condition. We should point out that in trending markets (which represent a majority of recent market history) the MACD is the superior indicator, according to our backtesting. During a trading market, however (as in most of 1994), the stochastics appears to give a better result.[5] Beginners will do well to use both indicators.

---

[5] A trending market is one in which a clear uptrend or downtrend is discernible. A trading market, also called a sideways or flat market, is virtually trendless.

The Alvim Stochastics

Luiz Alvim, a futures trader and colleague, has developed a unique two-stage application of the 21-5 stochastics, which we like to use. (Twenty-one refers to the length of time over which the stochastics is being calculated; 5 refers to the number of days of a moving average used to plot the stochastics reading.) After a positive breakout at the 25 percent line, Alvim recommends waiting until the stochastics crosses the 50 percent line upward (Exhibit 9.20). At that point, he enters half of his position. When and if the index crosses the 75 percent line upward, he enters the rest of his position. This application appears to give good results, perhaps because the delay ensures a continuation of the trend before more money is expended.

Alvim's selling strategy is to retrace his steps. After a negative breakout at the 75 percent line, he sells half his holdings, with the remaining position to be closed when the 50 percent line is crossed

Exhibit 9.20A   This chart shows a 10-month downtrend in Micron Technology.

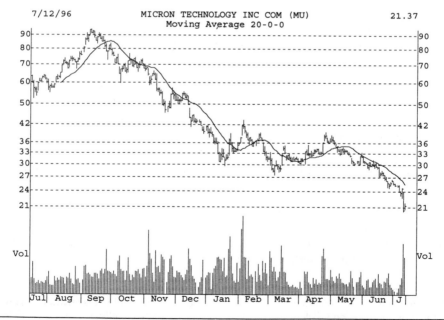

Exhibit 9.20B   This chart shows how the 10-month downtrend in Micron was well identified—and taken advantage of—by the Alvim Stochastics, because this indicator stayed below the 50 percent line most of the time.

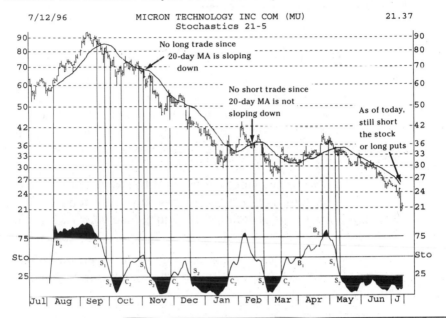

7/12/96   MICRON TECHNOLOGY INC COM (MU)   21.37
                                    Stochastics 21-5

B₁	Close second half of short	C₂	Close first half of short
	and buy first half of long	S₁	Close second half of long and
B₂	Buy second half of long		initiate first half of short
C₁	Close first half of long	S₂	Initiate second half of short

downward This prevents being taken completely out of a stock when the stochastics dips below the 75 percent line and then heads back upward, as often happens.

Like most investors, Alvim requires confirmation from other technical signals. Specifically, he requires:

- When entering a position, the 20-day moving average must be sloping upward when the stochastics crosses the 50 percent and 75 percent lines.

- When closing a position, the 20-day moving average must not be sloping upward but can be horizontal. This prevents an early exit

of a good move, which is the major disadvantage of using stochastics in trending markets. However, if the moving average
turns down after the stochastics crosses the 75 or 50 percent
lines, all open positions are closed.

WATCHING A WATCH LIST

Many investors keep a "watch list" of 25, 50, 100 or more stocks that they
would be willing to purchase on a strong technical buy signal. Knowing
when a buy signal occurs, however, can be a problem. There are three
possible solutions:

1. Run breakout searches (looking for MACD, stochastics, or basing-period breakouts) on just the stocks on your watch list. (The
   newest version of ProSearch allows you to use your own list of
   stocks for a search.)

2. Run breakout searches on stocks in general. When one of the
   stocks on your watch list turns up on a breakout search, you have
   your buy signal.

3. Turn your decision over to an expert system such as the AIQ
   TradingExpert™ from AIQ Incorporated. This system combines a
   number of technical trading rules to generate an expert rating for
   each stock in the system (the stocks can be loaded automatically
   from a ProSearch report). The expert rating predicts the likelihood that a stock will move or continue to move upward. The AIQ
   system is useful if you're following 100 or so stocks; it is of more
   interest to short-term traders than to longer-term investors who
   base their decisions on a stock's fundamentals.

Whichever method you use for entry signals, be sure to evaluate the stock
along the lines described in earlier chapters. If the stocks on your watch
list have already been evaluated, check other technical indicators for
confirmation.

TO RECAP . . .

Technical timing is the last step before purchasing the stock. The ideal
entry point is when either of the following conditions occurs:

- The stock gives a positive daily MACD breakout, especially one on good volume, with a positive weekly MACD. The buy signal should be confirmed with positive readings on the stochastic index (above the 25 percent line and moving upward) and trading bands (above the 30-day moving average headed upward). If the trading bands give one of the three positive signals described earlier, the MACD breakout would be especially strong.

- There is a preponderance of technical evidence. If there is no actual daily MACD breakout, go with the preponderance of evidence. This might be a positive reading on the daily and weekly MACD (that is, a recent positive breakout or the histogram is increasing if it is below the zero line), plus positive readings on the stochastics and trading bands.

The situations to avoid are technically overbought conditions or a failure swing at the top of the trading bands.

THE SEARCH FOR THE SUPERINDICATOR

For the dyed-in-the-wool technician, a number of technical analysis programs, such as MetaStock™, SuperCharts™ and Windows on Wall Street™ allow you to combine indicators for a unique effect and to create your own indicators. Be forewarned that creating your own indicators is extremely time consuming and can be expensive because of the extensive backtesting that is required. A significant amount of time and money must be expended to obtain the necessary data. Nonetheless, many are fascinated with the search for the superior indicator. If you have the time and the inclination, you may find this fun and potentially rewarding.

MEANWHILE, BACK AT THE RANCH . . .

We haven't forgotten the five finalists from our undervalued growth search. All these stocks were positive on the weekly MACD (a requirement of our original search), so they are all considered generally positive from a technical viewpoint. Therefore, in the following analysis, which was done on May 8, 1996, we are considering only the very short term. The question is: Do we buy the stock immediately or wait for better technical readings?

- Quanex looks somewhat attractive at this point (Exhibits 9.21, 9.22, and 9.23). It had a breakout in mid-April on the daily MACD and has been positive on the weekly MACD since early 1996. It has been climbing the trading bands since early in the year and continues to penetrate the upper band, which is very positive. The 21-5 stochastics index is in overbought territory. It has already broken through some short-term resistance at $21½. All in all, Quanex is in a strong technical position, but we would watch out for the long-term resistance at $24.

- OEA is weaker than it appears at first glance (Exhibits 9.24, 9.25, and 9.26). Despite the strong uptrend that began in February, its daily MACD is negative and the weekly MACD, while positive, is

Exhibit 9.21   Quanex is in positive territory on the daily MACD and has broken through short-term resistance at $21½. There appears to be longer term resistance at about $24.

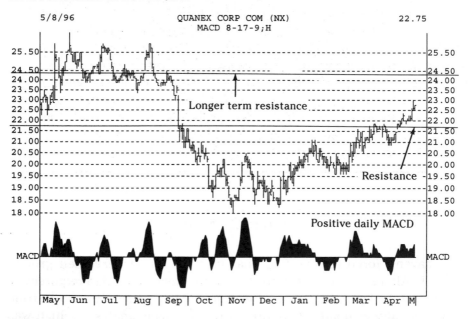

Exhibit 9.22   Quanex was climbing the trading band early in the year and has just penetrated the upper band. This a very strong pattern.

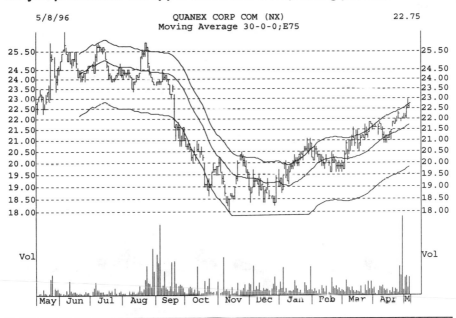

Exhibit 9.23   The 21/5 stochastics for Quanex is overbought.

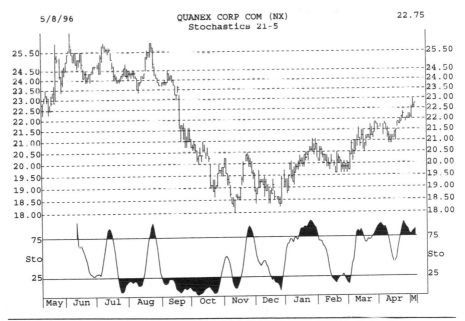

Exhibit 9.24 OEA's strong uptrend which began in February was broken in early May. The daily MACD is negative, even though the weekly MACD is positive.

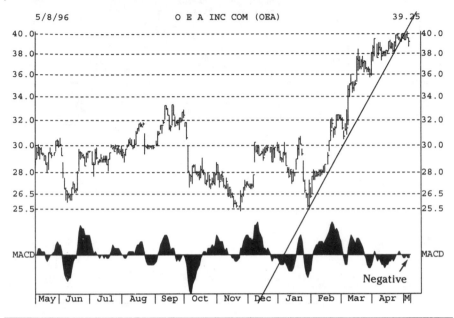

Exhibit 9.25 OEA had a negative failure swing in early April.

Exhibit 9.26   The 21/5 stochastics for OEA is overbought and weakening.

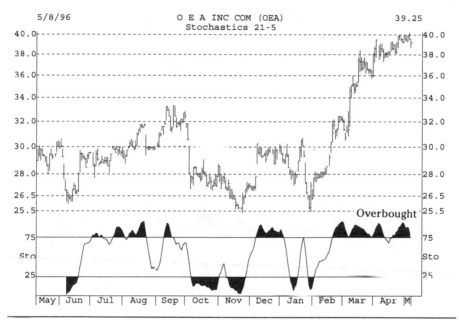

weakening dramatically. Moreover, the trading bands had a failure swing at the upper end of the band in early April, and the stochastics is overbought and weakening. We would consider this stock suspect at this point.

- ECI Telecom is technically weak (Exhibits 9.27, 9.28, and 9.29). Although it just had a positive (though rather weak) breakout on the weekly MACD, the daily MACD is negative; the trading bands had a failure swing at about $28; and the stochastics has just given a sell signal. There would appear to be significant support at $22, so we would probably wait to see what it does at that level. Note the resistance at about $26.

- Valero is giving conflicting signals (Exhibits 9.30, 9.31, and 9.32). Its weekly MACD is quite positive, but the daily MACD turned negative in early May. The trading bands appear to be finding support at the 30-day moving average after significant penetration of the upper band (which is positive), but the stochastics is very negative. There appears to be support at about $26, but at this point we would consider this stock neutral technically.

Exhibit 9.27 ECI Telecom failed to penetrate the short-term resistance at $26 and its daily MACD is negative.

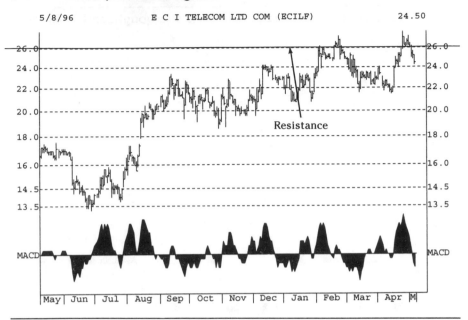

Exhibit 9.28 ECI Telecom had a negative failure swing in late April.

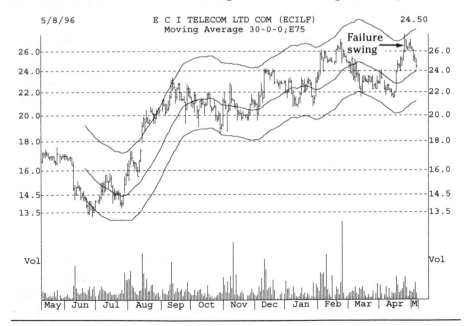

Exhibit 9.29   The 21/5 stochastics for ECI Telecom has just given a sell signal. Note the strong support at about $22.

Exhibit 9.30   Although the weekly MACD is still positive, Valero's daily MACD recently turned negative.

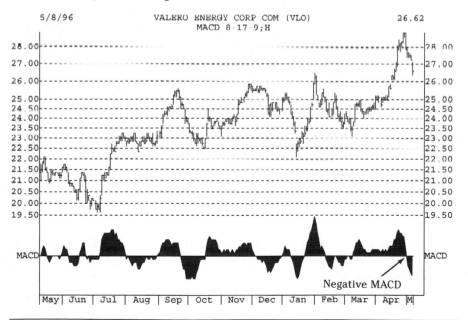

Exhibit 9.31 Valero significantly penetrated the top of its trading bands in April and is seeking support at the 30-day moving average. If it finds support and rebounds, that will be a very positive sign.

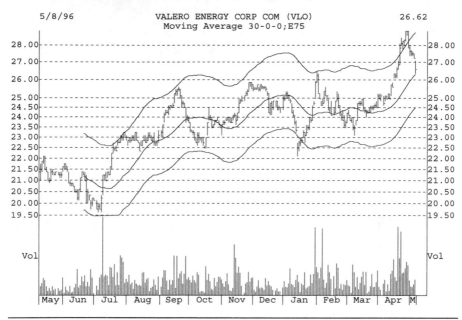

- King World Production is weak technically (Exhibits 9.33, 9.34, and 9.35). It just had a negative breakout on the daily MACD. The trading bands had a failure swing at $44, and the stochastics went negative a few days ago. This is not a good time to buy this stock.

None of the five stocks offers us a clear buy signal, although Quanex has a preponderance of evidence going for it. A long-term investor might go ahead and buy Quanex, although a short-term investor would wait for a clearer signal.

As you can see, stocks are not always ready when you are. But it is not important to buy the stocks at this moment, especially with the markets at a dangerously high extreme (as we'll see in Chapter 13). Tomorrow or a week from now, the same search will produce a different list of stocks, one of which might give all the right signals. That's why it is a good idea to keep a watch list of stocks that have been thoroughly evaluated.

Exhibit 9.32   The 21/5 stochastics for Valero is negative.

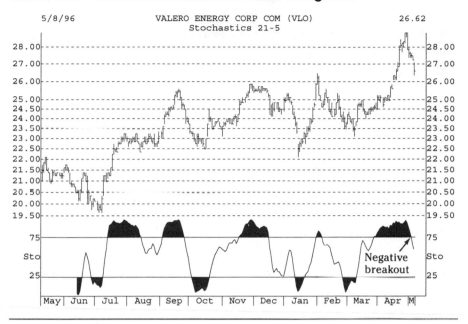

Exhibit 9.33   King World Productions recently had a negative breakout on its daily MACD (the weekly is positive).

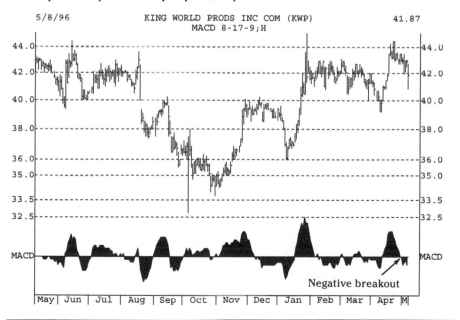

Exhibit 9.34   Trading bands for King World Productions show a negative failure swing at $44 in early April.

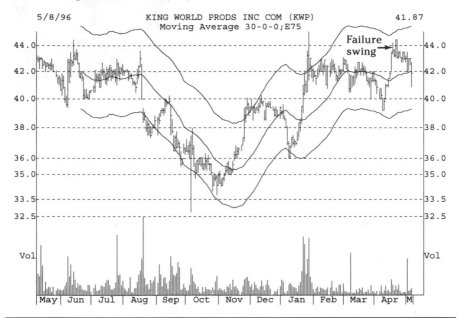

It increases the likelihood of finding a stock that is technically desirable when you are ready to buy.

YOU MUST REMEMBER THIS . . .

In stocks, as a romance, timing is important. Pay attention to the technical condition of the stock when you're ready to purchase it, but don't become obsessed with technical analysis.

- The MACD, in our experience, offers satisfactory exit and entry points, especially when confirmed by trading bands or a positive stochastics reading.
- It is recommended that you always trade in the direction of the weekly MACD.

Exhibit 9.35 The 21/5 stochastics for King World Productions recently turned negative.

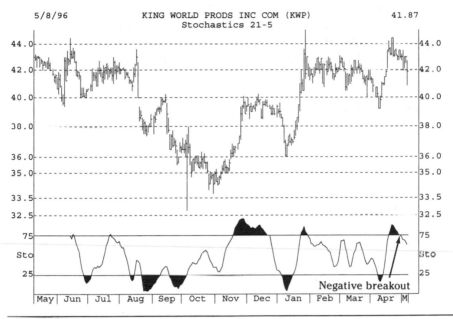

* In lieu of a clear-cut buy signal, go with the preponderance of evidence: positive readings on two or more indicators.

* Don't try to get large numbers of technical breakouts to agree. The effect is not cumulative. One valid signal is often as good as three, as long as it is confirmed by one other indicator.

* Technical timing is somewhat less critical to long-term investors who plan to hold stocks for six months to several years. Nevertheless, our backtesting has proven the value of technical timing: It often prevents getting caught in a meltdown.

* Trendline analysis with its support and resistance zones is used by many investors with good results.

* It may take several weeks for a stock to give an appropriate buy signal. If even one day has elapsed between your evaluation and the technical buy signal, double-check the current news and the S&P report for that stock. We operate in a dynamic market and

something could have happened to change your opinion of the stock.

- A number of publications have done exhaustive backtesting of technical indicators. One of the best is Colby and Meyers' *The Encyclopedia of Technical Market Indicators,* mentioned previously. Generally speaking, they concluded that technical indicators are helpful, with the MACD among the best.

Now let's move on to the art of the purchase.

10

THE ART OF
THE PURCHASE

Stock brokers were once the priests of Wall Street. They served as intermediaries between the market and the investor, dispensing research and advice and executing buy and sell orders. No stock trade could be made without their intercession. Now, with touch-tone telephones and personal computers, you can bypass the human element altogether. Nevertheless, most stock trades are processed through a registered broker. Your choice is between a full-service brokerage house or a discount broker, each of which has its advantages and disadvantages.

Full-service brokers usually offer access to their company's extensive research data (which can be very important), and some people simply feel more comfortable with a knowledgeable broker on the other end of the phone. Discount brokers offer lower commissions for investors who do their own research and feel comfortable making their own decisions. The differences between the two, however, have blurred in the past few years. Full service brokers have lowered commissions to more competitive levels, and many discount brokers now offer some access to research, charting, and analytical tools, as well as stock quotes and portfolio management tools. Some discount brokers offer very deep discounts with little service or information, which can be attractive if you have your own tools and information sources.

We recommend that you do a little comparison shopping. Ask your friends about their experience with each kind of broker. Call several full-service and discount brokerage houses, ask questions, and request sales literature. Then make your decision. Once you select a broker, he or she can help set up your account.[1]

The decision between a full service or discount broker may become less problematic if the differences between the two continue to blur. One important agent in this blurring of identities is online trading on the Internet.

ONLINE TRADING

Online trading is the buying and selling of stocks, funds, and other securities using a personal computer to enter the trades. It allows the investor to bypass a human stockbroker which reduces overhead for the brokerage firm which, in turn, cuts commissions. Discount brokers, who introduced electronic trading by touch-tone telephone years ago, pioneered online trading. Investors have eagerly embraced the concept, which gives them more control over their accounts and allows them to place trades 24 hours a day.

Technology analysts at Forrester Research in Cambridge, Massachusetts estimate that online investors have nearly 1.5 million accounts, and they predict that figure will reach 10 million by 2001.[2] The main reason for this explosive growth is the Internet. Many discount brokers offer direct trading from their Web sites, and some full service brokerage firms have a presence on the World Wide Web. It is likely the full-service brokers will move in the direction of online trading as the Internet continues to exert its influence on the lives of investors.

If you want to see what online trading is all about, play one of the investing games offered by some of the brokers on the Internet. You can test

---

[1] If you've never traded stocks, visit the American Association of Individual Investors on the World Wide Web (www.aaii.org). Their broker page offers articles on placing trades and working with brokers. The AAII site also has sections on investing basics, stocks, bonds, mutual funds, and portfolio management and a glossary that provides succinct definitions of basic investing terms.

[2] *The Forrester Report, Money & Technology: Brokers and the Web* (Cambridge, Mass: Forrester Research, Inc., September, 1966).

your skill at picking stocks and entering trades without risking any money!
A list of Internet addresses can be found in Chapter 16.

PLACING THE ORDER

Whether you place your order with a full-service broker, a discount broker, or make your trades online, here are a few hints to help you get
started:

- If a day or two has passed since the stage two analysis described
  in Chapter 8, recheck the current news for any story that might
  have an affect on the stock you wish to buy.

- Don't nickel and dime your entry point. Unless you are a very,
  very short-term trader, quibbling over a fraction of a point may
  only keep you out of a good stock. If you've done your homework,
  the stock you choose should stand a reasonable chance of increasing as much as 50 percent in less than a year. If it has had a
  positive technical breakout—which it will have if you're using the
  guidelines in this book—it should be moving upward. The fact
  that it moves another quarter or half a point while you're trying
  to buy it should only confirm that you've made the right decision.

- In most cases, use a market order rather than a limit order. A market order tells the broker to buy the stock at the going price; if the
  stock moves up before your order can be executed, you will pay
  the higher price. A limit order places conditions on the purchase,
  such as "Don't pay more than X." If a stock's fundamentals are
  good and the technical signal is right, the stock should be moving
  up smartly. Using a limit order is only advisable on thinly traded
  stocks (with an average daily volume of, say, fewer than 10,000
  shares) and only if you are buying several hundred shares.

- Don't try to buy on a "pullback," that is, don't use a limit order
  that tells the broker to buy only if the stock drops a quarter or an
  eighth of a point. If a stock pulls back, it is going in the wrong direction! This is a very common mistake of amateur investors. To
  repeat, if you've made a good selection, the stock should be moving up, and if you insist on seeing it drop before you buy, you may
  miss it altogether. Besides, if it starts heading down instead of up,
  it may mean your analysis was wrong.

TARGET PRACTICE

Part of the purchase decision is setting a price target for the stock you buy. (If you don't know where you're going, how will you know when you arrive?) Setting a target gives you a destination for your stock and a gauge against which to measure its progress. As the stock approaches the target, its risk/reward relationship changes dramatically, which can bear upon your decision to hold the stock or sell it. We'll talk about that in Chapter 12.

A target is not the same as your overall portfolio goal, which might be a return of 15 to 20 percent per year. Nor is it just some hopeful number plucked out of thin air. It is the price you expect the stock to achieve based on its historical performance.

You can base the target price on LSQ trading channels, trading bands, trendlines, or resistance levels (you might also use the target of a professional forecaster). In actual practice, we set a series of targets, using all four indicators to predict the stock's climb.

We've chosen Delta Airlines to illustrate how to set targets. Delta, you may recall, was used in Chapter 1 to show how an ordinary stock

---

Exhibit 10.1 A target based on Delta's long-term LSQ channel would be around $80 in the near term and around $100 in the long term.

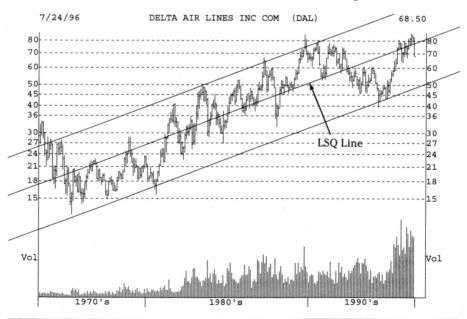

could be turned into an exceptional performer, although at the time of this writing, Delta has not generated a short-term buy signal. Nonetheless, it will serve as a useful example on target-setting.

Long-Term LSQ

The top of the long-term LSQ channel can be used with many stocks as a long-term target, because the LSQ line itself represents an average long-term price. With Delta (Exhibit 10.1), the LSQ line would represent a price of $80 or slightly above; to reach the top of the LSQ channel would be about $100. A comfortable near-term target, then, should be somewhat above $80 with a potential to reach a long-term goal of about $100. Either represents a handsome increase from the current price of $68.00.

Short-Term LSQ

Delta's short-term LSQ (Exhibit 10.2) reinforces its long-term LSQ. A target of $82 will simply get it back to the LSQ line; the longer-term potential is nearly $100.

Exhibit 10.2   Delta's short-term LSQ channel reinforces the targets of about $82 for the short term and $100 for the long term.

Resistance Levels

Normally, we would use a three-year chart to study resistance levels, but in Delta's case, a six-year chart is better (Exhibit 10.3). There is fairly substantial resistance at about $78 which goes all the way back to 1991, and very little resistance above that point (though there was minor resistance in mid-1996 at about $85). Incidentally, we would draw significant comfort from the fact that there is substantial support at $68, which is just below current (mid-1996) levels, and additional support at $64 and $60. We'll talk about support later in our discussion on setting stops.

Trading Bands

Delta's trading bands (Exhibit 10.4) are not positive, because there is a penetration of the lower band at the current price level. Nevertheless, we would expect the stock to move back up to about $78 before trading-band

---

Exhibit 10.3   A short-term target based on Delta's resistance level would be about $78. Notice the strong support at $60, which goes back for six years.

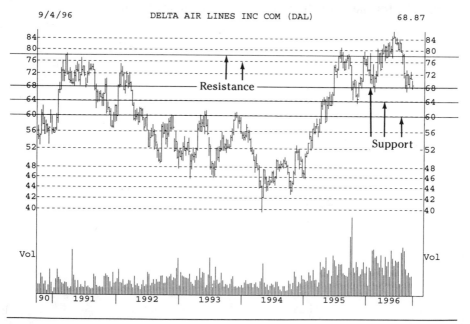

Exhibit 10.4   Delta's trading bands reinforce a short-term target of about $78.

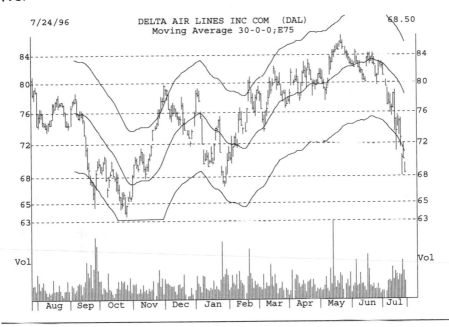

resistance sets in. This confirms the six-year resistance level at $78, which we see in Exhibit 10.3.

In light of the above comments, we might set the following series of targets for Delta. The first would be $78, about $10 above the current position. This is the first line of major resistance and should be a target for short-term investors and a good checkpoint for long-term investors.

A secondary target would be $85. At this level, Delta will have crossed above the LSQ line on both the short-term and long-term graphs. Keep in mind that, assuming continued growth, the LSQ line moves upward with time as the stock price increases. The price at which the stock will cross its LSQ line depends on when it gets there.

If Delta makes it beyond the $85 target, chances are excellent that it will move on up and approach the $100 level. At this level, however, risk becomes high and potential reward becomes minimal. It is unlikely, therefore, that we would set a reasonable long-term target much higher than $90, unless the stock makes a long, slow, gradual climb.

Our series of targets then are $78, $85, and $90. We will, of course, set protective stops as we reach each target in order to conserve our profits (as described below). When we talk about "The Positive Sell" in Chapter 12, we'll show you how to use computerized tools to assess the stock's progress as it moves toward its target.

SETTING STOPS

Stops can be used to limit your losses or protect your profits. There are *hard stops* and *mental stops*. A hard stop is a firm order to your broker to sell a stock if it drops to a specified level. Hard stops, in most cases, can help protect your downside, but they cannot protect you if a stock gaps down. A downward gap occurs when a stock opens well below its previous day's close or after a trading halt due to important news. For example, if a stock should close at $40 and open at $32, a hard stop at $37 would be bypassed. You would sell at $32. (A 20 percent gap, by the way, is not infrequent.)

A disadvantage of a hard stop is that it leaves no room for rethinking a decision. A broker is legally obligated to sell the stock if the price drops to or through a specified stop price. This can sometimes force you out of a stock before you're ready or at an unfavorable price. Sometimes, when a stock gaps, the market overreacts. When it discovers the news wasn't as bad as expected, the stock may rebound sharply, and if you want back in, you might have to pay more than the price at which you were stopped out. In addition, you'll have to pay commissions both ways.

We generally prefer mental stops. A mental stop is simply a reminder to yourself to consider selling a stock if it falls to a certain level. It enables you to reflect on market conditions and consider any extenuating circumstances before making a decision to sell. A mental stop can be entered as a "risk level" in some portfolio management programs.

When to Use a Mental Stop

There are two ways in which we use mental stops. We set an *initial* mental stop at the time of purchase to limit losses at the outset. Typically, we set this stop at approximately 15 to 20 percent below the purchase price (just below important support levels in this zone). In other words, we're suggesting that if we buy a stock at $20 and it drops to $17 or $16, we may have made a mistake. Whether or not the stock should actually be sold depends in part on what the market is doing. In essence, then, a mental stop simply tells us it is time to rethink our decision.

We also use mental stops to protect our profits. As the stock moves up, we keep a "protective" mental stop at about 15 percent below the stock price. As it moves closer to the target, we tighten the stop, setting it say, 10 percent below the price.

When to Use a Hard Stop

There are times when a hard stop is preferred. As a stock nears its target, we will set a hard stop about 5 percent below the current price or at an important support level. True, a dip in stock price will take us out of the stock, but at that point—with the stock near its target—we will be looking for a reason to sell; we won't need to rethink our decision. (We'll talk more about this in the next chapter under "The Positive Sell.")

We often use a hard stop at a major support level, whether or not the stock is near its target. For example, in Exhibit 10.3, Delta has very strong support at $68, it would be foolish to set a stop within a dollar of our entry price. However, there is also fairly major support at $64, which extends back over six years. We might set an initial hard stop somewhat below that level, say at $63. An investor with a little more tolerance for the downside might set a stop as low as $59, because $60 represents a powerful support level and was previously a major resistance level.

In the end using mental stops versus hard stops is a personal call. Sometimes, experience is the only way to learn which you prefer.

THE PURCHASE LOG

When you're trying to decide whether to sell a stock, it helps to know why you purchased it in the first place. Memories are fallible, which is why many investors keep a purchase log. When you review your purchase decision some weeks or months down the road, a purchase log can help illuminate where you made a mistake, if things go awry, or what went into a good decision if things go well.

A purchase log should contain any information used in finding and analyzing a stock and making your decision: the search report from the stage-one evaluation (the one with the circles and ×s); the report card from the stage-two evaluation, along with the back-up reports (company reports, news stories, earnings estimates); all stock graphs showing technical indicators, including those used for timing signals; and graphs of market indexes on the day of purchase. This information provides a valuable reference for tracking the stocks in your portfolio. For example, when one of your companies announces its earnings, you can compare them against the earnings estimates you relied on when buying the stock. If you don't keep the original estimates, you may have a hard time finding out what they were, because six months from now new estimates will have replaced the old ones in the database. Having the information in a purchase log greatly enhances your ability to make an informed decision to sell.

In addition, you may want to include handwritten notes on such things as: why stock A was chosen over stock B; how you felt about the market at the time of purchase (positive? wary?); what kind of mood you were in (optimistic? apprehensive?). Such information helps clarify what was going on externally and internally at the time you bought the stock.

A purchase log can also be used as a learning aid, to help you profit from both successes and mistakes. When you review your portfolio performance, you may wish to check out the stocks that didn't make the cut (in the evaluation process) to see if you did indeed select the right one. If it turns out that you didn't pick the best one, the purchase log may help you analyze why one stock did better than another.

Purchase logs can take almost any form: neatly labeled folders, a bunch of sheets stapled together, or a catch-all box in the corner of your office. One investor says he uses the finest leather-grained diary because it feels like money and makes him aware of how serious the process is. The wave of the future, of course, is the computerized purchase log, where all data collected electronically can be stored in an electronic file.

Whatever form it takes, a purchase log can be a very important tool, both for the sell decision and the learning process. The more information you have at review time, the more meaningful will be your lessons.

YOU MUST REMEMBER THIS . . .

The most important things to remember when buying a stock are:

- Find a broker who matches your needs and style of investing.
- Electronic or online trading can save you 10 percent or more on commissions, but it requires confidence in your skills and a large degree of comfort with the technology.

- Make sure you have checked the news within a day or so of purchase.
- Don't quibble over a fraction of a point when buying a stock.
- Don't try to buy on a pullback.
- Set a target for each stock in your portfolio.
- Set an initial mental stop 15 to 20 percent below the purchase price, and tighten the stop as the stock nears its target.
- Use hard stops judiciously.
- Keep a purchase log.
- Learn from your successes and your mistakes.

Once you purchase a stock, the job of monitoring it begins. That's part of the portfolio management process, which is the subject of the next chapter.

11

TAKING CARE
OF BUSINESS

Portfolio management is a lot like cultivating a garden. To reap a bountiful crop, you must select quality seeds, plant them at the right time, watch over them with care, weed out the sickly specimens, and harvest the vegetables at the peak of their flavor. To reap high returns from a portfolio of stocks, you must select quality stocks, buy them at the most propitious time, monitor them carefully, weed out mistakes, and sell them at a point of optimum return. Specifically, good portfolio management consists of six broad activities:

1. *Asset Allocation.* How much of your total assets should you invest in stocks at a given time? How much in cash? Should you consider bonds? Should you consider other alternatives?

2. *Market Analysis.* What is the general level of the market on a short-term basis? Is it so high you should cut back temporarily on your stock exposure? Is it so low that you should redouble your efforts to find more prospects?

3. *Diversification.* How many stocks should you own? In which industries? When should you buy them? Which searches should you use?

4. *Monitoring the Portfolio.* How will you monitor your stocks' progress toward their targets? What information will you review? How often should you review it? How much time will it take?

5. *The Sell Decision.* How do you know when to sell a stock? When should you let your profits run? When should you cut your losses? When should you substitute one stock for another?

6. *Evaluating Portfolio Performance.* How well is your portfolio doing? Are you keeping up with market averages? How do you stack up against comparable mutual funds? What can you do to improve?

In this chapter, we will discuss asset allocation, diversification, monitoring the portfolio, and evaluating performance. The selling process and market analysis will be treated separately in Chapters 12 and 13, because of the length of these discussions.

ASSET ALLOCATION: SLICING THE INVESTMENT PIE

Asset allocation determines the mix of assets that gives you, the investor, the best expected return for the amount of risk you are willing to take. Although we are concerned in this book mainly with stocks, asset allocation looks at the whole investment pie: U.S. stocks, international stocks, bonds, mutual funds, cash, and other investment possibilities. Asset allocation models have long been used by financial planners, but a couple are aimed at the individual investor. One is WealthBuilder,™ published by Reality Technologies, Inc. This program is exceedingly simple and easy to use, but it may have limited use for the serious investor. The other is an asset allocation program recently introduced by MacroWorld Research Corporation. This program, called Macro*World™ Investor, uses sophisticated statistical forecasting models in a dynamic environment, but it is accessible to the individual investor.

The Macro*World Investor uses Macro*World's highly respected forecasting system to generate investment signals and asset allocations. Briefly stated, the Macro*World system makes a massive mathematical analysis of all securities, major market indexes, industry groups, interest rates, commodity prices, and economic factors (even weather patterns) to find the best statistical forecasting model for every security, asset class, and industry. The database is updated every night with the day's new financial economic information, and the Macro*World system re-analyzes the data and updates its forecasts.

The Macro*World Investor, with its daily forecasts, is now available to the small investor through the Internet and through various Telescan products. All you have to do is select the types of assets in which you're interested, a short-term or long-term horizon, and one of five risk levels. Once these guidelines have been selected, the Macro*World Investor will examine its best forecasts for the specified time horizon for each security or asset you've selected and tell you the forecasted return, the forecasted risk, and the historic risk for each. Then Macro*World will search the universe of the assets identified as possibles, to determine the mix that should give the highest return for a level of risk that is less than the maximum risk specified.

The risk/return level is measured against the risk-free return of 3-month Treasury bills. Macro*World calculates the likelihood that the future return of any asset will be greater than the 3-month T-bill, given the risk level the investor has specified. If the asset's return is forecasted as less than the risk-free rate, it is labeled a "sell," warning the investor that it should be avoided. If Macro*World finds the confidence level[1] of the forecasted return is less than the investor's acceptable risk level, it is shown as neutral, indicating that no action, neither buy or sell, is recommended. Those securities that become candidates for the portfolio (the buys) have been found by Macro*World to have a high confidence level of offering a return better than the risk-free rate. The user sees a table that shows the risk category (buy, sell, neutral) for each asset class. For a buy, the recommended percentage mix of each asset or security is shown.

Those who wish to learn more about the inner workings of asset allocation should visit Macro*World's website on the World Wide Web (www.mworld.com).

In this chapter, we are considering only the slice of the investment pie that has been allocated to stocks. In a nod to asset allocation, however, we do provide guidelines in Chapter 13 for analyzing market conditions and adjusting your stocks-to-cash ratio at market extremes.

---

[1] Confidence level refers to the likelihood that the forecasted results will actually happen (based on quantitative variables used by the forecasting system). In other words, if the forecasted results actually occurred or were exceeded 75 times out of the last 100 times the forecast was made, the confidence level in that forecast would be 75.

BONDS AND MUTUAL FUNDS IN CYBERSPACE

Most asset allocation programs recommend that a portion of the investment portfolio go to bonds. For many investors, this means U.S. government bonds which, generally speaking, require analysis only with regard to the ideal maturity (i.e., term) of the bond, usually 2 to 30 years. Choosing among maturities is simply a matter of balancing interest rates and interest rate risk, which varies, based on the current interest rate level. However, the plethora of bond issues from municipalities and corporations present a much more daunting task for the investor.

In the past, information about municipal and corporate bonds was not readily accessible, but the Internet (again) is changing all that. There is a surprising amount of bond data at a Web site called Bonds Online (www.bonds-online.com), with other bond sites beginning to appear. As for analysis or search tools for bonds, there were none aimed at the individual investor (that we knew of) until the arrival of BondVu™, a real-time, Windows-based program by Capital Management Sciences, a company of Data Broadcasting Corporation. BondVu claims to offer single-security, fixed income analysis for bonds, as well as a search engine for its database of some 800,000 fixed income securities. We have not had the opportunity to examine this program, but BondVu has a home page on the World Wide Web and is looking for beta testers (www.bondvu.com). As an alternative to individual bonds, you might wish to investigate mutual funds that are dedicated to bonds.

As for technical analysis of mutual funds, there is some crossover between stock tools and mutual fund tools. Graphs can be plotted for mutual funds, although they are useful mainly in comparing the performance of one fund with another. Keep in mind that the price of a fund's shares is based on the aggregate of all the stocks in the portfolio and, therefore, not as susceptible to technical analysis.

A number of products aimed directly at mutual funds appear in the Source List at the back of the book. Chapter 16 tells you where to find mutual fund information on the Internet.

DIVERSIFICATION: PUTTING YOUR STOCKS IN DIFFERENT BASKETS

Asset allocation is about reducing risk. Considering only a portfolio of stocks, one way to reduce risk is to spread it over a number of stocks, a number of industries, a variety of market conditions, and a variety of searches.

Spread the Risk over a Number of Stocks

Diversification by number of stocks is a frequently debated topic. Some experts recommend as few as five stocks for a well-balanced portfolio; others recommend 20 or more. We tend toward the larger, rather than the smaller, portfolio because of the risk factor. With only a fraction of your assets in any one position, there is a more generous margin for error.

For instance, with five stocks in your portfolio, you're betting 20 percent of your total investment on each stock. If one of them should happen to gap down 50 percent, you will lose 10 percent of your money on just one position (stops can't protect against gaps). With 20 stocks, on the other hand, a 50 percent loss on one represents only 2.5 percent of your total investment.

The time it takes to manage a portfolio is, of course, a consideration. With computerized tools, a portfolio of 20 stocks should take a modest amount of time. (We have provided our list of daily, weekly, and monthly tasks at the end of this chapter.) We suggest you spread your risk over as many stocks as you can comfortably manage.

Spread the Risk over Several Industries

Diversifying among industry groups is another way to put your eggs in different baskets. A portfolio of 20 stocks could be spread over five to ten industry groups. Out of 200 industry groups, ten would represent only the top five percent.

There are several ways to achieve industry group diversification. You can use a search program to find the top performing groups and then search for stocks in those groups, as described in Chapter 14. You can find industry groups rankings from several sources on the Internet (see Chapter 16). You can use the Macro*World asset allocation program described earlier to select industry groups. Macro*World, at its most sophisticated level, can apply its statistical forecasting models to industry groups to determine their probable direction.

Spread the Risk over Time

Accumulating stocks over a period of time, rather than all at once, reduces risk through time diversification. By entering the market at different times under different conditions, you effectively average out market highs and lows and prevent an overcommitment at inappropriate times.

As you start to build your portfolio, we suggest you go slowly. Buy no more than two or three stocks a month (not necessarily at the same time). It may take a year or longer to complete your initial portfolio, but you will be reducing the market risk.

Use common sense, however. If the market is low in its LSQ channel (as described in Chapter 13) and is beginning to show upward momentum, you may wish to buy more stocks than usual. If the market is becoming extended, it might be a good idea to stop adding stocks until the market pulls back. Once you are fully invested, the five-step investing process that we've described in this book should take care of time diversification.

Spread the Risk with Different Searches

Computerized investing offers another important way to achieve diversification: You can vary the searches used to find stocks. For example, you might buy one stock from an insider buying search, one from a momentum search, and one from an undervalued growth search (or any other combination of your favorite searches). This would also allow you to have both a short-term portfolio (based on momentum stocks) and a long-term portfolio (based on insider buying searches and undervalued growth stocks). Varying your search strategies will in fact diversify the types of stocks in your portfolio, which will make you more neutral to market conditions.

As you can see, the components of diversification are intertwined. Industry-group diversification helps spread the risk among a number of stocks. Running different searches at different times helps spread the risk over different market conditions. The important point is to spread the risk.

THE PORTFOLIO MANAGEMENT PROGRAM

Managing a portfolio of stocks used to be an exceedingly laborious process. You had to check the stock prices in the newspaper and enter them by hand. You had to use a calculator to determine your gain or loss for the day, the week, the month, the year. You had to prepare by hand reports for accounting and tax reporting purposes. Now, with computerized portfolio managers, all this (and more) can be done with minimal time and effort.

Portfolio management tools have made great strides in the past few years, and there are now many excellent programs on the market. Some are stand-alone products, such as Quicken,™ published by Intuit, Inc., and CapTool,™ published by TechServe, Inc. Others are integrated with discount brokerage services, such as Fidelity Investment's Fidelity Online XPress™ or Charles Schwab's StreetSmart.™ Still others are supplemental to online services, such as various portfolio management services on Telescan. Most operate in a similar manner and include such features as:

- Tracking the sale and purchase of stocks and other securities.
- Daily update of stock quotes (if connected with online service).
- Alerts for new highs and lows, and when target or stop is reached.
- Tracking dividends, interest income, and stock splits.
- Maintaining related cash account with automatic debits and credits for each sale or purchase entered.
- Calculating profits and losses to date.
- Producing a variety of reports, including those needed for tax purposes.
- Maintaining multiple portfolios.

A portfolio management program is the basic tool you will need for tracking daily stock prices and for calculating the overall return of your portfolio. However, to monitor your stocks as described in the next section, you will need to use a few of the tools that you learned about in previous chapters.

MONITORING THE PORTFOLIO

Each stock should be monitored closely and evaluated periodically with regard to target levels, mental stops, risk/reward relationship, and negative events that might affect its potential. Situations change, and something could happen to invalidate the reasons for owning the stock. Monitoring routines are what trigger the sales decision, although the sales process itself is discussed separately in the next chapter. The importance of monitoring routines cannot be overemphasized. Without a systematic review, it is impossible to know early enough when a stock should be sold. A list of our daily, weekly, monthly, and quarterly tasks are summarized at the end of this chapter.

Monitoring Targets and Stops

Monitoring targets and stops is extremely important. Most portfolio management programs can generate an alert when a stock reaches a new high or low, or when a predetermined goal or risk level is reached. The latter can be used to track targets and mental stops. It's a good idea to set the target lower and the stop higher (in the program) than your actual targets and stops. This will enable the program to alert you when the stock *nears* one of these levels so you will have time to react accordingly. We'll talk more about this in Chapter 12.

Portfolio Alerts

It is advisable to have some kind of daily alert system to notify you of any news or information that might affect your stocks. Many sources on the Internet offer portfolio alerts (see Chapter 16). Zacks Investment Research, for example, will send you a daily email summarizing relevant changes to your stocks, including, among other information, the following alerts:

- Changes in the Zacks ranks.
- Changes in analysts' earnings estimates or buy/hold/sell recommendations.
- Earnings surprises.
- News headlines and stories from PR Newswire.
- Expected earnings release dates within the next two weeks.

Telescan Investment Platform offers an autoflag service that will alert you to various news and report releases each time you log on to their system. Septor,™ by Notable Technologies, offers alerts on an electronic pager, as well as through the Internet.

THE BOTTOM LINE

Monitoring your performance is one of the most important steps in portfolio management. You do this, in a sense, every time you update your portfolio and look at your overall return. But to judge your true performance, you need a basis of comparison. Clearly, if you're not keeping up with market averages or comparable mutual funds over a reasonable period of time, you would be better off buying mutual funds instead of stocks. If you follow the investing process that we advocate in this book, this shouldn't happen. In any case, it is important to know how you're doing.

Versus Market Indexes

If you compare your portfolio against a market index, use the one that most closely resembles your portfolio. Choose the Nasdaq index (NASD) or the Russell 2000 (RUT.X) if you are heavily invested in small cap stocks; use the New York Stock Exchange index (NYA) or the S&P 500 (SPX) if you have mostly large cap stocks.[2] If you have a mixture of both, try the Wilshire 5000 index (WIEIK). The performance of the index can be measured directly on the index graph. (By the way, be sure to enter any dividends and interest income into your cash account so they will be included in your portfolio return.)

Historically, the large cap indexes have gained about 10 percent a year and the Nasdaq, 12 to 14 percent per year. But that's not especially relevant on a quarter-by-quarter basis. For example, if the average Nasdaq stock is down 7 percent in a particular quarter and your portfolio is down only 3 percent, then, if your portfolio is primarily in Nasdaq stocks, you can assume you did well. Even though you're down for that quarter, you did better than the market and you should be pleased.

Versus Mutual Funds

Comparing your performance against a mutual fund is not as easy. First, you have to find a fund that parallels your objectives and risk tolerance.

---

[2] The terms "large cap" and "small cap" refer to the total market capitalization of a stock (total number of outstanding shares times market price per share). There are varying definitions, but the most common are: A large-cap stock has a total market capitalization in excess of $1 billion; a small-cap stock has a total market capitalization of less than 200 million.

The best way to do this is to use a mutual fund search product. Then check out the fund's performance on a graph and compare it with your return.

If you're doing better than comparable market indexes or mutual funds, give yourself a pat on the back. If you're not, don't rush to any conclusions. Give yourself another quarter or two before you conclude that you're wrong and they're right. If you find yourself outperformed for two consecutive quarters, you might want to take stock of the situation. Have you missed a sell opportunity because you don't review your portfolio often enough? Are you ignoring group rotation? Are you unwilling to take your losses and move on to something else?

It is important to ask these kinds of questions, but don't take your pulse too often. A quarterly review of this kind will suffice. You have to give your portfolio time to perform.

Fine-Tuning Your Investment Strategy

Investing is a learning experience as much as anything else. We suggest that you review your decision-making process once a quarter and fine tune your strategy as needed.

If you have kept a purchase log, as suggested in the previous chapter, compare the performance of each stock in your portfolio to that of the runners up that you rejected from the same search. Is your stock outperforming the others? You made the right choice. Is it lagging behind? Try to figure out why. The wise investor learns as much from mistakes as from successes.

TO-DO LISTS FOR MONITORING A PORTFOLIO

The monitoring and review process that we use is offered below for your consideration (and summarized in Exhibit 11.1). We use the same tools that were introduced in previous chapters. Based on a portfolio of 20 stocks, this process takes about 20 minutes a day, plus an hour once a week for weekly tasks, and another hour once a month for monthly tasks.

Daily To-Do List

- Update portfolio with current stock prices and review targets and stops.

Exhibit 11.1   Portfolio Management Checklist.

Activity	Daily	Weekly	Monthly	Quarterly
Update portfolio & review targets and stops.	x			
Check out portfolio alerts.	x			
Review all stock graphs with technical indicators.	x	x		
Run searches to generate new prospects.		x		
Review market conditions an asset allocation.			x	
Review quarterly earnings reports.			x	
Review new earnings estimates reports.			x	
Review company reports.			x	
Review insider trading.			x	
Review industry group graphs.			x	
Run industry group search.			x	
Review annual and quarterly reports.				x
Evaluate portfolio performance against market indexes or mutual funds.				x
Review decision-making process to fine-tune investing strategy.				x

- Check out any portfolio alerts.
- Review short-term technical indicators on each stock graph.

Weekly To-Do List

- Review long-term technical indicators for each stock.
- Run searches to replenish your watch list.

Monthly To-Do List

- Evaluate market conditions and asset allocation.
- Review quarterly earnings reports.

- Review earnings estimates reports.
- Review S&P MarketScope or Market Guide (or other company report).
- Review insider trading.
- Review industry group graphs and run an industry group search.

Quarterly To-Do List

- Review annual or quarterly reports.
- Evaluate performance against market indexes or mutual funds.
- Review decision-making process for each stock in portfolio and fine-tune search strategy.

THE FOLLY OF DOWN-AVERAGING

One of the biggest mistakes investors make is to buy more of a stock that has dropped in price. They down-average, hoping to lower their cost per share. But if a stock goes down after you buy it, there is at least one thought that should come to mind: *Maybe you made a mistake!* Maybe your analysis was faulty; maybe something negative happened to the company after you bought the stock. Whatever the reason it went down, you already have a position in the stock and now is not a good time to buy more. You may or may not want to sell just because it drops a little, but the number one rule of investing is (or should be): Never, never, never buy more of a stock that has dropped in price.

There is, of course, an exception to this rule. If you are intimately familiar with a company—for instance, if you work there or know someone who does—you may believe that the market is overreacting and any drop in price is temporary. If you're confident of your knowledge, act on it, assuming, of course, that your information is public and you are not violating insider trading rules.

YOU MUST REMEMBER THIS . . .

Good portfolio management is an indispensable element in the investing process.

- Diversify your portfolio by number of stocks, by market conditions (time), by types of searches, and by industry groups.
- Update your portfolio each day with current stock quotes and watch for price alerts.
- Monitor each stock on a daily, weekly, monthly, and quarterly basis.
- Keep abreast of market conditions.
- Never buy more of a stock that has gone down.
- Compare your portfolio's quarterly performance with a comparable market index or mutual fund.
- Fine-tune your investing strategy as needed.

Now let's move on to the positive and negative aspects of the sales process.

12

KNOW WHEN TO FOLD 'EM

Until a stock is sold, any profits are only paper profits and are susceptible to all the risks of the market. But knowing the best time to sell a stock is tricky. How do you know when to let your profits run? When to cut your losses and move on to something else? When to trade a good stock for an even better one? A good way to find the answers to these questions is to look at the stock's risk/reward relationship.

When we buy a stock, the potential reward is substantially greater than the potential risk, or we wouldn't buy it. Typically, we expect 50 to 100 percent on the upside and, hopefully, not more than 10 to 20 percent on the downside. When the potential risk becomes greater than (or even equal to) the potential reward, we start looking for a reason to sell. In fact, one of our most important trading rules is: *Never hold on to a stock when the downside potential is greater than the upside potential.* As a result, we sell a stock any time the risk/reward relationship that caused us to buy it in the first place becomes unfavorable. The actual events that trigger the sale may be positive or negative. (Positive and negative reasons to sell will become clear later in the chapter.)

WARNING SIGNS

To know if a stock is a sell candidate, you have to monitor your portfolio on a daily, weekly, and monthly basis, as described in the previous chapter. What you're looking for are certain technical warning signs or other events that have caused the stock's risk/reward relationship to change.

Technical warning signs—or sell signals—are generated by the same indicators that gave us our primary buy signals in Chapter 9: the MACD indicator, the stochastics index, trading bands, support and resistance levels, and trendlines. We don't necessarily act on every sell signal, but it does grab our attention and lead to a reassessment of the stock. We'll talk more about the positive and negative reasons to sell a stock and how we decide whether or not to act on a sell signal, but first, we will show you what the technical warning signs look like plotted on a stock graph.

Exhibits 12.1 through 12.8 show the technical indicators that we review on a daily and weekly basis for each stock in our portfolio. The warning signs are marked on the graph.

Exhibit 12.1   Nicor, Inc. shows a negative breakout on its daily 8/17/9 MACD.

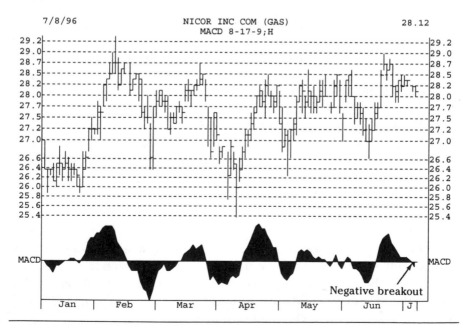

Exhibit 12.2 In July, at the time of its negative daily MACD breakout, Nicor's weekly MACD was positive.

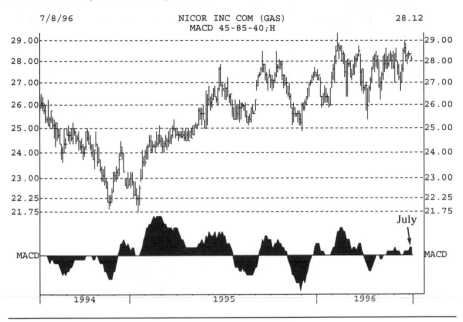

Exhibit 12.3 On July 8, BankAmerica Corp. had a negative breakout on the 14/5 daily stochastics.

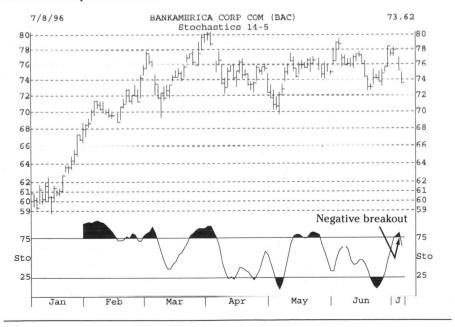

Exhibit 12.4   Philip Morris had a failure swing at the top of its trading bands in late February and subsequently plunged through its 30-day moving average through the bottom band.

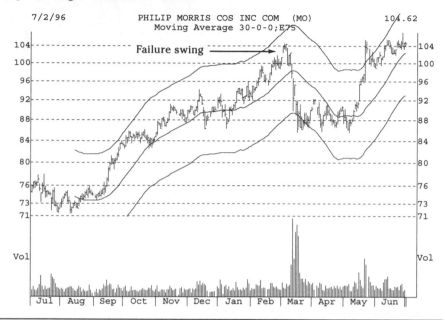

- *MACD Breakouts.* When the 8/17/9 daily MACD histogram dips below the zero line, it is considered a potential sell signal. Whether or not we sell depends on the weekly MACD reading and the distance the stock is from its target. In our example, Nicor gave a sell signal on its daily MACD in early July (Exhibit 12.1) but the weekly MACD was positive (Exhibit 12.2). We'll review this later when we discuss positive and negative reasons to sell.

- *Stochastics Index.* A sell signal occurs when the stochastics index crosses the 75 percent line downward. Exhibit 12.3 shows the daily 14/5 stochastics for Bankamerica Corp, which has just given a sell signal.

- *Trading Bands.* A failure swing at the top of the trading band, like Philip Morris in late February (Exhibit 12.4), or failing to find support at the 30-day moving average is an early symptom of weakening momentum.

Exhibit 12.5   Philip Morris also had a short-term trend break in early March 1996.

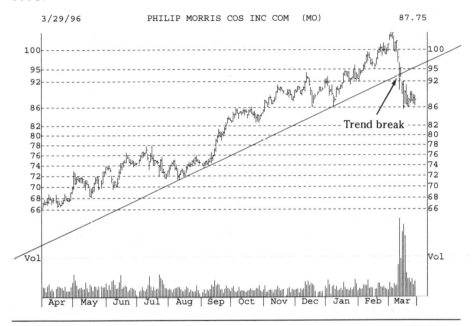

- *Trendline Break.* When a stock falls below a rising trendline (Exhibit 12.5), the uptrend is probably over and a downtrend is likely to begin. Keep in mind that stocks exhibit a short-term trend and a long-term trend. Which trendline break you consider important depends on whether you are a short-term or long-term investor.

- *Resistance Level Reached.* When a stock hits a strong resistance level and fails, as AT&T did in early 1996 (Exhibit 12.6), it is time to reassess the situation, especially for short-term traders.

- *Support Level Breach.* A well-defined support level that doesn't hold, as shown in Exhibit 12.7, should be taken as a warning sign. How much credence to give this warning sign depends on the strength of the support level. As stated earlier, the more times a stock has reached a support level and rebounded, the stronger or more well defined that support is, and thus the more alarming a breach of that support.

Exhibit 12.6 AT&T shows strong resistance at about $67.

Exhibit 12.7 Intel Corp. broke through a strong support level in December 1995.

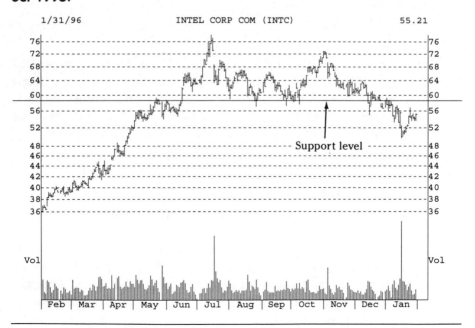

Exhibit 12.8   In early February, 1996, Merck & Co. showed a divergence between the rising stock price and the MACD graph. This is an example of an upward trendline being broken combined with a divergence in the MACD indicator as the stock reached a new high. A good time to sell.

- *Trend Break with a Divergence Between the Stock Price and the MACD.* Seasoned investors consider trend breaks even more significant if there has been a divergence near the trend break between the stock price and a technical indicator, such as the MACD. For example, in Exhibit 12.8, Merck reached a new high in early February, but the MACD did not reach its earlier peak set in January. This is considered a more ominous trend break than if the divergence had not occurred.

We would take any of these technical patterns as a warning to reassess the stock. Whether or not we sell the stock would depend on how close the stock is to its target, whether or not a more desirable stock (with a better risk/reward relationship) is waiting in the wings, and whether there are other positive or negative reasons to sell the stock.

THE POSITIVE SELL

When a stock nears its target, we start looking for reasons to take our profits and move on to something else.[1] Why? Because riding a stock all the way to the target price could be flirting with danger. The closer a stock gets to the top of its long-term or short-term price channel, the more resistance it is likely to meet and the more likely the trend will reverse. In other words, as a stock nears its target, the level of risk increases and the potential reward diminishes.

Obviously, we are not the only ones who know this. Wall Street analysts also use technical indicators to assess the risk/reward potential of a stock. If an analyst believes a stock is becoming overpriced and says so publicly, the stock will very likely fulfill that prophecy and might gap down on the next day's opening. Then it will be too late for investors like us to play sell-signal games with technical indicators.

So when the stock is about halfway between its LSQ line and the top of the channel, we will set a tight stop to protect our profits and start looking for a reason to sell. We call this a *positive sell.*

Technical Triggers

If a stock is near its target, we'll pull out on any sign of technical weakness in the stock. We monitor all the short-term technical indicators described earlier—MACD, stochastics, trading bands, trendlines, resistance levels—and a sell signal by any of them would give us a reason for a positive sell.

Keep in mind, however, that technical sell signals indicate that momentum has shifted. If momentum does not shift—if none of these sell signals occur—we may let a stock run to the top of the LSQ channel. This frequently happens during bullish market periods with high momentum stocks. Nevertheless, we would still keep an eye out for other positive reasons to sell.

Fundamental Triggers

Another positive reason to sell is if the P/E ratio nears an all-time high or significantly exceeds the industry average. Either is a harbinger of potential overvaluation.

---

[1] Targets are discussed in Chapter 10. In brief, a target can be the top of the long-term or short-term LSQ channel, the top of the trading bands, or just below a strong resistance level.

One way to determine the relationship of the current P/E ratio to the stock's historical P/E is to overlay a P/E ratio channel on the stock graph. If the stock is near the upper boundary of the channel, as Atmel Corp was in mid-1993 and mid-1995 (Exhibit 12.9), the relative P/E is at an all-time high. In both cases, Atmel took a sharp dip in price. Telescan's valuation report also gives the stock's relative P/E ratio. (This report is called the Pro-Search Criteria Report in the Windows version of Telescan.) A comparison to the industry P/E can be found in a Zacks earnings estimates report.

Protective Stop Trigger

As described in Chapter 10, we keep a protective mental stop 15 to 20 percent below the current stock price. As the stock moves toward the top of its LSQ channel, we tighten the stop to about 10 percent below the stock price. When the stock gets close to the top of the channel, we switch to a

Exhibit 12.9   A P/E over/undervaluation channel is overlaid on a stock graph of Atmel Corporation. Notice the points of relative overvaluation and relative undervaluation, according to the P/E ratio.

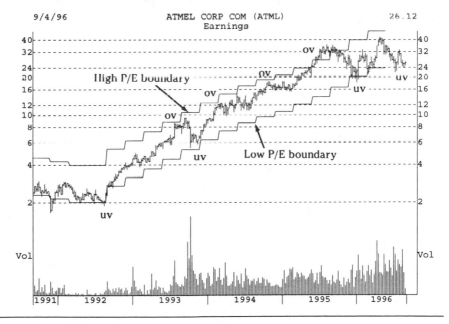

ov – overvalued
uv – undervalued

5 percent hard stop. If the stock falls below this hard stop, we have an automatic positive sell.

Risk/Reward Trigger

Another positive reason to sell is that a stock on our watch list, with a better risk/reward relationship, gives a buy signal. In that case, we'll sell the stock that is near its target and buy the new stock. We'll show you an example under "Trading Places" below of how this has worked for us.

It doesn't really matter which of these triggers you use; if you're looking for a reason to sell, one signal is as good as another. What complicates this issue just a bit is that the target normally will not be a permanent number. It moves with time.

Moving Targets

Keep in mind that the target price for the stock is usually close to the top of the LSQ channel (or for short-term investors, close to the top of the trading band). With high-growth stocks, however, both the LSQ line and trading bands move upward. Thus, your target can move upward as well.

Imagine a case in which a company's earnings grow steadily at 25 percent per year. It is possible that it would stay properly valued at the center of the LSQ channel on its climb. If so, the price would increase approximately 25 percent per year without the stock ever becoming fundamentally or technically overvalued. In such a case, we would increase the target about 25 percent a year. Unfortunately, this is rare.

TRADING PLACES

A comparison of risk to reward is the key to trading one stock for another. A stock at the top of its long-term LSQ channel may have only a few points of likely gain but potentially many points to fall. That's a lot of risk for a small reward. We see no reason to hang on for those last few points if a stock with a better risk/reward potential has just given a good technical buy signal. That's what our watch list is for. These are stocks that have already gone through our two-stage evaluation process and are awaiting a technical buy signal. If a stock on the watch list is particularly attractive, we won't wait for a sell signal on a portfolio stock that is near its target. We'll simply sell it and buy the new stock.

We use this risk/reward analysis regularly. One of the best examples in our portfolio was our Computer Associates/Intel switch in 1993. Computer Associates, you may recall from Chapter 2, was one of our single highest-profit investments, returning more than 200 percent profit in less than two years. In January 1993, it had approached the top of its LSQ channel, and it was clear that the downside potential was more than the upside potential. Intel, on the other hand, had the opposite characteristics: little downside potential and significant upside potential. So we sold Computer Associates and bought Intel. Subsequently, Computer Associates dropped more than 20 percent and Intel climbed to new highs. Although Computer Associates eventually rallied and did quite well in 1995 and 1996, we made the right trade at the time, based on the ratio of risk to reward.

Trading a good stock for a better one is a lot like trading an aging baseball player for a hot young rookie. The old veteran may still have a few hits left, but he could also retire next year and leave you holding the bat. The rookie, on the other hand, may have the makings of a superstar who could bat .300 for many, many years. Based on the risk/reward potential, we would not hesitate to trade the veteran for the rookie. The same goes for stocks.

THE NEGATIVE SELL

Stocks do not always live up to our expectations. Sometimes, things just don't work out.

When we purchase a stock, we base our decision on a number of specific conditions exhibited by the stock at that time (that's what the two-stage evaluation process in Chapters 7 and 8 was all about). If one or more of those conditions deteriorate, we will generally sell the stock. We call this a *negative sell*.

Here are some negative events that might cause us to sell a stock:

- The stock falls and hits a stop. If you set a mental stop at 20 percent below the purchase price and the stock hits that stop, it is time to reassess the situation. That's the purpose of a stop.

- A significant downward revision is reported in earnings estimates. This is one of the surest predictors of a drop in stock price, and a strong signal to get out.

- The company announces disappointing earnings for a quarter. Ask yourself whether or not you would have bought the stock had you been able to see that quarter's earnings. If not, either sell now or watch the stock closely and evaluate next quarter's results.

- The company announces other bad news. Bad news can take myriad forms. It could be an admission that the company can't meet its earnings projections or maybe a lawsuit has been filed that could have a material impact on the company or perhaps the CEO has resigned. You'll recognize bad news when you see it. The problem with acting on bad news is that the damage may have already been done. The market will probably have already taken the negative event into consideration by the time it becomes news, so if the consequences are short term, the fallout may have already occurred. You will need to assess whether the event may have a long-term effect on the company.

- There is a large increase in insider selling. If the president or other officers sell half their holdings, that is not a good sign. Such rampant insider selling is a sign that they perhaps know something you don't, which is a good reason to sell. Do consider the industry, however. In technology stocks, for example, a modest amount of insider selling is not a cause for alarm. These companies often attract employees with stock options, which are viewed as part of their salary. Selling shares acquired through the exercise of options is common in this industry and shouldn't be viewed with alarm.

- The industry group loses momentum. One of our requirements for buying a stock is that it must be in a high-ranking industry group. When the group loses momentum and appears to be rotating downward (see Chapter 14), it is time to consider selling.

- The stock generates a technical sell signal far from its target. Earlier, we said that whether or not we act on a technical sell signal depends on how far the stock is from its target. It also depends on whether you are a short-term or long-term investor. A long-term investor probably won't worry about technical signals when the stock is far from its target, except for a negative weekly MACD. They're in for the long haul. Short-term investors, however, may consider selling on any negative weekly (or even daily) technical breakout and then buy back the stock when it turns upward, assuming the fundamentals have not changed. In a published study on the MACD indicator,[2] we concluded that selling on a weekly MACD breakout avoided most significant drops, except when a stock gapped down (which is difficult to protect against). The point is, when a trusted technical indicator produces a sell signal, it is at least time to reassess the situation.

Daily monitoring of your portfolio is critical. Without it, one of these negative events might zap your stocks before you have time to act.

YOU MUST REMEMBER THIS . . .

Nothing is more detrimental to your bottom line than being in love with the companies you own. The question you must continually ask yourself is, "Would I buy this stock with what I know about it today?" The minute the facts don't support your original decision, it is time to reassess the situation. Loyalty is great in romance, but it can be deadly in the stock market.

Keep these things in mind when reviewing your portfolio:

- There are positive and negative reasons to sell a stock. Know what they are.
- Set stops to protect your profits as a stock moves toward its target.
- When a stock nears its target, consider selling on any short-term technical sell signal or an extended P/E ratio.
- Consider trading a stock near its target for one with a better risk/reward relationship.
- Keep a watch list of stocks that have been through the evaluation process. Use this inventory to trade up and to replace stocks that you sell.
- Monitor your stocks daily so you'll be aware of negative reasons to sell.

---

[2] Kassandra Bentley, *MACD: An Indicator for All Seasons* (Houston: Teleostan, Inc., 1988).

- Don't let your emotions control your decision to sell.
- Don't be afraid to take a loss.

This chapter has rounded out the five-step cyber-investing process as it applies to stocks. We have taken you through identifying prospects, analyzing them, timing the stock purchase, monitoring a portfolio, and timing the stock sale. But we skipped over a couple of procedures that are part of monitoring a portfolio: keeping up with industry groups and the market in general. We will address these topics in the next two chapters.

13

WHAT BIG
BAD MARKET?

"The market goes up, the market goes down." That was the wry response of Robert Rubin, Treasury Secretary during the first Clinton administration and former chairman of Goldman Sachs, when asked about the latest gyrations on Wall Street. That pretty well sums it up. No one really knows where the market is going, not even the experts. Tune in to *Wall Street Week* or CNBC any day of the week. For every guru proclaiming disaster, there are two touting buying opportunities.

In fact, when the great majority thinks the market is going up, the smart money says it will go down, and vice versa. But even that rule is difficult to follow. Much of the time the market goes sideways, where it is difficult to tell up from down.

The point is, if you're going to invest in stocks, you'll have to get used to market fluctuations and not panic every time the Dow wiggles. If your investing strategy is built on value investing and if you follow a disciplined investing process that uses technical timing signals and industry group rotation to take you into and out of stocks, as we suggest in this book, the gyrations of the market should be relatively inconsequential.

This is not to say you should ignore the market. When the market is extremely high (overbought) and susceptible to a correction, you may want to convert more stocks to cash. When the market is extremely low (oversold), you may want to step up your rate of investment to take advantage of buying opportunities.

The trick is learning to recognize market extremes. In early 1995 the Dow had just broken the 4,000 barrier, which had a lot of people wringing their hands and predicting the market's demise. But, as we demonstrated in the first edition of this book, the Dow was not dangerously high at that time (based on its historical trading channel), nor were the broader indexes. In fact, the Dow soared straight through the 5,000 barrier less than a year later and kept right on going. When we first wrote this chapter in mid-July 1996, it was a different story. The Dow was at 5,600 and at the top of its long-term LSQ channel (see Exhibit 13.1). So were the broader indexes. All would have been viewed as dangerous extremes. A week later, there was a nasty little correction that had the market quaking in its boots. But the market recovered and roared past the 6,000 mark just three months later.

Exhibit 13.1   In early 1996 the Dow had reached dangerous territory at the the top of its long-term LSQ channel. A 200-point correction occurred in midsummer.

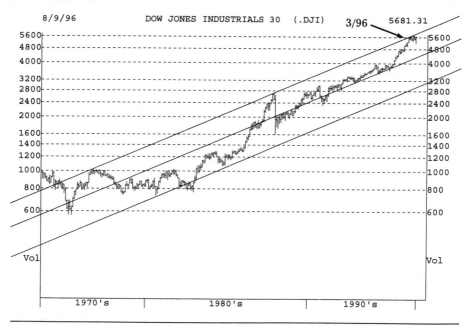

MARKET COMMENTARY FROM THE PROS

Newsletters that offer market commentary by experts are a way to supplement your own evaluation of the market. In general, these experts comment on near-term market direction based on their interpretation of government economic indicators, sentiment data, and technical indicators. Remember, though, the experts don't always agree on the direction of the market. Study their analyses and techniques; then choose the ones with whom you feel most comfortable. A list of some of the newsletters available on the Internet appears in Chapter 16.

So how do you know when to ignore the Chicken Littles and when to run for cover? By looking at the market through the same technical lenses we used to evaluate stocks (plus a couple designed especially for group indexes).

Remember, though, the market doesn't operate in a vacuum. It is affected by interest rates, economic conditions, corporate earnings and dividends, and other market fundamentals. Although a fundamental evaluation of the market is more complicated than a technical analysis, we will touch on it briefly at the end of this chapter.

WHICH MARKET IS THE MARKET?

Before you can analyze the market, you have to decide which market to analyze. Usually, when people talk about the market, they're referring to the Dow Jones Industrial Averages, or the Dow. But with only 30 blue chip stocks, the Dow is much too narrow to be truly meaningful. There are other indexes that give a broader picture of the market.

The New York Stock Exchange index represents about 3,000 of the larger capitalized stocks; the S&P 500 more or less parrots the New York index. The S&P 500, by the way, is weighted for capitalization, which means the higher capitalized stocks carry more weight in the index averages. The Nasdaq index (with about 5,100 stocks) and the Russell 2000 represent the smaller cap stocks. Use the one that most closely represents your portfolio, or for a broader view, use both the New York Stock Exchange index and Nasdaq, as we do.

TECHNICAL LENSES

Many technical indicators are just as appropriate for analyzing market indexes as for analyzing stocks. In essence, they are like X-rays that let you see through the current confusion of the market to its bare-bones reality. We would caution you, however, that technical analysis is much less precise when applied to the market than when applied to stocks. The bottom line with market analysis is the "preponderance of evidence" rule: Go with the majority of the signals.

Two of our favorite indicators for market analysis are LSQ lines and the MACD indicator.[1] In addition, specialized indicators have been developed for analyzing the particular oddities of market indexes. We'll look at one called the overbought/oversold indicator.

The LSQ Lens

Market extremes become very clear when viewed through the lens of our old friend, the LSQ line.

A market index, like a stock, moves in a predictable range around its long-term and short-term LSQ lines. Most of the time it stays somewhere in the middle of the LSQ channel, but as the market becomes overbought or extended, the indexes will edge toward the top of the channel. This happened in mid-summer 1996. Before the mid-summer market correction, the New York Stock Exchange index and the Nasdaq both hit a dangerous extreme on their long-term and short-term LSQ channels (Exhibits 13.2 through 13.5). In mid-July, both indexes dropped precipitously toward the LSQ lines on their long-term graphs. On the short-term graphs, the New York index fell through the LSQ line and the Nasdaq plunged all the way to the bottom of its channel.

These indexes clearly signaled that the market was likely to turn down. Had you been paying attention, you would have been sitting safely on the sidelines during the correction that followed during the week of July 17.

---

[1] Trendlines, trading bands, and stochastics are also popular tools for market analysis. Use these just as you would for stocks, as described in earlier chapters. There are also other indicators (which we think are unnecessary), such as on-balance volume, rate of change, and the newly popular candlestick charts. If you care to experiment with them, they are adequately defined in users manuals of technical analysis programs or in books on technical analysis.

Exhibit 13.2 The Nasdaq market reached the top of its long-term LSQ channel in early summer before falling to the LSQ line in the midsummer correction.

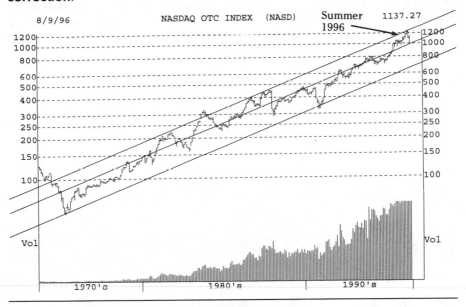

Exhibit 13.3 The New York Stock Exchange index never reached the top of its long-term LSQ channel before the midsummer correction, although it was somewhat extended.

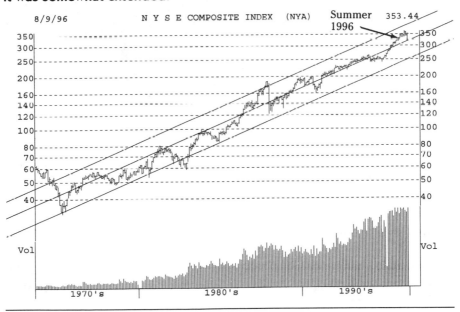

Exhibit 13.4   The short-term LSQ channel shows the Nasdaq market index just below the LSQ line in early August 1996, after plunging almost to the bottom of the channel. The weekly MACD is negative, showing an oversold condition.

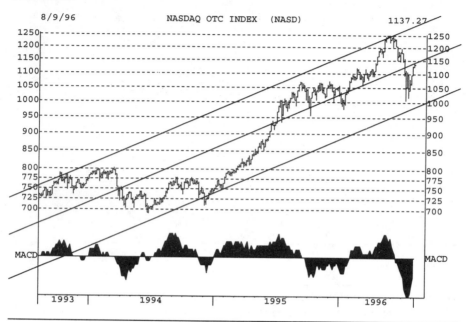

By the way, a market index at the top of its LSQ channel is at a more dangerous extreme than a stock at the top of its channel. Why? Because it is much more difficult for an entire market to break out of a long-term trading channel. The odds of a reversal are greater than a stock in a similar position.

What should you do when the market is near the top of its LSQ channel? First, look at another market index to see if its LSQ position is any better. If you usually follow the New York Stock Exchange, look at the Nasdaq, and vice versa. They do not always move together. For example, in the summer of 1996, the Nasdaq market reached a short-term high of 1260 which put it at the very top of its long-term LSQ channel, whereas the New York Stock Exchange index, at 360, was marginally above its LSQ line. In the summer correction, the Nasdaq fell much more sharply than the New

Exhibit 13.5   The New York Stock Exchange index closed above the LSQ line on August 9, after dipping below it in July. Like the Nasdaq, the weekly MACD is negative, showing an oversold condition.

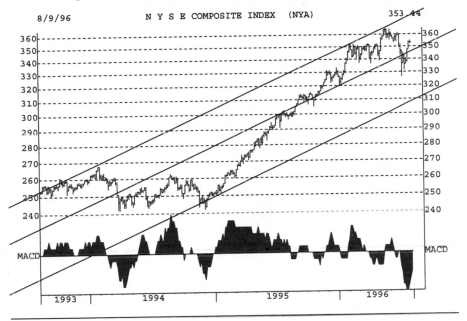

York index, and, by the end of the year, the Nasdaq had gained only a total of 4 percent, whereas the New York index gained about 10 percent.

The MACD Lens

It is also important to take a look at market momentum, which helps assess the strength or weakness of the current trend. A good technical lens for this is the weekly MACD indicator. It views momentum in two ways. First, it shows the deterioration of market momentum, which tells you that the market is topping. Second, the MACD's classic sell signal—when the MACD histogram crosses the zero line downward—is a sign of a forthcoming correction.

In July 1996 both the New York Stock Exchange index and the Nasdaq had turned negative on the weekly MACD (Exhibits 13.4 and 13.5), and both fell considerably farther after the MACD breakout.

The Overbought/Oversold Lens

Another way to evaluate the market is to look at the ratio of advancing to declining issues. How many stocks are going up compared with the number of stocks going down? The overbought/oversold (OB/OS) indicator was designed especially for group indexes for this purpose. Telescan plots the net of advancing and declining issues for the past 10 days (on graphs of four years or less) or the past 10 weeks (on longer-term graphs).

Exhibit 13.6 shows the OB/OS for a 10-year graph of the New York Stock Exchange index. As you can see, the OB/OS gave very clear signals for two great buying opportunities—after the October 1987 crash and in late 1990. The signal given in mid-1994 produced only a modest gain, but the buy signal in December of that year heralded the extraordinary bull market of 1995.

We have found the oversold signals from the OB/OS indicator to be more reliable than the overbought signals. To assess overbought

Exhibit 13.6   The overbought/oversold indicator is shown on a 10-year graph of the New York Stock Exchange index. Note the four buy signals in late 1987, late 1990, mid 1994, and late 1994.

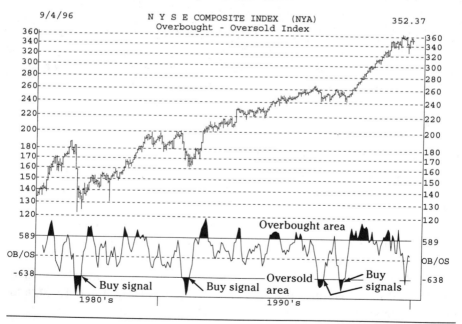

THE BROWN BREAKOUT RATIO

Another interesting gauge of *short-term* market direction is the Brown Breakout Ratio (BBR).* The BBR uses ProSearch to find the ratio between positive and negative breakouts based on a momentum oscillator. Briefly stated, breakout searches are run on three market surrogates (optionable stocks, the New York Stock Exchange stocks, and Nasdaq stocks). Then a calculation is made of the total number of positive breakouts (previously oversold stocks) and the total number of negative breakouts (previously overbought stocks) in each market. The ratio of the positive breakouts to negative breakouts is the BBR. For example, a BBR of 7 to 3 is a positive reading; a BBR of 3 to 7 is a negative reading.

A divergence between the BBR and the direction of the market is the key. On a day when the market goes up but the BBR is negative (more negative breakouts than positive breakouts), that's a sign the market is topping and a downturn is imminent. In other words, even though the market is going up, there are more people taking profits than there are bargain hunters, so the market is likely to turn down.

Conversely, if the market has been going down for some time and suddenly the BBR turns positive (more positive breakouts than negative), that's a sign that the decline is over. The profit takers have wound down, and the bargain hunters are out in full force, so an upturn is likely.

The BBR provides a much clearer *short-term* signal than LSQ channels or other technical indicators plotted on a stock graph. It has given us some of the most consistent and important indications of significant turnarounds after a sharp rise or fall in the market. It has not, however, been particularly effective in sideways markets.

For sideways markets, we use an alternative indicator that measures the traffic "across the border" of the momentum oscillator's overbought and oversold territories. If more stocks are moving into the oversold territory than into the overbought territory, that's a sign of continuing bearishness, and vice versa: If more traffic is moving into the overbought rather than the oversold area, that's a sign of bullishness. Again, a divergence between the indicator and the market is the important sign. We are continuing to evaluate the effectiveness of this indicator.

---

* David L. Brown and Mark Draud, *The Brown Breakout Ratio: Market Timing Indicator* (Houston: Telescan, 1992).

conditions, we would rely more on the LSQ line and a fundamental evaluation of the market.

FUNDAMENTALLY SPEAKING

The market, as we said earlier, does not operate in a vacuum. It is affected by a whole slew of economic conditions and by certain market fundamentals. We don't have the space to go into the economic indicators here, but we will take a moment to talk about a simplistic kind of fundamental market evaluation.

As the market moves above its LSQ line, you need to take a hard look at market P/E ratio, market price-to-book value, and market dividend yield.[2] How high is market P/E and price-to-book value compared with historical figures? How low is dividend yield compared with historical figures?[3] What kind of interest rates can you get from competing fixed income investments, such as bonds? If bond yields are low, the market can absorb higher-than-normal P/E ratios and price-to-book values and lower-than-normal dividend yield. Why? Because low bond yields aren't as likely to lure investors away from the market.

Conversely, if bond yields are high, the market can take a beating despite reasonable P/Es, book value, and dividend yields. There is a sort of flight to safety as money exits the stock market for attractive and safer bond yields.

Essentially, a fundamental evaluation compares the effective yield on stocks to the yield on bonds. We're talking about earnings yield on stocks, not dividend yield. Earnings yield (also called market earnings yield) is the inverse of the P/E ratio: A P/E of 20 would equal a 5 percent earnings yield; a P/E of 24 would equal an approximate 4 percent earnings yield. Earnings yield usually bears some relationship to the yield available on bond rates, because they both compete for the same dollars. So it is not surprising that they move more or less in sync. Although earnings yield is not paid out in cash dividends, it provides an approximate

---

[2] These figures are the averages for the market as a whole and can be found in major financial publications, such as *Wall Street Journal, Investor's Business Daily,* or *Barron's.*

[3] Dividend yield has become less meaningful because of the general reluctance of companies to pay dividends and the actual policy of many large companies, such as Intel and Microsoft, of *not* paying dividends. The investing public seems to be ambivalent about the subject.

return for comparison purposes (though clearly not as certain as a bond coupon in the mail.)

In effect, stocks and bonds are involved in a tug of war. During the past 20 years, bond yields have ranged from a high of 4 percent to a low of 0.5 percent above market earnings yield. At the higher end of the range, money flows out of the riskier stocks into bonds; at the lower end, money flows out of bonds and into stocks. Obviously, then, stocks are relatively undervalued when the bond yield approaches market earnings yield; they're relatively overvalued when the bond yield exceeds market earnings yield by 3 to 4 percent.

A look at the market environment in early 1994 might be instructive. The average market P/E ratio then was 24 (an all-time high for the S&P 500); this was equal to an effective earnings yield of 4.2 percent. Under normal conditions, this would have been a danger signal for the market. But interest rates had been steadily declining throughout 1993. By January 1994, the long bond rate (for 30-year bonds) was below 5¾ percent (near an all-time low) and represented only a 1.5 percent premium to market earnings yield. Certificates of deposit offered even lower returns than bonds, so people were looking for some place other than cash or bonds to put their money. Therefore, despite the high P/Es in early 1994, the market continued to make some headway. By November, the long bond yield had risen to 8.2 percent, but market earnings yield, due to improved corporate earnings, had advanced to 6.7 percent.

In mid-summer of 1996, as this chapter was being written, the long bond yield was approximately 7 percent and the market earnings yield was a little over 6 percent, representing the lower end of this range. Thus, it was more bullish than bearish for stocks. However, a pervasive feeling in the marketplace that bond rates could rise sharply was putting pressure on stocks.

Two other examples might shed more light on this issue. In late 1982, the market was at a low, with market yield at 12.5 percent versus a Treasury-bond yield of 12.9 percent. With almost no premium involved, stocks staged a great rally with the Dow gaining some 400 points over the next several months. On the other hand, at a market high in October 1987, market yield was 5.3 percent whereas Treasury-bond yield was 9.1 percent, very close to its all-time high premium. We all know what happened soon thereafter—the crash of '87!

The point is, the effective yield on stocks must be close enough to the effective yield on bonds to justify taking the extra risk in stocks to obtain the rewards of potential growth.

UP P/E, DOWN P/E: THE EFFECT OF INTEREST RATES ON MARKET P/E

The rise and fall of interest rates can affect P/E ratios, irrespective of earnings growth. The following table shows the approximate effect of interest rates on P/E ratio for various earnings growth rates. Other interest levels would, of course, dictate lower or higher P/Es.

Market Interest Rate	Long-Term Earnings Growth Rates	Rational P/E
6%	10%	18
6	15	24
6	20	33
6	30	58
6	40	78
8	10	15
8	15	20
8	20	27
8	30	48
8	40	82
10	10	12
10	15	17
10	20	23
10	30	40
10	40	68
12	10	10
12	15	14
12	20	19
12	30	33
12	40	57

The logic behind this seesaw of interest rates and P/E ratio is competition for investment dollars. Generally, the market requires about four percent more from equity investments—such as stocks with their earnings risks—than for risk-free government securities. So as interest rates rise, money flows out of stocks into less risky bonds and CDs, which causes P/E ratios to fall in general. Conversely, falling interest rates provide a strong impetus to buy stocks and can cause P/Es in general to rise. When P/Es rise or fall because of interest rates, it has nothing to do with the earnings growth rates of companies.

Individual investors can't do anything about market interest rates. However, you can be aware of how current P/Es relate to historical P/Es so that you can judge for yourself the risk in the market.

This type of market analysis is often confusing to a beginning investor or even to some seasoned investors. Just keep in mind that there is a significant relationship between market P/E and market interest rate, and the time to pay attention is when the difference between them is bumping into historical highs and lows.

WHEN TO CONVERT STOCKS TO CASH

When the market is extended, it is prudent to consider the composition of your portfolio. Should you convert any stocks to cash? If so, when and how much?

If you are using the cyber-investing process described in this book—buying fundamentally attractive stocks and monitoring them closely for technical signals—the process should take care of itself during normal market conditions. As the market becomes extended, the process itself should move you more heavily into cash. However, this process will not work as well for all investors.

Exhibit 13.7 This grid shows the approximate levels of investment when the market is in various positions in its short-term and long-term LSQ channels. For example, if the market index is above its long-term LSQ line but below its short-term LSQ line, you would be between 20 and 60 percent invested. Where exactly you might fall within this range would depend on whether you're a short-term or long-term investor and whether the weekly MACD is negative or positive. Short-term investors will gravitate toward the lower end of the ranges when the weekly MACD is negative; long-term investors will gravitate toward the higher end of the ranges when the weekly MACD is positive.

Long-Term LSQ Channel	Percentage Invested			
Near top	20–60%	15–50%	15–40%	10–30%
Above LSQ	25–70	20–60	20–60	15–50
Below LSQ	30–90	25–80	25–70	20–60
Near bottom	50–100	35–90	30–80	25–70
	Near bottom	Below LSQ	Above LSQ	Near top
	Short-Term LSQ Channel			

Momentum players, for instance, are very susceptible to market extremes, because momentum stocks tend to have very high P/E ratios that can get corrected in a hurry if the market peaks. Long-term investors are also susceptible because they do not use technical signals as aggressively as do short-term investors. Without these signals, there is little to prompt long-term investors to move into cash at market highs—unless most of their stocks happen to be reaching their targets at the same time, which is not very likely.

We have prepared a somewhat simplistic grid (Exhibit 13.7) as a guideline for stock-versus-cash allocation during market extremes. (Long-term investors may wish to utilize an asset allocation program to accomplish this function.) The grid is based on long-term and short-term LSQ lines and a weekly 8/17/9 MACD. As the market's LSQ lines become more and more extended, the chart indicates a bias toward cash, especially when the MACD is negative. The percentages are general goals, not hard-and-fast rules.

In the end, your ratio of stocks to cash must be based on your own risk tolerance, on the short-term or long-term nature of your portfolio, on the use or nonuse of industry group rotation, and—as always—on common sense.

YOU MUST REMEMBER THIS . . .

It goes without saying that the market cannot reach new highs without going through old highs. Yet a common mistake investors make (even some experienced ones) is to panic and convert their stocks to cash whenever a new high is reached in the Dow or other index. This is one of the surest ways to miss the great market rallies. The key is to consider the current position of the market in relation to its long-term trend. Otherwise, you could end up sitting on the sidelines in the new millennium when the Dow breaks 10,000.

Here's a handy checklist to keep your market fears in check:

- About once a month, evaluate a market index that mimics your portfolio. Look at the short-term and long-term LSQ channels, along with a technical indicator or two. Consider the market P/E in light of bond yields. If all these are average, don't worry.

The Nasdaq index (NASD) or Russell 2000 (RUT.X) are good indexes for mimicking a small-cap portfolio; choose the New York Stock Exchange index (NYA) or the S&P 500 (SPX) if you have mostly large-cap or blue chip stocks.

- Here are two danger signals to watch for when evaluating the market: (a) the market moves to the high side of its LSQ channel or (b) the *difference* between bond yield and market yield approaches its former highs. If either of these events occur, it is time to consider converting some of your stocks to cash.

- The effective yield on bonds has to be enough greater than the effective yield on stocks to justify giving up the potential growth in the stock.

- Don't panic when the Dow goes through 7,000, 8,000 or any other barrier. It is just a number.

- Keep your emotions in check, especially when listening to the market gurus.

- Go with the preponderance of the evidence.

The market is notoriously difficult to predict. None of the technical indicators is foolproof; no market theory is infallible. But with cyber-investing tools and a little common sense, there is no reason why you can't be among the ranks of the smart investors. Moreover, if you watch your industry groups closely (as described in the next chapter), you can afford to be wrong about the market.

14

THE IN CROWD

Stocks within a particular industry are affected in similar ways by market and economic conditions. Viewed as a group, they behave like a miniature market index and can, therefore, be tracked and analyzed much like a market index. That is why companies that serve the investing public created industry groups.[1]

The importance of industry groups is the way they rotate into and out of favor with institutional investors. This rotation, which we have mentioned in previous chapters, can be very beneficial to the small investor.

There is nothing magic about industry group rotation. It happens because institutional investors—mutual funds, pension funds, and large brokerage houses—control the great bulk of money in today's market (an estimated 70 percent of all trading). Competition for investment dollars is fierce, which creates a demand for short-term performance to boost their quarterly statements. As a result, institutions track industry groups with the tenacity of Scotland Yard. They employ analysts who study demographic trends, economic cycles, and other factors, and try to predict which industry groups have the brightest prospects for near-term growth.

---

[1] Industry groups were created by companies that serve the investing public, such as Standard & Poor's, *Investor's Business Daily,* and others. These companies classify the approximately 9,000 listed stocks into 75 to over 200 industry groups. A service that uses only 75 groups might lump pharmaceuticals, medical supply companies, and medical equipment manufacturers into one group, whereas another service might make each of these a separate industry group.

Once an opportunity is clearly identified, one institution after another begins to accumulate shares in the top companies of the industry. This creates something like a tidal wave that drives up stock prices and P/E ratios within the group. Such a group is said to be rotating upward or "into favor."

Some months or years later, a favored industry's earnings potential will peak or become diminished, or the shares of the group will be considered fully priced or overpriced. When that happens, institutional money will begin to flow out of that group and related stock prices and P/Es will fall. Such a group is said to be rotating downward or "out of favor."

And so it goes. The rotation is not an orderly one, with one group after another rotating upward single file. Instead, there may be 10 to 20 groups or more in favor during a bull market, and maybe four or five groups during a bearish period. Over time, most industry groups will have their day in the sun.

WHO'S IN? WHO'S OUT?

Industry groups are important to the investor who wants to reap the benefits of a group that is rotating upward. Computerized search tools allow us to find positively rotating industry groups early in their rotation. We can see how each group is ranked against all other groups, in which direction it is rotating, and the strength of its momentum.

Once we identify the top industry groups, the next step is to search for stocks that are rotating upward within the selected industries. This

---

ROUND AND ROUND THEY GO . . .

Investors Business Daily has published a chart entitled "35 Years of Best Industry Groups." The chart is a fascinating study of industry group rotation. Some groups stay in favor over several years. This is partly because economic trends that drive a rotation can last a very long time, but it also has to do with the slowness with which institutional investors move. We've included a sampling from the chart to give you an idea of how and why industry groups rotate. As you can see, there are bullish groups even in bear markets!

A Sampling of Top Performing Industry Groups over History as Published by *Investor's Business Daily*.

Bull Markets	Industry Group	Reason for Ascendancy According to Investor's Business Daily	% Increase Over Period of 2 to 4 Top Stocks
7/94–9/95	Computer software	Expanded use of Internet; improved functionality of multimedia applications.	416%–1,165%
7/92–9/95	Semiconductor manufacturing	PC boom; strong demand for smaller, faster chips.	1,129%–2,731%
10/91–10/93	Oil & gas products	More favorable supply/demand relationship for natural gas.	143%–433%
5/90–1/92	Biotech industries	Actual and anticipated development and approval of new drugs.	473%–782%
4/88–10/89	Cable TV	Deregulation.	164%–300%
2/88–7/90	Telecommunications	Modernization of networks and increased competition caused by the breakup of AT&T.	203%–500%
8/84–10/87	Cable TV	New programming and strong subscriber gains.	210%–314%
Bear Markets or Sideways Markets			
1/78–11/80	Electronics	Increased demand from computer, telecommunications, aerospace, and automation industries.	500% to 904%
8/76–9/78	Hospitals & nursing homes	Medicare payments; increased efficiency of investor-owned facilities.	210% to 309%
2/73–8/74	Gold	Increased inflation, monetary turmoil, political unrest.	285% to 331%
4/71–5/72	Mobile homes	Increased development of mobile home parks; increased availability of financing.	143% to 433%

Source: Courtesy of *Investor's Business Daily* Library, P. O. Box 661780, Los Angeles, CA 90066.

228

rotation of stocks within a rotating industry group is also a function of institutional favor.

When an institution decides to move into a group, it typically starts to accumulate shares of the top company in the group. (Deciding which is the top company is often a subjective judgment.) As more institutions move in, the price and P/E ratio of the number one stock rise, which makes the stock less attractive. Consequently, institutional money flows into the number two stock, and so on down the line.

For example, if the semiconductor industry should rotate into favor, the first institutions to make a move might buy Intel (generally recognized as the leader). If the trend toward that industry should gain momentum, other institutions might also buy Intel, which clearly would cause an upward trend in Intel's stock. At some point, however, Intel might seem overpriced, compared with other stocks in the industry; then other stocks in the industry, such as National Semiconductor or Advanced Micro Devices, might begin to look like bargains and attract the institutional money.

This is an oversimplification. In reality, the rotation is much less precise. Some stock is going to be the favorite, but in many groups the second favorite stock will rotate closely behind the number-one stock. In other groups, there might be one outstanding performer that rotates far ahead of a cluster of runners-up, which rotate together.

THE INDUSTRY GROUP SEARCH

Industry-group searches are similar to stock searches; they use many of the same indicators and can be done with the same stock search program. The primary difference in constructing the search is that industry groups are selected as the search universe, rather than stocks.

One search we use frequently is shown in Exhibit 14.1. All of the indicators were used in the various stock searches in Chapter 5.

- The group rank indicator is used to eliminate all groups that are not ranked among the top 60 percent of all groups; then it will rank the groups in descending order.

- Four group rank change indicators will favor those industry groups that are moving up the fastest over the past one to 13 weeks; these indicators are weighted to favor groups with a recent move.

Exhibit 14.1 An industry group search for industries with positive momentum.

Indicator	Action/Weight
Group rank (GrpRK)	Eliminate all groups under a rank of 40
Group rank (GrpRk)	Rank stocks by highest scores/60%
Group rank change—1-Week (cGRP1)	Rank stocks by highest scores/100%
Group rank change—3-Weeks (cGRP3)	Rank stocks by highest scores/80%
Group rank change—6-Weeks (cGRP6)	Rank stocks by highest scores/60%
Group rank change—13-Weeks (cGP13)	Rank stocks by highest scores/40%
LSQ deviation—3-year (3LDv)	List only
LSQ deviation—5-year (5LDv)	List only
LSQ deviation—10-year (10LDv)	List only
LSQ deviation—15-year (15LDv)	List only
LSQ deviation—Maximum (MaxDv)	List only
Relative performance—1-day (1-Dy)	List only
Relative performance—1-week (1-Wk)	List only
Relative performance—3-weeks (3-Wk)	List only
Relative performance—6-weeks (6-Wk)	List only
Relative performance—18-weeks (18-Wk)	List only

- Five LSQ deviation indicators and five relative performance indicators (used to list information) will reveal where a group is within its trading channel and the level of its recent performance.

It is important to use both the *group rank* indicator and the various *group rank change* indicators. The group rank indicator tells how the group compares with other groups; a rank of 70 is obviously higher than a rank of 60. But that doesn't tell us whether the group is on the way up or on the way down. The group rank change indicators tell us this.

Search Results: The Innies and the Outies

Exhibit 14.2 shows the top 20 industry groups with positive momentum on the date of the report. These results are based on the relative movement of an industry with respect to the other industries. The group rank

Exhibit 14.2   The top 20 industry groups with positive momentum on July 26, 1996, based on the search criteria in Exhibit 14.1.

```
1> .OFU    – Office Furniture widx                                    .OFU
     GrpRk  = 113.0    (99)    GrpRk  = 113.0    (99)    cGRP1 = 0.2      (94)
     cGRP3  = 6.3      (99)    cGRP6  = 4.0      (99)    cGP13 = 11.5     (99)
     3LDv   = 17.6     (89)    5LDv   = 2.7      (69)    10LDv = 8.6      (63)
     15LDv  = –3.4     (51)    MaxDv  = –22.7    (15)    1-Dy  = 99.7     (16)
     1-Wk   = 99.0     (57)    3-Wk   = 109.5    (98)    6-Wk  = 107.6    (96)
     18-Wk  = 123.9    (92)

2> .FPA    – Pawnshops widx                                           .FPA
     GrpRk  = 110.3    (98)    GrpRk  = 110.3    (98)    cGRP1 = 1.1      (98)
     cGRP3  = –0.4     (93)    cGRP6  = 1.1      (98)    cGP13 = 4.7      (99)
     3LDv   = 21.4     (90)    5LDv   = 6.2      (77)    10LDv = N/A      (  )
     15LDv  – N/A      (  )    MaxDv  = – 29.5   (11)    1-Dy  = 101.9    (81)
     1-Wk   = 104.3    (95)    3-Wk   = 100.0    (81)    6-Wk  = 100.8    (75)
     18-Wk  = 112.3    (87)

3> .BSB    – Banking / Savings Banks TSCN-                            .BSB
     GrpRk  = 103.0    (89)    GrpRk  = 103.0    (89)    cGRP1 = 0.8      (98)
     cGRP3  = 0.9      (97)    cGRP6  = 0.2      (97)    cGP13 = –1.7     (89)
     3LDv   = 1.5      (63)    5LDv   = 3.2      (71)    10LDv = 68.5     (91)
     15LDv  = N/A      (  )    MaxDv  = 58.7     (93)    1-Dy  = 100.6    (63)
     1-Wk   = 100.7    (87)    3-Wk   = 98.8     (68)    6-Wk  = 100.5    (73)
     18-Wk  – 102.8    (75)

4> .TCI    – Tobacco / Cigarettes TSCN-Wid                            .TCI
     GrpRk  = 106.8    (96)    GrpRk  = 106.8    (96)    cGRP1 = –0.2     (92)
     cGRP3  = –1.3     (85)    cGRP6  = –0.5     (90)    cGP13 = 8.3      (99)
     3LDv   = 0.4      (54)    5LDv   = 31.8     (91)    10LDv = –2.9     (37)
     15LDv  = –20.4    (27)    MaxDv  = –16.5    (20)    1-Dy  = 100.5    (60)
     1-Wk   = 98.9     (56)    3-Wk   = 95.5     (54)    6-Wk  = 95.7     (53)
     18-Wk  = 112.6    (87)

5> .BSL    – Banking / Savings and Loan TS                            .BSL
     GrpRk  = 102.5    (79)    GrpRk  = 102.5    (79)    cGRP1 – 2.0      (99)
     cGRP3  = 1.4      (99)    cGRP6  = 0.1      (94)    cGP13 – 1.1      (96)
     3LDv   = –1.2     (44)    5LDv   = 3.4      (71)    10LDv = 20.0     (75)
     15LDv  = –4.5     (50)    MaxDv  = –3.5     (43)    1-Dy  = 102.3    (84)
     1-Wk   = 100.3    (85)    3-Wk   = 96.6     (60)    6-Wk  = 97.8     (62)
     18-Wk  = 102.2    (73)

6> .COT    – Cosmetics & Toiletries TSCN-W                            .COT
     GrpRk  = 105.1    (94)    GrpRk  = 105.1    (94)    cGRP1 = –0.4     (91)
     cGRP3  = –0.9     (87)    cGRP6  = –0.2     (92)    cGP13 = –0.9     (90)
     3LDv   = 1.2      (61)    5LDv   = 9.4      (80)    10LDv = 2.2      (49)
     15LDv  = 10.0     (66)    MaxDv  = 45.2     (91)    1-Dy  = 99.4     (14)
     1-Wk   = 101.2    (89)    3-Wk   = 99.1     (69)    6-Wk  = 100.4    (72)
     18-Wk  = 107.7    (83)

7> .DET    – Drugs-Generic and OTC / Ethic                           .DET
     GrpRk  = 103.4    (89)    GrpRk  = 103.4    (89)    cGRP1 = –0.5     (89)
     cGRP3  = –0.9     (87)    cGRP6  = –0.9     (87)    cGP13 = 2.0      (97)
     3LDv   = –1.9     (40)    5LDv   = 26.0     (90)    10LDv = 11.6     (67)
     15LDv  = –6.5     (47)    MaxDv  = –5.6     (37)    1-Dy  = 99.6     (16)
     1-Wk   = 98.8     (55)    3-Wk   = 95.8     (55)    6-Wk  = 97.9     (62)
     18-Wk  = 100.5    (60)
```

(Continued)

Exhibit 14.2   (continued)

8> .AMC   – Aerospace / Major Contractor   .AMC
    GrpRk = 105.2   (94)   GrpRk = 105.2   (94)   cGRP1 = −0.3   (91)
    cGRP3 = −2.2   (80)   cGRP6 = 0.1   (94)   cGP13 = −1.8   (86)
    3LDv = −2.4   (38)   5LDv   = 12.5   (83)   10LDv = 41.7   (85)
    15LDv = 37.0   (81)   MaxDv = 22.3   (86)   1-Dy = 101.3   (76)
    1-Wk = 99.2   (59)   3-Wk   = 94.7   (48)   6-Wk = 100.3   (72)
    18-Wk = 101.2   (65)

9> .HCF   – Home Furnishings / Carpets, F   .HCF
    GrpRk = 101.6   (70)   GrpRk = 101.6   (70)   cGRP1 = 0.4   (95)
    cGRP3 = −0.5   (93)   cGRP6 = 2.3   (98)   cGP13 = 3.7   (98)
    3LDv = 5.8   (77)   5LDv   = −17.5   (18)   10LDv = −17.4   (17)
    15LDv = −31.3   (14)   MaxDv = −22.4   (16)   1-Dy = 104.5   (92)
    1-Wk = 101.0   (88)   3-Wk   = 94.8   (49)   6-Wk = 96.3   (56)
    18-Wk = 99.0   (49)

10> .FLE   – Finance / Leasing TSCN-Widx   .FLE
    GrpRk = 104.2   (91)   GrpRk = 104.2   (91)   cGRP1 = −1.2   (76)
    cGRP3 = 0.7   (94)   cGRP6 = −0.6   (90)   cGP13 = 1.3   (96)
    3LDv = 7.3   (79)   5LDv   = 11.2   (82)   10LDv = 24.0   (77)
    15LDv = 20.1   (73)   MaxDv = 5.5   (74)   1-Dy = 99.8   (17)
    1-Wk = 99.5   (64)   3-Wk   = 98.1   (66)   6-Wk = 98.2   (64)
    18-Wk = 101.9   (71)

11> .BAN   – Banking / Commercial TSCN-Wid   .BAN
    GrpRk = 102.1   (77)   GrpRk = 102.1   (77)   cGRP1 = −0.7   (88)
    cGRP3 = −0.8   (93)   cGRP6 = −2.1   (85)   cGP13 = −2.5   (86)
    3LDv = −0.5   (48)   5LDv   = −6.2   (35)   10LDv = 14.7   (70)
    15LDv = 20.6   (74)   MaxDv = 29.5   (88)   1-Dy = 100.9   (70)
    1-Wk = 99.6   (65)   3-Wk   = 97.6   (64)   6-Wk = 97.6   (61)
    18-Wk = 101.4   (67)

12> .FRE   – Receivables widx   .FRE
    GrpRk = 110.6   (98)   GrpRk = 110.6   (98)   cGRP1 = −0.7   (88)
    cGRP3 = 1.3   (98)   cGRP6 = −4.2   (65)   cGP13 = 9.2   (99)
    3LDv = 11.7   (85)   5LDv   = 53.9   (95)   10LDv = 17.0   (72)
    15LDv = −4.7   (50)   MaxDv = 3.4   (70)   1-Dy = 98.8   (10)
    1-Wk = 98.8   (55)   3-Wk   = 102.9   (94)   6-Wk = 103.6   (93)
    18-Wk = 127.6   (93)

13> .FCG   – Food / Candy, Gum TSCN-Widx   .FCG
    GrpRk = 101.5   (70)   GrpRk = 101.5   (70)   cGRP1 = 2.8   (99)
    cGRP3 = 2.8   (99)   cGRP6 = 3.4   (99)   cGP13 = −4.3   (71)
    3LDv = 3.8   (72)   5LDv   = 1.6   (65)   10LDv = −0.4   (42)
    15LDv = −16.4   (33)   MaxDv = −14.7   (22)   1-Dy = 100.3   (55)
    1-Wk = 104.4   (95)   3-Wk   = 101.5   (92)   6-Wk = 104.4   (94)
    18-Wk = 93.4   (26)

14> .RCL   – Rail Equipment/Car Leasing Wi   .RCL
    GrpRk = 100.3   (61)   GrpRk = 100.3   (61)   cGRP1 = 2.8   (99)
    cGRP3 = −1.0   (86)   cGRP6 = 0.2   (97)   cGP13 = 4.2   (99)
    3LDv = −8.6   (22)   5LDv   = −13.1   (23)   10LDv = −6.9   (29)
    15LDv = −6.3   (47)   MaxDv = 9.1   (78)   1-Dy = 102.5   (85)
    1-Wk = 99.3   (60)   3-Wk   = 92.5   (35)   6-Wk = 95.8   (53)
    18-Wk = 98.1   (44)

Exhibit 14.2   (continued)

15> .REA   – Real Estate Invest. Trust TSC   .REA

GrpRk = 101.5	(70)	GrpRk = 101.5	(70)	cGRP1 = −0.8	(82)
cGRP3 = −1.4	(84)	cGRP6 = −0.6	(90)	cGP13 = 0.6	(95)
3LDv = 2.8	(69)	5LDv = −3.4	(42)	10LDv = 12.8	(68)
15LDv = 7.5	(63)	MaxDv = 19.7	(85)	1-Dy = 100.0	(44)
1-Wk = 99.1	(58)	3-Wk = 98.1	(66)	6-Wk = 99.5	(67)
18-Wk = 100.8	(62)				

16> .TLS   – Leaf / Snuff widx   .TLS

GrpRk = 101.5	(70)	GrpRk = 101.5	(70)	cGRP1 = −0.8	(82)
cGRP3 = −1.5	(82)	cGRP6 = 2.3	(98)	cGP13 = −0.6	(90)
3LDv = 2.3	(67)	5LDv = 9.6	(81)	10LDv = −22.7	(13)
15LDv = −27.5	(18)	MaxDv = −25.6	(13)	1-Dy = 100.1	(49)
1-Wk = 102.0	(91)	3-Wk = 96.9	(61)	6-Wk = 99.4	(67)
18-Wk = 104.7	(79)				

17> .CAG   – Chemicals / Agricultural TSCN   .CAG

GrpRk = 100.8	(65)	GrpRk = 100.8	(65)	cGRP1 = −0.9	(79)
cGRP3 = 2.0	(99)	cGRP6 = 3.5	(99)	cGP13 = −0.2	(91)
3LDv = −7.8	(23)	5LDv = 10.2	(81)	10LDv = 22.3	(76)
15LDv = 72.2	(90)	MaxDv = 86.7	(96)	1-Dy = 101.4	(77)
1-Wk = 98.3	(48)	3-Wk = 99.2	(70)	6-Wk = 99.3	(67)
18-Wk = 94.8	(30)				

18> .UWA   – Utilities-Water TSCN-Widx   .UWA

GrpRk = 101.2	(67)	GrpRk = 101.2	(67)	cGRP1 = −1.0	(78)
cGRP3 = 0.8	(95)	cGRP6 = −0.3	(91)	cGP13 = −1.3	(89)
3LDv = 8.5	(81)	5LDv = 5.2	(75)	10LDv = 11.8	(67)
15LDv = −11.7	(40)	MaxDv = −19.6	(18)	1-Dy = 100.1	(49)
1-Wk = 98.5	(51)	3-Wk = 100.0	(81)	6-Wk = 103.1	(92)
18-Wk = 102.8	(75)				

19> .FBM   – Bakery/Mill/Sugar widx   .FBM

GrpRk = 113.7	(99)	GrpRk = 113.7	(99)	cGRP1 = 0.6	(95)
cGRP3 = −4.2	(61)	cGRP6 = 3.9	(99)	cGP13 = 15.2	(99)
3LDv = 15.5	(87)	5LDv = 23.1	(89)	10LDv = 15.0	(70)
15LDv = −12.7	(39)	MaxDv = −30.7	(11)	1-Dy = 100.3	(55)
1-Wk = 100.1	(83)	3-Wk = 94.9	(49)	6-Wk = 102.4	(88)
18-Wk = 114.6	(88)				

20> .OIN   – Oil & Gas / International TSC   .OIN

GrpRk = 102.6	(80)	GrpRk = 102.6	(80)	cGRP1 = 1.4	(74)
cGRP3 = −0.7	(93)	cGRP6 = −0.8	(87)	cGP13 = −5.0	(70)
3LDv = 1.7	(64)	5LDv = 6.0	(76)	10LDv = 9.6	(64)
15LDv = −1.8	(53)	MaxDv = 3.2	(69)	1-Dy = 100.2	(53)
1-Wk = 98.4	(49)	3-Wk = 96.4	(59)	6-Wk = 99.1	(66)
18-Wk = 103.5	(77)				

Source: ProSearch 5.0, courtesy of Telescan, Inc.

percentile tells you where the group is ranked at this time; the 99th percentile is the highest ranking. To determine whether a group is rotating upward or downward, look at both the score and ranking percentile for the rank change indicators. Any negative score means the group was rotating downward in that period.

Also, consider how much room there is for movement. On the search report, the LSQ deviation indicators tell you where the industry is in relation to its LSQ line. Here, a negative score means it is below the LSQ line, which is good, because it has room to move up.

The purpose of this evaluation is to pinpoint those groups that seem to be rotating the most positively at this time and have the most room to move. The office furniture group (.OFU) ranked number 1 is excellent. Not only is it in the 99th percentile in group rank, it is in the 99th percentile in four out of five measurements of group rank change. That means it has just recently rotated to the top spot. Furthermore, despite its recent strength, the group is still 22 percent below the LSQ line on the long-term LSQ deviation indicator, and 3 percent below the LSQ line on the 15-year indicator. It has plenty of room to grow.

Another interesting group is number 13, food/candy/gum (.FCG), which appears to have just begun to move rapidly. Although it is only in the 70th percentile in group rank, the group rank change indicators show that it has been rotating upward (in the 99th percentile) over the past 1, 3, and 6 weeks. It also has plenty of room to grow according to the LSQ deviation indicators: It is about 15 percent below the long-term LSQ line and 16 percent below the 15-year LSQ line.

Watch out for groups that are rotating the wrong way. The cosmetics & toiletries industry (.COT) is in the 94th percentile, but all of the group rank change indicators are negative, which means it is rotating downward in all four time periods. Obviously, we would eliminate that group from the list, as well as tobacco/cigarettes (.TCI), banking/commercial (.BAN), aerospace (.AMC), and oil & gas/international (.OIN) for the same reason.

This list can be narrowed somewhat further by eliminating groups that have high LSQ deviation scores or the least impressive recent performance. The following groups are the best six out of this list of 20:

Office Furniture (.OFU)

Banking/savings and loan (.BSL)

Drugs/generic and OTC (.DET)

Home furnishings/carpets (.HCF)

Food/candy/gum (.FCG)

Utilities/water (.UWA)

Our next step would be to look at a price-and-volume graph of each group, just as we do with stocks.

The Industry Group Graph

A price-and-volume graph gives a clear view of the current direction and historical trends of an industry. Industry groups cycle between high valuation and low valuation, much like stocks, so some of the same technical analysis tools can be used. We use the same ones that we used in the previous chapter to analyze market indexes: LSQ lines, the MACD indicator, and the overbought/oversold indicator.

Exhibit 14.3   The office furniture industry group has a very positive weekly MACD reading and a favorable position on the LSQ channel.

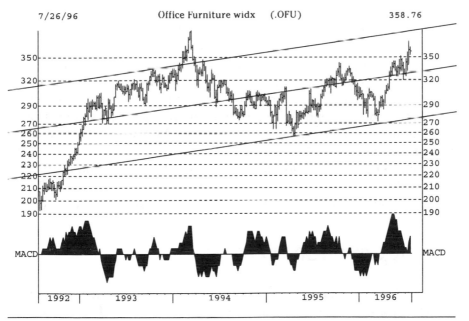

Exhibit 14.4   The office furniture industry group is at the bottom of its long-term LSQ channel with lots of room to grow.

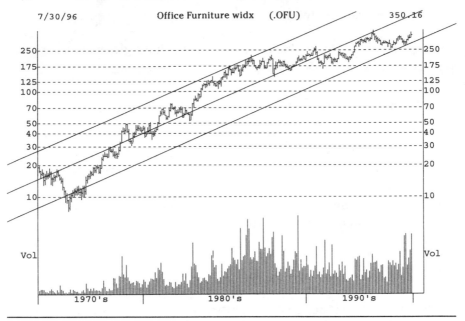

Exhibits 14.3 and 14.4 shows the long-term and short-term LSQ channels for the top-ranked group from our search, the office furniture industry. A weekly MACD is plotted on the short-term graph. These graphs support the positive momentum of this group. It has had steady growth from around $15 to nearly $300 over the past 25 years, a 20-fold growth. On the date of the graph, the group had just come off the bottom of the LSQ channel. It can increase in value nearly 25 percent and only reach the LSQ line itself. We would consider that quite attractive. In addition, the weekly MACD is positive and the short-term chart also looks good.

TOP STOCKS IN TOP INDUSTRIES

Now you have a list of industry groups rotating into favor. What do you do with it? Find a stock that is rotating upward within one of the groups.

One way to do this is to run a momentum stock search and limit the search to stocks within the top industries that you've identified.[2] The high momentum stocks in those industry groups will appear on the search report. You could also run an undervalued growth search on the top industries to find stocks with high growth potential.

When we ran the undervalued growth search from Chapter 5 on the six industries selected from the industry group search (in late July 1996), only four stocks were returned:

Washington Federal Inc. (WFSL)

Wrigley, William Jr. Co. (WWY)

Shaw Industries, Inc. (SHX)

Ladd Furniture, Inc. (LADF)

This should not be surprising because in the summer of 1996, the market had just completed one of its greatest advances in history. It is difficult to find stocks that are selling below their LSQ lines when the search is limited to high momentum industry groups. It would be important to study stocks from a search like this to determine why they have not "joined the crowd." It is possible they could be unappreciated companies that simply haven't made their move yet.

You can also identify excellent companies within a single industry group by searching that group for the most fundamentally sound stocks. For example, you might rank the companies within an industry by their ability to generate returns on sales, assets, and equity, as well as a host of other fundamental criteria. Exhibit 14.5 shows such a ranking for the banking/savings and loan group. Much can be gained by studying one of these reports and comparing the performance of companies in the same industry.

WHAT GOES UP . . .

Industry groups rotate downward as well. If you monitor your portfolio closely, you shouldn't get caught in a group that is going the wrong way.

---

[2] Limiting stocks to particular industries is a simple procedure in ProSearch. First, specify the industries that you want to use. Then, before submitting the stock search, select the search universe as "stocks in specified industries."

Exhibit 14.5   The top 25 stocks in the banking/savings bank industry group on July 26, 1996, ranked by return on sales, assets, and equity.

Criteria	Criteria Values
Return on sales	High 100%
Return on assets	High 100%
Return on equity	High 100%

1> OBT   – ORIENTAL BANK & TRUST P R COM   .BSB
  ROS = 20.6   (96)   ROA = 1.7   (71)   ROE = 18.9   (90)

2> FFED   – FIDELITY FEDERAL BANCORP COM   .BSB
  ROS = 16.4   (94)   ROA = 1.3   (69)   ROE = 26.1   (95)

3> HPBC   – HOME PORT BANCORP INC COM   .BSB
  ROS = 21.3   (96)   ROA = 1.7   (71)   ROE = 15.2   (85)

4> GBCI   – GLACIER BANCORP INC COM   .BSB
  ROS = 19.7   (96)   ROA = 1.5   (70)   ROE = 16.0   (86)

5> NYB   – NEW YORK BANCORP INC COM   .BSB
  ROS = 15.8   (94)   ROA = 1.1   (68)   ROE = 19.8   (91)

6> VFFC   – VIRGINIA FIRST FNCL CORP COM   .BSB
  ROS = 14.3   (93)   ROA = 1.1   (68)   ROE = 16.3 .   (87)

7> HOMF   – HOME FED BANCORP INDIANA COM   .BSB
  ROS = 15.2   (94)   ROA = 1.1   (68)   ROE = 15.0   (85)

8> FSPG   – FIRST HOME SAV BANK INC COM   .BSB
  ROS = 13.1   (92)   ROA = 1.0   (67)   ROE = 15.7   (86)

9> FMSB   – FIRST MUTUAL SAVINGS BANK COM   .BSB
  ROS = 12.5   (91)   ROA = 1.0   (67)   ROE = 15.2   (85)

10> MAFB   – M A F BANCORP INC COM   .BSB
  ROS = 12.6   (91)   ROA = 0.9   (67)   ROE = 15.6   (86)

11> PBCT   – PEOPLES BANK BRDGPORT CT COM   .BSB
  ROS = 15.5   (94)   ROA = 1.0   (67)   ROE = 14.1   (83)

12> BANC   – BANKATLANTIC BANCORP INC CL B   .BSB
  ROS = 14.2   (93)   ROA = 1.0   (67)   ROE = 14.0   (83)

13> HARL   – HARLEYSVILLE SAVINGS BANK COM   .BSB
  ROS = 12.8   (92)   ROA = 0.9   (67)   ROE = 13.4   (82)

14> CFB   – COMMERCIAL FEDERAL CORP COM   .BSB
  ROS = 10.8   (89)   ROA = 0.8   (66)   ROE = 15.0   (85)

15> WSB   – WASHINGTON SAV BANK F S B COM   .BSB
  ROS = 11.3   (90)   ROA = 0.9   (67)   ROE = 12.5   (80)

16> PBCI   – PAMRAPO BANCORP INC COM   .BSB
  ROS = 18.0   (95)   ROA = 1.4   (70)   ROE = 9.0   (74)

Exhibit 14.5 (continued)

17> ROSE	– T R FINANCIAL CORP COM			.BSB		
ROS = 11.9	(91)	ROA = 0.8	(66)	ROE = 12.7	(81)	
18> WAMU	– WASHINGTON MUTUAL INC COM			.BSB		
ROS = 12.5	(91)	ROA = 0.9	(67)	ROE = 11.8	(79)	
19> FFRV	– FIDELITY FNCL BANKSHARES COM			.BSB		
ROS = 11.9	(91)	ROA = 0.9	(67)	ROE = 11.8	(79)	
20> HSBK	– HIBERNIA SAV BANKS BOSTON COM			.BSB		
ROS = 11.3	(90)	ROA = 0.8	(66)	ROE = 12.7	(81)	
21> GROV	– GROVE BANK COM			.BSB		
ROS = 10.2	(88)	ROA = 0.7	(65)	ROE = 13.0	(81)	
22> PSBK	– PROGRESSIVE BANK INC COM			.BSB		
ROS = 12.5	(91)	ROA = 0.9	(67)	ROE = 10.5	(76)	
23> BKUNA	– BANKUNITED FNCL CORP CL A			.BSB		
ROS = 15.6	(94)	ROA = 1.0	(67)	ROE = 9.4	(74)	
24> FGHC	– FIRST GEORGIA HOLDING INC COM			.BSB		
ROS = 10.3	(89)	ROA = 0.8	(66)	ROE = 11.3	(78)	
25> NWSB	– NORTHWEST SAVINGS BANK COM			.BSB		
ROS = 13.0	(92)	ROA = 1.0	(67)	ROE = 9.3	(74)	

This report is based on mathematical calculations and, as such, no investment decision should be based solely on its conclusions.

Source: ProSearch 5.0, courtesy of Telescan, Inc.

It is instructive, however, to see what can happen to a perfectly sound stock if its industry group falls out of favor. The medical industry is a good example of the rise and fall of an industry group.

The Health Care Scare

During the late '80s and early '90s medical stocks were growing at 15 to 30 percent or more a year (Exhibit 14.6), and P/E ratios ranged from 20 to 100 or more (recall U.S. Surgical in Chapter 2). But by early 1994 these same stocks were selling for P/Es of 10 to 12. Why? Because the specter of health care reform unnerved investors who feared the high growth rates couldn't continue.

The rotation away from medical stocks started even before the 1992 presidential election. Widespread concern about spiraling medical costs had created a general feeling that there would be margin pressure in medical products companies. So investors began to pull out. P/Es for

Exhibit 14.6   In mid-1996 the medical instruments group was at the top of its LSQ channel.

the entire industry fell from an average of 30 to below 15, and stock prices tumbled 30 to 80 percent—*even though earnings for many of the companies were increasing by 10 to 15 percent or more.*

A classic example of a solid performer that got caught in a downward spiraling group is St. Jude Medical Corporation. Before 1992, St. Jude had a P/E ratio of 25 to 30, which it deserved, based on the previous seven years' earnings growth. Its earnings increased from 30 cents in 1989 to $2.32 in 1993, more than 60 percent per year compounded. But when the rotation away from medical stocks began in mid-1991, St. Jude's stock price fell from the mid-$50s to the mid-$20s by the end of the year, and its P/E fell from 28 to 13 (Exhibit 14.7). Ironically, St. Jude's earnings had not gone down. Granted, earnings flattened out because government posturing put margin pressure on the company, but St. Jude remained the dominant player in its industry.

By the summer of 1994, medical stocks were so undervalued that investors began to move back in. At that time, the Clinton health care reform act was in deep trouble and there were rumblings of more moderate

Exhibit 14.7   St. Jude shows a steady increase in earnings in the early 1990s accompanied by a steep decline in price due to disenchantment with the medical industry. A recovery that began in mid-1994 peaked in early 1996.

solutions, so investors began to focus on the higher quality issues within the medical group (whose P/Es were at historically low levels). By late fall the medical industry was headed toward full recovery, with St. Jude leading the way. Even though earnings were flat, St. Jude rose from $27 in July 1994 to about $40 in mid-November (presplit prices).

The recovery was short-lived. In early 1996 the entire medical industry was hit with another wave of fear about the developments in health care. This time the decline was fueled by the dramatic growth of HMOs and drastic cost-cutting measures required by medical companies to maintain profit margins.

And so it goes. Industry groups move into and out of favor, and facts don't count for much when rumors and fears take hold. It is the market's *perception* that counts. When institutions flee an industry because of fears, real or imaginary, about its future, stocks in that group may take a beating even though earnings continue to rise. Eventually, if the industry doesn't go into a secular decline, the industry group will likely start rotating upward again.

YOU MUST REMEMBER THIS . . .

Industry group rotation helps the small investor swim with the tide, rather than against it.

- Use your computerized tools to find the industry groups that are rotating into favor.
- Use stock search tools to find stocks that are rotating upward within positively rotating groups.
- Find the leaders in an industry by ranking stocks in that group by their fundamental performance (such as return on sales, return on equity, and return on assets).
- After you've found the best stocks within a rotating industry group, be sure to evaluate them as described in earlier chapters.
- What goes up must come down. Stay abreast of what's happening to the industry groups of stocks you own. When a group starts to weaken, it is probably time to clear out.
- Long-term growth of earnings is important, but the perception of future earnings is the key to price growth.
- The industry group search and the search for stocks in an industry ranked by fundamental performance are on the Telescan diskette that accompanies this book. See the Quick Start Guide for how to use them.

15

OPPORTUNITIES IN OPTIONS

Options. You either love 'em or you hate 'em. They create a flush of excitement in some investors and a rush of fear in others. If you're one of the former, you'll be pleased to know there are computerized tools to help you tame those puts and calls.[1] If you're one of the latter, we'll show you a way to do a little low-risk speculation that could result in some spectacular profits.

Options are derivative securities, which means they track the performance of the underlying stock. The advantage of trading options is the higher reward potential for fewer dollars risked. The disadvantage is the higher risk that comes with the limited duration of the option: If the underlying stock does not move before the expiration date of the option, the entire premium will be lost.[2] Volumes have been written on the subject of options, and we won't attempt even a cursory treatment here. We'll

---

[1] A put gives the option holder the right to sell a specified number of shares of stock at a fixed price on or before a given date. A call gives the option holder the right to purchase a specified number of shares of stock at a fixed price on or before a given date. (A glossary of option terms is available on the Internet at the Wall Street City Web site (www.wallstreetcity.com).

[2] Premium refers to the difference between the price of an option and its intrinsic value.

just preach to the choir by mentioning a couple of computerized tools that make option trading a whole lot easier.

There is, for example, an options search tool designed specifically for options (such as Telescan's Option Search, which is part of the Cyber-Investing Kit). It allows you to specify requirements for price, performance, volume, and volatility; it lets you stipulate the technical patterns of both the option and the underlying stock; and it helps you find the optimum spread and straddle opportunities for a given stock. Like stocks, the options will be ranked on the search report in order of how well they fit your search strategy.

Other option tools include valuation programs that use complex mathematical formulas, such as the Black-Scholes formula,[3] to measure an option's inherent overvaluation or undervaluation. (All formulas are transparent to the user, which means the programs are not difficult to use.) Option valuation programs can also be used to estimate decay rates of premiums, evaluate spreads, and perform other sophisticated option analyses, such as determining the ideal option position for taking advantage of a projected stock move.

A more thorough discussion is beyond the scope of this book, but the rest of this chapter will show you how to dabble in options with a bit of low-risk speculation.

LOW-RISK OPTIONS: AN OXYMORON?

Recall in Chapter 5 how we extolled the virtues of following the insiders' lead?[4] Another way to do this is with options.

Investors often purchase speculative options in anticipation of an event that might cause a sharp rise in the price of the underlying stock. Such an event might be a merger or acquisition that is under negotiation; it might be the release of a new product that has been under development; or it could be anything that might positively affect earnings, which is not yet known by the general public. Rather than purchase the stock, a shrewd investor can purchase large quantities of speculative options at a

---

[3] The Black-Scholes formula is a method for arriving at the theoretical value of an option, based on the underlying stock price, volatility, and the number of days left until option expiration.

[4] Insiders, in this case, may simply be individuals, such as employees of investment bankers, accounting firms, or law firms, who are aware of an emerging event in the company and not necessarily officers or directors.

fraction of the cost of the stock itself. For example, 100 shares of IBM would have cost $11,500 in late summer 1996, whereas an at-the-money option to purchase 100 shares of IBM ranged from $200 to $1,100.

We have observed that many major corporate events over the past several years have been preceded by unusual option activity. With computerized option search and analysis tools, we can discover this kind of speculation for very little money. The rewards, as you will see, can be substantial, and if the speculative event falls through, the option holder stands to lose relatively little.

Is this illegal? Not for the outsider. If insiders are trying to profit from information that has not yet been made public, their actions may be considered illegal. But the information we use to find *their* speculative option activity is public information, and we are not insiders!

Three option graphs from 1994 will show the dramatic possibilities of speculative option trading. The numbers following the month indicate the strike or exercise price. In other words, the September 17.5 call means the option holder would have the right to buy x-number of shares of Syntex Corporation for $17½ on or before the expiration date of the option.

- Exhibit 15.1 shows a September 17.5 call for Syntex Corporation. From February through mid-April of 1994, the volume fluctuated between zero and 400 contracts a day. Then, it shot up to over 1,000 contracts in one day. If you had observed this activity the next day and purchased just 10 contracts for about $900, you would have owned a position that was worth over $5,800 about a week later, an increase of over 600 percent.

- Exhibit 15.2 shows a September 35 call for H. J. Heinz. In late July, the volume jumped from virtually zero to over 500 contracts in one day and to over 1,000 contracts two days later. Within the next three days, you could have bought 10 contracts for less than $400. In less than three weeks, ten contracts were worth about $3,500, an increase of almost 1,000 percent.

- Exhibit 15.3 shows an October 65 call for American Cyanamid. In early July, the volume steadily increased from very low levels to more than 150 contracts, dropped off, and then repeated the same pattern. Any time during the first half of July, you could have bought ten contracts for between $2,500 and $3,000. By the third week of July, ten contracts were worth more than $25,000 and by mid-August, almost $35,000.

Exhibit 15.1 This Syntex call shows the emergence of unusual volume and the subsequent sharp rise in price.

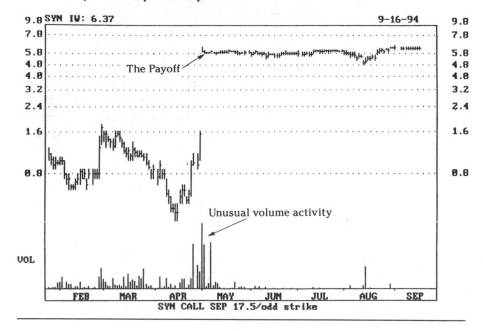

SYN CALL SEP 17.5/odd strike

Exhibit 15.2 This H. J. Heinz call shows the emergence of unusual volume and the subsequent sharp rise in price.

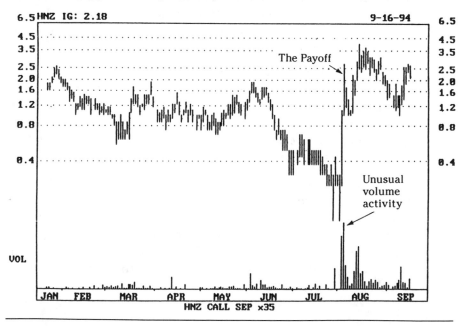

HNZ CALL SEP x35

Exhibit 15.3   This American Cyanamid call shows the emergence of unusual volume and the subsequent sharp rise in price.

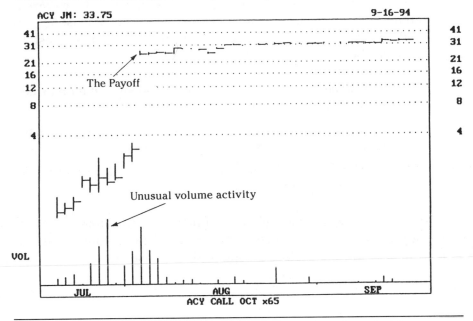

ACY JM: 33.75   9-16-94

The Payoff

Unusual volume activity

VOL

JUL   AUG   SEP
ACY CALL OCT x65

As you can see, these are very exciting investments. Even if you had bought only one contract—which you could do in most cases for a couple of hundred dollars   you could have had outstanding gains. There are pitfalls, which we'll talk about later, but the potential reward of this kind of low-cost speculation makes it fun, if nothing else. The best news is that there is a computerized search that will identify these opportunities for you as they occur.

THE OPTION SEARCH

To find speculative situations like those described, we will design a search to look for options with unusual volume activity. Specifically, we want a very high ratio of current 1-day average volume to 14-day average volume, together with enough daily volume to indicate that the current volume is significant. For example, it would not be significant if an option that has averaged 1 contract a day suddenly goes to 6 contracts a day. On the other hand, it would be significant if an option that has averaged 30 contracts a day suddenly goes to 100.

To find such options, we will first narrow the universe of the search. We will require that the options have a current volume of at least 50 contracts and an average of at least 10 contracts per day over the past 14 days. We'll use the following indicators:

- *Today's volume indicator* will eliminate all options that didn't trade at least 50 contracts on the day of the search.

- *14-day average volume indicator* will eliminate all options that have not averaged at least 10 contracts per day over the past 14 days.

- *Put or call indicator* will allow us to eliminate puts. (We are looking for positive speculation here.)

Next, we will score and rank the options. The indicators just mentioned are minimum requirements. We are actually looking for much larger numbers. We want to see an option that has been averaging 20 or

---

AT THE MONEY, IN THE MONEY, OUT OF THE MONEY . . .

These terms have to do with how close the strike price of the option is to the current price of the underlying stock.

"At the money" refers to an option (a put or call) whose strike price is about the same as the current stock price.

An "in-the-money" option is either (a) a put whose underlying stock price is below the strike price or (b) a call whose underlying stock price is above the strike price. These are obviously higher priced than at-the-money or out-of-the-money options.

An "out-of-the-money" option is either (a) a put whose underlying stock price is above the strike price or (b) a call whose underlying stock price is below the strike price. Out-of-the-money options are the least expensive, and the further out of the money they are, the less expensive they are. So, you don't necessarily have to buy the option where all the activity is; you could buy one further out of the money. You would not make as much money, but you wouldn't be taking as great a risk, either.

30 contracts and suddenly trades 400, 500, or even 1,000 contracts in one day. This would be a clear sign of speculative activity and would bear careful scrutiny. So we'll have the program rank the options from high to low according to the ratio of the current day's volume to the 14-day average volume and the amount that the option is out of the money. We'll use the following indicators and ask for the highest scores.

- 1-to-14-Day Average-Volume Ratio
- Dollar out-of-money indicator

Regarding the dollar out-of-money indicator, the further the calls are out of the money, the better the indication of speculative activity. Why? Because far out-of-the-money options will prove to be valuable *only* if the stock makes a very substantial move. In-the-money calls, on the other hand, are frequently used by regular purchasers to accumulate the shares for nonspeculative purposes, which wouldn't necessarily indicate unusual activity in the stock price.

Finally, we will select several indicators to retrieve information that we'll use to make the final selection (see Exhibit 15.4). Because this search is highly speculative and out of the mainstream of a long-term, prudent investing process, we don't want to take the space to explain these indicators here. Most are self-explanatory; others are adequately defined in Telescan's Options Search program. This search, by the way, is on the Telescan diskette that accompanies this book.

CHECK IT OUT

Once you have a list of options, find those with the highest one-day volume and the largest ratio of 1-to-14 day average volume. Then look at their price-and-volume graphs for a graphic representation of the speculative activity.

Next, print a list of the option quotes for the underlying stocks that look the best. (Option quotes are available through the Internet and other online sources.) This list is helpful in two ways. First, it lists the option symbols so you can look up other options near the same time frame and strike price to see if they reflect unusual activity as well. Second, if you decide to speculate, you can use the list to select a lower-priced option that is further out of the money than the ones that showed up on the option search report.

Exhibit 15.4   This is the search strategy for speculative calls.

Indicator	Action/Weight
Today's volume (Vol)	Eliminate all options with fewer than 50 contracts
14-day average volume (AvgVl)	Eliminate all options that have not averaged at least 10 contracts per day for 14 days
Put or call (P/C)	Eliminate all puts.
1-day-to-14-day average volume ratio (1/14V)	Rank options by highest scores/100%
Dollar out of money ($/Mon)	Rank options by highest scores/80%
Bid (Bid)	List only
Asked (Asked)	List only
Last trade (LTrade)	List only
Stock close (StkCl)	List only
Black-Scholes value (BSVal)	List only
Delta (Delta)	List only
Gamma (Gamma)	List only
Theta (Theta)	List only
Vega (Vega)	List only
Implied volatility/statistical volatility —20-day (IV-20)	List only
Percent over/undervalued (%O/U)	List only
Relative performance-stock/ 1-Day (1-Dy)	List only
Relative performance-stock/ 1-Week (1-Wk)	List only
Relative performance-stock/ 3-Week (3-Wk)	List only
Relative performance-option/ 1-Day (1DyOp)	List only
Relative performance-option/ 1-Week (1WkOp)	List only
Relative performance-option/ 3-Week (3WkOp)	List only
Open interest (OpInt)	List only
Total volume/total open interest (TVTOI)	List only
Put/call open interest (P/COI)	List only

Finally, try to determine the reasons for the speculative activity. Check the news and other reports on the underlying stock. Rumors of a merger or acquisition may or may not have reached the news media, or there could be something going on besides a pending takeover. For example, unusual activity in an in-the-money call may mean nothing at all. Some investors add to their position in a stock by purchasing in-the-money calls rather than buying the stock outright (which may protect them if the stock goes down). The high volume could also be merely the "unwinding" of previous option positions. You'll need to do a little detective work to track this down. Here's how.

Inspect a six-month or nine-month graph and pay attention to the price of the transactions on the day in question. If the volume reflects buying, the option price would be going up; if it reflects selling, the option price would be going down. If the volume indicates selling, look back over earlier periods and see if the volume spread over a day or two equals the volume in question. If so, it probably is the unwinding of a previous position and, therefore, nothing to get excited about. Usually, these are fairly obvious. What we want are cases similar to those described earlier in this chapter. The bottom line of this kind of activity is that a very small amount of risk can generate a handsome reward indeed, if we do our homework.

YOU MUST REMEMBER THIS . . .

Option trading is very speculative, and there are several places where you could go wrong.

- There may be no speculation at all. The unusual volume could be the unwinding of an earlier purchase, or it could be part of a routine stock acquisition program. Buying out-of-the-money options protects against the latter.

- Your option could expire before any increase in price occurs. Speculation in options sometimes occurs long before any corresponding activity in the stock.

- The anticipated event may fail to take place. Mergers and acquisitions often fall through; product releases may be delayed; expected earnings often don't materialize. Any number of factors could prevent the underlying stock from rising to speculated heights in the time frame allowed by your particular options.

- Even if the anticipated event should occur, it may not be greeted with the enthusiasm hoped for by the original speculators. Both you and they could lose.

Nonetheless, opportunities exist for low-cost option speculation. Just use reasonable care, and treat this activity as a hobby—one with some very good monetary rewards when you happen to be right.

16

WELCOME TO THE WORLD WIDE WEB

In the past two years, there has been a virtual explosion of information on the Internet related to the stock market and investing in general. When we wrote the first edition of this book two years ago, there were only a handful of investing-related Web sites and those had only minimal content. Now there are more than 200, the most important of which have significant content.

In this chapter, we will attempt to organize the investing information on the Internet as it applies to our five-step cyber-investing process. This is not meant to be a comprehensive guide to investing on the Internet or a review of the Web sites mentioned. Rather it is meant to help you find sites that have information or services for each of the five steps. Once there, you can explore the site at your leisure. You'll find that each site is packed with much more information than is listed here. If we have omitted a site that you've found to be helpful or failed to list it under the appropriate step, we apologize.

Much of the information on the Internet is free, although most of the investing Web sites offer much of their proprietary information on a subscription basis. You'll usually find at least a free tour at each site, a guest account to let you try out the services, or a trial subscription that is free for a limited time. The only way to judge any of these services is to roam freely around the site and determine if the subscription prices make sense for you.

One drawback to the Internet at this time is its often excruciating slowness. Unless you have a 28.8 baud modem or faster, it may feel like you are crawling, rather than jumping, from one Web page to another. In addition, there seem to be rush hours on the information superhighway when traffic between Web sites backs up (evenings, weekends, and holidays), which can slow down even the fastest modem. (The best time to surf the net seems to be in the wee small hours of the morning.) Eliminating the graphics will speed things up a bit, but this also makes for rather dull viewing. Eventually, faster modems and competitive pricing of ISDN lines (communication lines dedicated to the Internet) will solve the slowness problem.

A Web site, by the way, is located by its URL (Uniform Resource Locator), which is the equivalent of a street address. In these pages, the URL follows the first mention of a Web site, and an alphabetical listing of URLs appears at the end of this chapter.

PROSPECTING FOR STOCKS

The World Wide Web has much to offer for the first step of the cyber-investing process, from mere lists of stocks based on different criteria to stock picks from market gurus to simple screening services to at least one full-blown search engine. As always, we would caution you to evaluate any stocks you may find before buying them.

- *Investor's Hotline* (http://www.wallstreetcity.com/hotline) presents interviews by market experts who may offer stock tips as well as market commentary.

- *MarketEdge* (http://www.marketedge.com) is the Web site from Thomson Financial Services. Its "Top Performers of the Month" lists the top 20 stocks for large-, middle-, and small-cap stocks whose performance is ranked by various criteria. They also have a screening service that allows you to screen the stocks in their database with any of 18 different variables. There is also a subscription-based "Stock of the Day" from MarketEdge president Bob Gabele.

- Newsletters that offer stock picks by a variety of experts can be found at *INVESTools, NETworth, PAWWS Financial Network,* and *Wall Street City.*

- *Standard & Poor's* (http://www.stockinfo.standardpoor.com) has a subscription-based MarketScope@Home®, which offers lists of stocks in the news, stocks touted by the media, investment ideas, and lists of buy, sell, or hold recommendations on its STARS-rated stocks.

- *Stock Smart* (http://www.stocksmart.com) offers lists of best and worst performers in large-cap, mid-cap, small-cap, and micro-cap stocks (the latter with less than $50 million in market capitalization). You can also get a daily list of the most active stocks on the New York, American, and Nasdaq exchanges broken down by percentage winners and losers and volume leaders. A unique prospecting tool is their list of IPOs and mergers. The entire site is free.

- *Wall Street City* (http://www.wallstreetcity.com), developed by Telescan, Inc., is an investing supersite that offers a cornucopia of prospecting tools, including what appears to be the only (at this time) full-blown search engine on the Internet. To begin with, there are a number of free lists of stocks, such as those with high revised projected earnings and best and worst stocks in several categories. (A "Free" icon lets you know which features are free.) There are several lists from S&P MarketScope: Five Star stocks, Platinum portfolio stocks, Fair Value portfolio stocks (all based on S&P ratings), IPOs, and takeover candidates. There are lists of stocks favored by analysts, insiders, and institutions. There are lists of stocks that have technical breakouts, basing pattern breakouts and new high/low breakouts. Then there are a variety of search engines. Mini-search engines retrieve lists in stocks in some 21 predefined categories. Something called "Quick Search" takes you through a series of filter screens that allow some user-input. A full-fledged search engine called Esearch uses a variety of earnings estimates, earnings surprises, and earnings revisions as search criteria. But the *pièce de résistance* of the Internet prospecting tools is the ProSearch search engine which contains all the power and features of the original ProSearch that we've described in this book: some 250 user-customizable criteria (of which you can use as many as 40 in one search), and three search modes: elimination, ranking, and list-only, with the results of the search ranked in order of best fit.

- *Zacks Investment Research* (http://www.zacks.com) offers, through its "Analyst Watch on the Internet," the Z100 list of stocks that are based on Zacks' Ranks.

RESEARCH AND ANALYSIS

Step 2 of the cyber-investing process is the technical and fundamental evaluation of stocks. The Internet offers little of the former, but a considerable amount of latter.

Technical Evaluation

Many investment sites on the Internet offer stock graphs with preplotted indicators such as moving averages, but only one, at this time, offers true technical analysis.

- *Charts by CPCUG InvestSIG* (http://www.cpcug.org) is the Web site of a special interest group of the Capital PC Users Group. It has dozens of charts (including candlestick charts) for intraday, daily, weekly, and long-term stock indexes, as well as charts on individual stocks.
- *Silicon Investor* (http://www.techstocks.com) has charts that compare technology stocks with the Nasdaq composite.
- *Wall Street City* offers stock graphs for any of some 9,000 stocks and market indexes. Time horizons available are 1, 2, 5, and 10 days; 1 and 6 months; 1, 2, 5, and 10 years, and maximum length (which can include as much as 20 years of data). True technical analysis, using ActiveX stock graphs with a variety of technical indicators and user-defined parameters, is available at Wall Street City using the Microsoft Internet Explorer.

Fundamental Evaluation

With regard to fundamental analysis, the Internet offers many sources. Some of the following sites offer stock graphs with an occasional preplotted technical indicator, but mainly they provide fundamental research materials. Again, some of the information is free, but most is available only through subscription.

- Most *brokerage firms* that offer online trading also offer to their brokerage customers various research services, such as news and company profiles. These are listed in the next section under "Trading Stocks."
- *Dow Jones News/Retrieval* (http://bis.dowjones.com) offers a searchable database (by subscription only) of the major daily

newspapers; SEC full text filings; insider trading transactions; earnings estimates from Zacks Investment Research; and reports from Standard & Poor's, Dun & Bradstreet, Media General, Investext, and Disclosure. It also offers transcripts of more than 70 radio and television news shows. At this writing, you can take a tour of Dow Jones News/Retrieval at the Web site, but special software (downloadable at the site) must be used to access the Dow Jones database. America Online subscribers can use the Dow Jones database on AOL.

- *EDGAR* (http://edgar.stern.nyu.edu) is a government database of SEC filings on more than 8,000 issues, including 10K's, 10Q's, and other official reports. The EDGAR database is also available from Disclosure (http://www.disclosure.com), EDGAR Online (http://www.edgar-online.com), and other sites.

- *MarketEdge* has news headlines and company reports from Thomson Financial Services.

- *Multex Systems, Inc.* (http://www.multexnet.com) offers analysts' research reports to subscribers at its own Web site and through various other providers, such as Wall Street City.

- *PAWWS Financial Network* (http://pawws.com) has Hoover company reports.

- *PRARS* (http://www.prars.com), sponsored by The Public Register and Annual Report Services, is a free service that offers annual reports by mail. Requests are processed within 24 hours.

- *Quote.Com* (http://www.quote.com) offers a subscription-based service that includes news headlines from Reuters Newswire and others; company profiles from Standard & Poor's, Trendvest, and Disclosure; earnings estimates from Zacks Investment Research and Nelson's; insider trading reports from Vicker's; and annual reports from the EDGAR government database.

- *Reuters Money Network* (http://www.moneynet.com) offers comprehensive company reports that are updated daily.

- *Stock Smart*'s free site offers financial news from U.S. and foreign markets, corporate earnings reports, news about initial public offerings, corporate mergers, stock splits, and dividends. They also have a "Company Catalog" that gives you a brief overview of each public company.

- *Standard & Poor's* offers company reports, earnings announcements, industry reports, news stories, and insider trading reports.

- *Wall Street City* has a searchable news database (supplied by Reuters Newswire and Comtex), and a number of reports that can be retrieved by company name or stock symbol, including Market Guide company reports, S&P MarketScope company reports, Macro*World Price Forecasts, Vickers insider trading reports, Zacks II earnings estimates reports, quarterly earnings reports, and technical and valuation data reports. When you retrieve a stock graph you get statistics for that company on more than 70 fundamental and technical categories, and, particularly noteworthy, a "Telescan Ranking" report that shows you the stock's percentile rank and color-coded bar graph for short-term and long-term growth rank, value rank, technical rank, analyst rank, insider rank, fundamental rank, momentum rank, and volume rank. These ranks are a great way to analyze a stock quickly or if you're a beginning investor.

- *The Wall Street Journal Interactive Edition* (http://interactive2.wsj .com) is a cornucopia of business and world-wide news, and each article is accompanied by links to related articles and Web sites. It also has a "Company Briefing Book" which gives a brief profile of a company and any related articles in the Journal's recent files.

- *Zacks Investment Research* offers virtually everything you want to know about earnings estimates through its "Analyst Watch on the Internet" (for a fee). It also has a free index to research reports.

BUYING AND SELLING STOCKS

Buying and selling stocks (steps 3 and 5 of the cyber-investing process) has almost become commonplace on the Internet, with almost 20 discount brokers vying for your trades. In addition to offering real-time quotes for placing the trade, the brokers shown here offer one or more of the following services (the deeper the discount, the fewer supplemental services): portfolio tracking, historical quotes, stock graphs, and company research. Most Web sites that have online trading offer guest accounts; some have investment games that let you play at trading, which is good practice for the real thing. The commissions range from $9.95 a trade to about $40, but commission schedules can get rather complicated, depending on the number of shares traded and the supplementary services offered by the broker. You might want to visit several sites before settling down with any one broker.

- Accutrade   http://www.accutrade.com
- American Express InvestDirect   http://www.americanexpress
                                             .com/direct
- Ceres Securities, Inc.   http://www.ceres.com
- Charles Schwab & Co.   http://www.schwab.com
- CompuTEL Securities   http://www.rapidtrade.com
- Datek Online   http://www.datek.com
- eBroker   http://www.ebroker.com
- E*Trade   http://www.etrade.com
- Fidelity Brokerage Services   http://www.fid-inv.com
- Howe Barnes Investments, Inc.   http://pawws.com/Broker
  (The Net Investor)   /How
- Investex Express On-Line   http://www.investexpress.com
- Jack White & Co. (PATH Online)   http://pawws.com/Broker/Jwc
- K. Aufhauser and Company   http://www.aufhauser.com
  (WealthWEB)
- Lombard Investment Center   http://www.lombard.com
- National Discount Brokers   http://pawws.com/Broker
  (NDB Online)   /Ndb
- Pacific Brokerage Services   http://www.tradepbs.com
- PC Financial Network   http://www.pcfn.com
- Quick & Reilly   http://www.Quick-Reilly.com

The following full service brokerage firms have Web sites, although they do not (currently) offer online trading. Some allow you to access your own account on the Web. Some sites have a variety of learning tools, usually free, including calendars of investor seminars sponsored by the brokerage firm.

- A.G. Edwards   http://www.agedwards.com
- J.P. Morgan   http://www.jpmorgan.com
- Merrill Lynch   http://www.ml.com
- Oppenheimer & Co.   http://www.oppenheimer.com
- PaineWebber   http://www.painewebber.com
- Prudential Securities   http://www.prusec.com
- Smith Barney   http://www.smithbarney.com

PORTFOLIO MANAGEMENT

The Internet offers many resources for step 4 of the cyber-investing process, portfolio management, which includes asset allocation, portfolio updates, stock alerts, market analysis, and industry group analysis. Virtually every site mentioned thus far offers stock quotes, news, market updates, and some form of market analysis. The online trading sites just listed offer some type of portfolio tracking and updates. The Macro*World Investor, mentioned in Chapter 11, will soon be available at Wall Street City.

The following discussion is restricted to those sources that offer stock alerts, market commentary and analysis, and industry analysis.

Stock Alerts

In Chapter 10 we talked about the importance of keeping abreast of news about the stocks in your portfolio. Here's a list of Internet resources that offer automatic alerts for a portfolio of stocks. Most are subscription-based.

- *Dow Jones News/Retrieval* has a service called "CustomClips," which scans more than 1,600 trade and industry publications for news about your stocks.

- *MarketEdge* has stock alerts for such things as price changes, earnings surprises, revisions in earnings estimates, upgrades or downgrades in broker consensus recommendations, insider trading activity, and short interest ratio changes.

- *Quote.Com* offers stock price alarms via e-mail.

- *Septor on the Web* by Notable Technologies (http://www.notable .com), offers wireless stock price and volume alerts and news alerts via a PC or alphanumeric pager.

- *Stock Smart* offers a paging alert so that price or volume triggers entered in a Stock Smart portfolio will beep you when the pre-defined level is reached. (You'll need an alphanumeric pager for this.)

- *Wall Street City* has news and price alerts, plus alerts of new Zacks II earnings estimates reports. It also has a unique feature called "Scan My Portfolio," which shows for each stock in a portfolio the short-term and long-term technical rank, fundamental rank, analyst rank, momentum rank, volume rank, and insider rank. The portfolio scan also shows if any of the stocks had a technical breakout or basing pattern breakout.

- *The Wall Street Journal Interactive Edition* offers a customized "Personal Edition" through which they will alert you to news on companies you wish to follow.
- *Zacks Investment Research* will send you daily portfolio alerts via e-mail through its "Analyst Watch on the Internet."

Market Commentary and Industry Group Analysis

Some form of market commentary or analysis is offered at many different sites on the Net, including many of the online trading sites; a fewer number offer specific industry group analysis. Market index charts and industry group charts are available from any service that offers charting capabilities. Here are some noteworthy sources.

- *Dow Jones News/Retrieval* offers a weekly snapshot of the top economists and traders' expectations for equity, currency, and debt markets.
- *Investor's Hotline* has monthly interviews and commentary with three top market experts.
- *MarketEdge* updates its "Market Monitor" four times a day, which includes, among other things, a summary of headlines affecting the stock market; analysis of the day's important stories; and intraday updates on market indexes. MarketEdge also offers, free of charge, Bob Gabele's market "Tip of the Day" and a weekly schedule of economic events and announcements. Analyst reports are available on major industry sectors.
- *Stock Smart* offers daily, weekly, and monthly lists of best performing industry groups (and subindustry groups) with the percentage change. You can jump from any group or subgroup to a list of stocks in that group and from there to a company fact sheet on a specific company.
- *Wall Street City* features a customizable market snapshot that displays the current day's graph for the Market index of your choice and a recap (including advances and declines) of the New York Stock Exchange, American Stock Exchange, and Nasdaq, plus your choice of more than 200 market indexes. A market commentary by Mark Draud (co-editor of The Cyber-Investing Newsletter) is updated twice a day. A schedule of economic events and announcements is posted weekly. As for industry groups, this site has the most comprehensive content on the Internet, at this time. There is

a color-coded bar chart of all industries that ranks their performance for 1 day; 1, 6, 18, or 26 weeks; or 1, 3, or 5 years. Click on one of the bars to bring up a 1-year price-and-volume graph for that industry, overlaid with a daily advance/decline line and a 6-day daily high-low graph. A color-coded bar chart ranks the performance for the stocks in that group.

MUTUAL FUNDS ON THE NET

Here are some of the places to find information on mutual funds.

- *Dow Jones* has performance reports on mutual funds.
- *EDGAR* has a Mutual Fund Reporting section with SEC filings on more than 2,000 mutual fund groups. These are also available through the Disclosure Web site.
- *MarketEdge* offers reports on individual funds, plus a MarketEdge 1-to-10 rating. It has mutual fund quotes; alerts; a monthly listing of top performers; a screening capability with 12 key variables; and a monthly summary of mutual fund activity, funds to watch, and emerging trends.
- *Morningstar, Inc.* reports can also be found at INVESTools (http://www.investools.com) and Reuters Money Network. They are also available through America Online (in the Personal Finance section) and from CompuServe (Go: PUBONL).
- *NETworth* (http://networth.galt.com) offers a directory of mutual funds, recent and historical fund prices, lists of top performers in various categories, a fund search service, and Morningstar mutual fund reports.
- *Stock Smart* offers a free search mechanism for mutual funds, fact sheets on over 5,000 mutual funds, and lists of the best and worst weekly and monthly performers in several categories. It has a list of the 20 largest mutual funds based on net asset value (NAV) with percentage change in NAV. It also ranks the performance of over 5,000 mutual funds against similar fund types and the S&P 500, and provides an annual list of the top 50 best performing funds. All free.
- *Wall Street City* offers a bona fide search engine for mutual funds that allows you to combine any 40 of 82 different criteria and use three different search modes. It also has lists of best and worst performers, lists of S&P's top-rated closed end funds, and newsletters devoted to mutual funds. There are mutual fund reports and

links to mutual fund Web sites. Telescan ratings of mutual funds will soon be added to this site.

BONDS ON THE NET

Bond quotes are available from many of the online trading sources listed above. However, we found only two sites that offered substantial information on bonds.

- *Bonds Online* (http://www.bonds-online.com) has a robust site with extensive market information for tax-free municipal bonds, treasury and savings bonds, corporate bonds, and bond funds. They also offer questions and answers about bonds from "The Bond Professor."
- *MarketEdge* has news on municipal bonds supplied by *The Bond Buyer,* a current calendar of new municipal issues, and a tutorial about municipal bonds for new investors. They also offer news on the debt market, including macro-economic events and trends, trading in the federal debt market, and the economic calendar mentioned previously.

GLOBAL INVESTING ON THE NET

To sophisticated investors, world markets have long represented diversification and a way to spread the risk among diverse economies. Now the international arena is opening its doors to the individual investor via the World Wide Web, which is awash with information on international securities.

International Stock Quotes

Stock quotes on market indexes and some international stocks can be obtained from many of the sites mentioned earlier (especially brokerage firms), and from America Online, CompuServe, and Prodigy. Moreover, international exchanges themselves are just a mouse click away. Data Broadcasting Corporation's DBC Online (http://www.dbc.com) has a comprehensive list of hyperlinks to foreign exchanges.

Foreign Exchange Rates

A major difference between domestic and global investing is currency risk. Because stocks and indexes are traded in local currency, the global investor must stay abreast of fluctuations in a country's currency. Foreign exchange rates are available at most Web sites that offer international stock quotes and at many of the sites offering market analysis or research tools.

Global Market Analysis

Selecting the right country is as important in global investing as selecting the right stock. The global investor must stay abreast of changes in a country's economy. The Internet is the ideal medium for this. Most foreign exchanges have their own Web sites with various economic data; many international banks, service companies, and media have sites devoted to their countries. We lack the space to cover these in detail here, but will do so in our forthcoming book about investing resources on the Internet. Here we can only offer a sampling of sites that feature global news or market analysis.

- *Barron's* (http://www.barrons.com), the *New York Times* on the Web (http://www.nytimes.com), and the *Wall Street Journal* Interactive Edition (http://interactive2.wsj.com) all feature world news.

- *CNN Financial Network* (http://www.cnnfn.com) has market and currency reports from European, Asian, Australian, and South American markets.

- *Fortune Magazine* (http://www.fortune.com) has a special report on the Pacific Rim under its Special Issues/Lists section.

- *I/B/E/S Financial Network* (http://www.ibes.com) provides earnings forecasts for companies in 47 countries.

- *I.D.E.A.* A currency and economic outlook on a country-by-country basis will soon be offered by Wall Street City as a result of its agreement with Independent Economic Analysis (I.D.E.A.) of London. I.D.E.A., which collaborates with the London School of Economics to produce reports on the emerging markets of Asia and Latin America, is a world leader in currency and economic forecasts. Its services were previously available only to the world's highest volume trading rooms.

- *INVESTools, NETworth,* and *Wall Street City* have newsletters devoted to global investing.

- *M.A.I.D./Profound* (http://www.maid-plc.com) has comprehensive country reports, economic forecasts, and analyses of world markets from leading publishers. See the Countryline section under Sources.

- *Wall Street City's* International section offers a market snapshot of the world's major markets, which includes a graph of a market index, plus market commentary. You can get end-of-day international stock quotes for each market (there's a symbol look-up feature); you can plot stock graphs, and you can plot them in U.S. dollars or the currency of the country. There are also foreign exchange rates here, along with the ability to plot currency graphs.

Global Prospecting Tools

Three noteworthy prospecting tools for international stocks are newsletters, country indexes, and American Depository Receipts (ADRs).

- *Newsletters* devoted to global markets can provide insights into a country's economy as well as tips on specific investments. INVESTools, NETworth, and Wall Street City have extensive newsletter collections.
- *Country indexes,* available from Macro*World (at the Wall Street City site) are excellent international prospecting tools. A country index includes various foreign stock baskets, which are groups of stocks that represent the economy of a particular country.
- *ADRs* are foreign companies that are traded in U.S. dollars on domestic exchanges, thereby avoiding the problem of currency risk. An extensive list of ADRs can be found at DBC Online and at many of the brokerage Web sites.
- *Morningstar International Stocks OnDemand* has a searchable database of more than 700 stocks in 36 global markets. It is available at the INVESTools Web site.

Global Corporate Research

Information that provides comfort to the investor about the fundamental value of a company—earnings estimates, research reports, corporate reports by independent services—is still scarce, although it is beginning to trickle onto the Internet.

- *Disclosure* offers a Canadian database, a Global Researcher, and Worldscope, which profiles international companies.

- *Dow Jones* has profiles of the top 1000 Saudi Arabian companies.
- *M.A.I.D./Profound* (http://www.maid.plc.com) has the most extensive coverage of industry reports and broker research reports on foreign companies.
- *Standard & Poor's* offers its MarketScope corporate profiles for Canadian and European public companies.
- *Stock Smart* offers a unique "Industry Watch" feature on its World Markets page. Click on a country name to display a bar chart showing the performance of the industries within that country. Click on an industry name to see a list of companies in that industry. Click on a company name to display the stock price and other data on the company. Stock Smart has announced it will soon add profiles on over 9,000 worldwide stocks in 40 countries.

Global investing is the wave of the future. As the Internet continues to blur the boundaries between Main Street, USA and the rest of the world, we predict that individual investors will begin trading stocks in international markets as effortlessly as do the professionals. If you learn the tools and techniques for investing in the domestic markets, you'll be ready to play in the global arena when the time comes.

YOU MUST REMEMBER THIS . . .

The Web sites mentioned in this chapter are in transition as we write this, although that will probably always be the case. The beauty of the Internet is that it is dynamic. It will always be in a state of flux with a continuous stream of new Web sites and new information.

One way to keep up with what's new on the World Wide Web is to learn to use the major indexing sites, such as Excite, Infoseek, Lycos, Magellan, and Yahoo. Another way is to visit The Cyber-Investing Center (http://www.cyberinvest.com) where we will undertake to keep you up to the minute with new investing sites as they relate to the 5-step cyber-investing process.

Whatever you do, log in, stay tuned, and surf on, because the future of cyber-investing *is* the Internet.

ALPHABETICAL LISTING OF KEY INVESTING WEB SITES

Note: Broker sites are listed on page 259.

America Online	http://www.aol.com
Barron's Online	http://www.barrons.com
Bonds Online	http://www.bonds-online.com
CNN Financial Network	http://www.cnnfn.com
CompuServe	http://www.compuserve.com
The Cyber-Investing Center	http://www.cyberinvest.com
Data Broadcasting Corporation	http://www.dbc.com
Disclosure	http://www.disclosure.com
Dow Jones	http://bis.dowjones.com
EDGAR	http://edgar.stern.nyu.edu
EDGAR Online	http://www.edgar-online.com
The Financial Center Online	http://www.tfc.com
Fortune Magazine	http://www.fortune.com
I/B/E/S	http://www.ibes.com
INVESTools	http://www.investools.com
Investor's Hotline	http://www.wallstreetcity .com/hotline
Macro*World Investor	http://www.sfnb.com
M.A.I.D./Profound	http://www.maid-plc.com
MarketEdge	http://www.marketedge.com
Multex Systems, Inc.	http://www.multexnet.com
NETworth	http://www.networth.galt.com
The New York Times on the Web	http://www.nytimes.com
PAWWS Financial Network	http://pawws.com
PRARS	http://www.prars.com
Prodigy	http://www.prodigy.com
Quote.com	http://www.quote.com
Reuters Money Network	http://www.moneynet.com
Septor on the Web	http://www.notable.com
Standard & Poor's	http://www.stockinfo .standardpoor.com
Stock Smart	http://www.stocksmart.com
Telescan, Inc.	http://www.telescan.com
Wall Street City	http://www.wallstreetcity.com
The Wall Street Journal Interactive Edition	http://interactive2.wsj.com
Zacks Investment Research	http://www.zacks.com

17
THE CYBER-INVESTING TOOLS OF TOMORROW

The world of cyber-investing continues to expand and evolve. Some of the cyber-investing tools and services that we called "tools of tomorrow" in the first edition of this book, did in fact make their debut during the past two years.

- Search optimizers can now identify the indicators that would have been the most helpful in selecting winning stocks in past markets. (Telescan's ProSearch 5.0.)

- Company reports, such as earnings estimates and company profiles, can now be retrieved automatically based on search results. (Telescan's ProSearch 5.0.)

- Asset allocation programs that use dynamic models are now available for the individual investor. (The Macro*World Investor described in Chapter 11.)

- Online trading is flourishing on the Internet as discount brokers slash commissions to attract investors. The complex buy and sell orders mentioned in the first edition are being offered by at least one online brokerage firm (Accutrade for Windows).

- Sophisticated wireless products can now interact with pagers or cellular telephones to give special intraday alerts, such as when a stock makes a significant move counter to the market. Septor, produced by Notable Technologies, LLC, is a noteworthy example.

- EDGAR, the government database for SEC documents filed by public companies and mutual funds, is available on the Internet. Several Web sites offer intelligent EDGAR retrieval systems.

- Interactive communication with public companies, brokers, and Wall Street analysts has been initiated to a limited extent on the Internet through forums, roundtables, and e-mail. Such communication will no doubt become a staple of Internet Web sites.

Other tools still under development or simply envisioned at the present time include the following:

- A "search builder" is under development that will be able to create a custom search in response to straightforward questions about investment goals, such as your attitude about risk and return.

- Electronic filing systems will allow you to store diverse graphs and research data on a single stock in an electronic folder, thus doubling as a purchase log.

- Technical analysis software will use a form of artificial intelligence to improve its ability to recognize chart patterns that have proven successful in the past.

- 3D graphics and other advanced graphic tools will increase the amount of information that can be communicated by graphs, as well as improve their visual appeal.

- Specialized information, such as government statistics for economic or industry analysis, will be more easily accessed via the Internet.

- Educational opportunities in the investment field will become interactive on the Internet.

- Mutual fund analysis programs will become more sophisticated, more specialized, and more global.

- Fundamental information on international stocks will become more accessible, tightening the individual investor's grasp on global investing.

- Hypertext or smart text, which allows an Internet user to jump instantaneously from one spot to another within a document or from one Web site to another, will be expanded to enhance financial documents. For example, you would be able to jump from a balance sheet item to the proper explanatory footnote or from financial data within a text to percentile rankings of that data.

- Automatic portfolio valuation based on asset allocation and other tools should become possible. Sophisticated modeling techniques should be able to forecast near-term and midterm performance of a portfolio. These techniques already exist or are within the current range of modern computers.

- Intelligent agents for investing on the Internet are not far away. Also called smart agents, these programs scan Web sites in search of user-defined information and deliver reports or summaries of what they find. Applied to investing, such agents could monitor your portfolio, assimilate the portfolio valuation, recommend any action to be taken, and provide a short list of new opportunities based on your stated preferences *and* on the agent's assimilation of your reaction to its previous recommendations! Agent technology, which is already in existence, should usher in a whole new era for investors and lead to more market efficiency.

Some of these tools of tomorrow are close to completion; others are in the first stage of development; and a few are still in the vision stage. All, however, are within the realm of today's technology.

YOU MUST REMEMBER THIS . . .

Tomorrow's cyber-investing tools will make today's tools look like tinker toys. The tools of the future will undoubtedly be more powerful and more sophisticated, but they will begin where today's tools leave off. You will still need to find the stocks that have the best chance for growth and evaluate them thoroughly. You will still need to consider the risk/reward relationship when buying and selling stocks. You will still need to manage your portfolio carefully to ensure the greatest possible return on your investments. The investing process and tools described in this book are a good place to start.

If you're daunted by the thought of venturing into cyberspace with actual money at stake, start with paper trades and a dummy portfolio. Once you gain confidence in the technology and in your decisions, you can begin investing for real. Just remember that *discipline* is what distinguishes successful traders from the rest of the crowd. They find a methodology that works for them and they have the discipline to stick with it.

Remember, too, that you have the nimbleness of the individual investor and the computerized tools of the professional. If you use these advantages properly, you too can make excellent returns on Wall Street.

THE
CYBER-INVESTING
KIT

To provide a hands-on experience with cyber-investing tools, the publisher of *Cyber-Investing* has arranged for you to have free access for 30 days to the Telescan 3.0 System. This powerful investment software is a virtual cyber-investing toolkit that contains the search tools, technical analyses tools, and research tools used in the 5-step investing process described in this book. A detailed description of the contents of the kit follows.

FREE SOFTWARE

Software for Telescan 3.0 System is free on the diskette in the back of this book. Telescan 3.0 is a complete system of information and tools for the computerized investor. It includes price and volume charts, technical indicators, fundamental indicators, news stories, company reports, earnings estimates, and search tools for stocks, options, and mutual funds. A description of the various components follows.

30 Days of Free Online Access

Access to the Telescan 3.0 System is free for 30 consecutive days after you call Telescan to obtain a password and user ID number to activate the software, which is described in the next section. Local telephone access is available for most U.S. cities. A long distance call is required to access the Telescan database outside the continental United States.

PC Requirements

The Telescan 3.0 System requires the following hardware and peripheral equipment:

IBM PC (286 or faster) or 100% compatible computer

MS DOS 2.1 or higher

640K Memory

Hard disk; EGA, or VGA board

Hayes Smartmodem (2400 baud or higher) or 100% compatible

Mouse (optional)

Printer (optional)

To Activate Your Software

To activate your software, call Telescan Customer Service at 1-800-281-4357 to receive your local access telephone number, user ID number, and password. Install the program and complete the log-on setup screen according to the instructions in the Quick Start Guide at the end of this section.

Toll-Free Customer Service

Telescan customer service may be reached in the following ways:

Toll-free telephone: 1-800-281-4357

Regular telephone: 1-713-588-9700

Fax: 1-713-588-9797

Telescan e-mail: Select Telescan Mail from the Program Menu (described in the Quick Start Guide.)

Customer service hours are:

Monday–Friday: 7:30 A.M. to 11:00 P.M., Central Time

Saturday: 9:00 A.M. to 6:00 P.M., Central Time

Upgrade to Telescan for Windows®

An upgrade to Telescan for Windows® 3.1 or Windows® 95 is available at a discounted price of $79.95 (excluding the search products). A Windows upgrade that includes ProSearch is also available.

THE TELESCAN 3.0 SYSTEM

The Telescan 3.0 system offers a wealth of statistical and textual information on more than 300,000 securities, market indexes, and currencies. The database contains current online quotes (with 20-minute delay); historical price and volume data dating back to 1973; more than 80 technical and fundamental indicators; insider trading information; news from Reuters and PR Newswire; and fundamental information on listed stocks, such as company profiles, insider trading, earnings estimates, stock forecasts and other special reports. Following is a description of the components included with your 30-day free trial.

Telescan Analyzer

Telescan Analyzer is the charting and analysis component of the 3.0 System. (It was used for the stage-two evaluation in this book, plus the market and industry group analyses.) It allows you to

- Access historical price and volume charts on stocks, industry groups, market indexes, mutual funds, options, and futures.
- Retrieve current stock quotes (delayed 20-minutes) for the NYSE, AMEX, and NASDAQ and Canadian exchanges.

- Perform technical and fundamental analysis.
- Retrieve news and a variety of text reports.

ProSearch 4.0

ProSearch 4.0 is the stock search program used in the stock and industry group searches in this book. (The ranking search in Chapter 5 requires ProSearch 5.0, which is available with the Windows upgrade but is not available for DOS.) ProSearch 4.0 offers over 200 fundamental and technical indicators for defining a search request; predefined search requests, including the ones described in this book; and an online database that is updated daily. Intraday searches are available.

Zacks Earnings Estimates

Zacks Investment Service compiles earnings estimates from thousands of research analysts for approximately 5,000 companies. (A sample report appears in Chapter 8.) Zacks reports are free during your 30-day trial.

Company Profiles from S&P and Market Guide

Company profiles from Market Guide and Standard & Poor's (such as the one in Chapter 8) are available without charge during your 30-day trial.

Mutual Fund Search

Mutual Fund Search offers 82 search criteria designed exclusively for mutual funds. It uses Telescan's mutual fund database of more than 2,000 mutual funds, which are classified by investment objective and fund type. Searches are free during your 30-day trial.

Options Search

Options Search offers 120 search criteria designed exclusively for options. It uses Telescan's online database of more than 35,000 options on stocks and indexes, and more than 300,000 option combinations (spreads and saddles). The program was used to find the speculative calls in Chapter 15. Searches are free during your 30-day trial.

Online Investment Newsletters

Investment newsletters can assist you in market analysis, as well as point you toward specific securities and emerging industry groups. During your 30-day trial, you may sample without charge more than 20 popular market letters covering stocks, options, mutual funds, market trends, and more. This includes the *Cyber-Investing Newsletter* by David Brown, Mark Draud and Paul Alvim, which is based on the five-step cyber-investing process in this book.

TeleScan Seminars

Telescan regularly offers investment seminars throughout the country, including seminars on cyber-investing and searching for high-growth stocks. As a *Cyber-Investing* book purchaser, you will receive discounted admission to all seminars for one year from the activation of your Telescan software. Seminar schedules are listed in the What's New section of Telescan 3.0 (the first screen you see when you log on). You may also call Telescan Customer Service at the numbers listed previously for information on seminars.

A QUICK START GUIDE TO TELESCAN 3.0

The Telescan 3.0 software comes with 30 days of free access to the Telescan database. Your 30 days begin with your first log-on.

BEFORE YOU BEGIN

Before you can log onto the Telescan System, you must do the following:

1. Call Customer Service at 1-800-281-4357 to obtain your local access number, user ID number, and password.

2. Install the software as described below.

3. The first time you log on the database, you will be asked to enter some general information to ensure that your account is set up properly for your free trial.

4. If you log on the Telescan database during prime time hours or if you request a report or service that carries a surcharge, you will be asked for credit card information for billing purposes. The prime-time charge is $0.94 a minute.

To Continue Using Telescan after the 30-Day Free Trial

At the end of your free 30 days, you will see a list of Telescan's monthly billing options when you log on. To activate your account at that time, choose a billing plan at the online prompt and enter the requested credit card information.

INSTALLING THE TELESCAN 3.0 SYSTEM

Before attempting to install the Telescan software, be sure that your computer meets the minimum system requirements listed previously. If you need assistance installing the program, please call Telescan's Customer Service.

To install Telescan:

1. Insert the Telescan 3.0 diskette in the a: or b: drive.

2. If using the a: drive, at the A:\> DOS prompt, type a:\install and press Enter.

   If using the b: drive, at the B:\> DOS prompt, type b:\install and press Enter.

3. The Telescan System will be located in a newly created directory on your hard drive called tele30>.

4. After the program is installed, you will see the following graphics card selections:

   1 EGA Color

   2 VGA Color

   3 Exit to DOS

Select the number for your type of graphics card. You will advance to the offline Telescan screen.

5. You must complete the log-on setup screen, described next, before going online.

Note: To access the program in the future, type **cd\tele30** to change to the Telescan directory; then type **t.**

Log-On Setup

1. Call Telescan Customer Service at 1-800-281-4357 and identify yourself as a Cyber-Investing customer. You will be given:

   - The local telephone number of your communications carrier, which will be used to access Telescan's online database. Be sure to specify your baud rate.
   - A user ID number.
   - A password.

2. Select Log-on Setup from the System Menu on the menu bar.

3. Complete the Log-on Setup screen as follows:

   Baud Rate: Select the baud rate of your modem.
   Access: Specify the communications carrier for your area.

   - SprintNet serves most U.S. metropolitan areas.
   - Datapac serves Canadian residents only.

   Com Port: Select the com port to which your modem is connected. If you select COM-X, you must specify the Interrupt number and HEX address.

   ID# and Password: Enter your user ID number and password as obtained from Telescan. *Note: Enter your password in all capital letters.*

   Phone Number: Enter your local access telephone number as obtained from Telescan. *Note: Do not use hyphens, dashes or spaces.* Keep in mind the following when entering a phone number:

   - Enter T for Touchtone dialing or P for Pulse.
   - If 9 or any other access code is required for an outside line, be sure to enter it, followed by a comma. Example: T9,5551234
   - Enter the area code if the local access number is in a city different from your area code; precede the area code with a 1. Example: T17135551234 or T9,17135551234

Modem Program: Reserved for networked computers. Call Telescan Customer Service for assistance.

4. Click Save and press Alt+S to save the log-on parameters or press Escape.

5. Perform a modem test by choosing Modem Test from the System Menu. If the modem is properly connected, you will see a confirmation.

You are now ready to use the program.

Note: Basic navigational commands and hot keys appear at the end of this chapter.

USING TELESCAN ANALYZER

Telescan Analyzer offers stock quotes, price-and-volume graphs on all securities, and complete technical and fundamental analysis. In Telescan 3.0, the Telescan Analyzer Menu is found offline at the Program Menu. Online, it appears on the menu bar.

Each time you log on you will see a "What's New" screen, with information about Telescan's products and services. To escape this screen, make a menu selection.

To Retrieve a Graph

To retrieve the first graph online:

1. Choose New Graph from the Analyzer Menu, or press Ctrl+G.

2. At the Stock prompt, type the symbol for the security and press Enter. *Note: Security symbols must be entered in uppercase letters.*

3. To retrieve subsequent new graphs online, press G and enter the security symbol.

Other Graph functions:

- To plot technical or fundamental indicators on a graph, make a selection from the Indicators Menu.
- To save the displayed graph, press S.
- To print the displayed graph, Press P.

- To plot a different time span for the displayed graph, use the button bar at the top of the graph or press the following keys:

Time Span	Keys
Days, 1–10	Alt+F1 through Alt+F10
Months, 1–10	F1 through F12
Years, 1–9	1 through 9
10 years	10
Maximum time span	=

To Look Up a Stock Symbol

If you don't know a stock symbol, you may look it up online.

1. Select Text Services from the Program Menu.
2. Select Symbols Menu from the Text Services Menu.
3. Select Symbol LookUp.
4. Type in the partial or full name of the security and click Send or press Alt+S. The security symbol will appear on the screen.

To Create an AutoRun File

AutoRun files are used to retrieve multiple graphs quickly for viewing offline. First, create a file of security symbols with desired technical or fundamental indicators (called an AutoRun file) and then perform an AutoRun. To create an AutoRun file:

1. Offline, select Edit AutoRun from the Analyzer Menu. You will see a blank Edit AutoRun screen.
2. Click on the Add button or press Alt+A.
3. A window will open which contains text boxes for the security symbol, name (optional), and time span, plus a list of indicators. A yellow arrow will point to the active box. Use the mouse or the Tab key to move the arrow between the different boxes.
   - If you do not know the symbol, use the online Symbol LookUp described in the previous section.
4. Be sure to save your selections.
5. Repeat these steps for the next security you wish to include.

To Perform an AutoRun

To perform an AutoRun:

1. Select Log On from the System Menu or press Ctrl+O.
2. Select Start AutoRun from the Analyzer Menu. After AutoRun is complete, you may view or print the graphs offline.
3. Select Log-off from the System Menu or press Ctrl+O.

To Print and Save Saved Graphs

To view graphs offline:

1. Open the graph file by pressing Ctrl+G or selecting One Graph from the Analyzer Menu.
2. To view the graphs, use the PgDn or PgUp keys (or left and right mouse buttons).

To print saved graphs (and those retrieved by the AutoRun):

1. Open the graph file, *offline,* as above.
2. To print the displayed graph only, press P.
3. To print selected graphs:
   - Mark the graphs you wish to print by displaying the graph and pressing Alt+T.
   - Select Start AutoPrint from the Analyzer Menu or press Ctrl+V to print the tagged graphs.
4. To print all graphs in the file:
   - Select Tag All Graphs from the Analyzer Menu or press Ctrl+T.
   - Select Start AutoPrint from the Analyzer Menu or press Ctrl+V.

To Retrieve News and Company Reports

Telescan's news database and company reports, such as S&P Market-Scope, Market Guide, and Zacks earnings estimates, may be accessed (on-line) in two different ways:

1. *With a graph displayed:* Select Special Reports from the Indicator Menu; then select the desired report.

2. *Without a graph displayed:* Select Text Services from the Program Menu; then select Special Reports; then select the desired report and enter the security symbol when prompted.

To Access Online Newsletters

To access an online market letter:

- Select Newsletters from the Text Services Menu *online*. A list of currently available newsletters will be displayed.
- Double-click the letter preceding the desired newsletter or press the corresponding letter key and then press Enter.
- You will see a sample newsletter or a list of dates of the most recent issues. If the latter, double-click the letter preceding the desired date, or press the corresponding letter key and then press Enter.

To Print or Save Articles or Reports

Saved articles and reports are stored in the File Manager as text files.

- To review an article or report offline, open the File Manager as described in the following section.
- To print a displayed article or report (online or offline), click Print or press Alt+P.
- To save an article or report, click Save or press Alt+S and enter a file name when prompted.

To Use the File Manager

Saved files may be found in the File Manager under the appropriate File Type. To retrieve or view a saved file:

1. Select File Manager from the System Menu.
2. Click the File Type button or press the Tab key to move the yellow cursor to the desired file type. A list of files for that category will be displayed in the window.
3. To open a file, highlight it and click Open or press Alt+O or Enter.

When a saved file is opened, it will be displayed in the appropriate window.

To Find the Searches Described in This Book

Open the File Manager and click the ProSearch File Type button. Searches are listed as follows:

Name of Search	Description of Search in Book
CYBER-INS	Insider Trading Search—the expanded search that was backtested in Chapter 6
CYBER-UVG	Undervalued Growth Search from Chapter 5
CYBER-MO	Momentum Search from Chapter 5
CYBER-IG	Industry Group Search from Chapter 14
CYBER-ROA	Stocks in Specified Industries from Chapter 14

To use the Option Search in Chapter 15, open the File Manager and click the Options Search button. The search will be listed as CYBER-OPT.

To Use Telescan E-Mail

1. Log on and select Telescan Mail from the Program Menu.
2. Click on the desired department, or use the Tab key.
3. Type the message, then click on Mail-Send or press Alt+M.
4. The system will tell you if the mail was delivered successfully.

If you have a message, you will see a prompt that you have unread mail. To read it, select Telescan Mail from the Program Menu. Then click Receive or Press Alt+R to display the message.

USING PROSEARCH

If you have not previously logged on to the database, you must do so in order to activate ProSearch. Choose Log On from the System Menu. When you see the What's New screen, press Escape. Select Log Off from the System Menu. ProSearch will be highlighted in white on the Program Menu if it has been activated.

Searches may be created offline or online but must be submitted online. You may use up to 40 criteria in a search.

To Create a Search

You may create a search offline or online.

1. Select ProSearch from the Program Menu or press Ctrl+S. The ProSearch screen will appear, with a list of indicators to be used as search criteria in the left window.

2. Scroll through the indicators to find the one you wish to use. The definition of the highlighted indicator will appear in the upper right window.

3. Double-click or press Enter to select the highlighted criteria.

4. A window will open, allowing you to specify the search mode for the indicator.

   - Choose *Absolute* to eliminate stocks from the search universe based on the raw score of the indicator. Enter minimum and maximum values. (Press Enter at the fields for absolute minimum or maximum values.)

   - Choose *Rank* to eliminate stocks from the search based on the percentile rank of the indicator. Enter minimum and maximum values.

   Note: All stocks outside the minimum and maximum ranges will be eliminated from the search.

   - Choose *Relative* to score and rank the stocks. This allows you to search the universe of stocks to find the optimal issues that best fit your criteria, and rank them in the order of best fit. Select the desired weighting percentage to indicate the importance of the indicator to your strategy.

   - Choose *List Only* to retrieve information without affecting the search.

   Note: You may use the Absolute and Relative modes or the Absolute and Rank modes for the same indicator.

5. After you select a search mode, click Save or press Alt+S, and you will return to the initial ProSearch window.

6. Repeat the above steps for each indicator you wish to use.

To Save a Search

To save a search, select Save from the System Menu and enter a filename when requested. *Be sure to save the search if you created it offline.*

To Submit a Search

To submit a search you must log on to the Telescan database.

1. Select Log On from the System Menu or press Ctrl+O.
2. Online, select File Manager from the System Menu.
3. Click the ProSearch File Type button or press Alt+P. The saved ProSearch files will appear in the window.
4. Highlight the saved file you wish to use and click Open or press Alt+O. The search will appear in a ProSearch window.
5. Click Submit or press Alt+S to open the Submit Search screen. Complete the information on this screen as follows:
   - *Title:* Enter a title if you wish one to appear on your search report.
   - *# Securities:* Enter the number of stocks you wish to see on the search report. 10 is the default; the maximum is 200 or fewer, depending on the number of indicators used in the search.
   - *Search:* These buttons allow you to specify the search universe: Stocks, Optionable Stocks, Mutual Funds, Industry Groups, or Stocks in Specified Industries. The latter should be used only if you first select industry groups, as described later.
   - *Back Test:* Select Yes if you wish to backtest a search; then enter the test parameters. *Months Back* refers to start date for the backtest; *Days for Return* refers to the time period over which you wish to test the results.
   - *Report Format* and *Report Data:* These refer to various formats for the printed report. The default is Standard, which lists both the absolute value and percentile rank.
6. Click Submit or press Alt+S to submit the search. In a few seconds you will see the search report in a text window. Use the Down Arrow key to scroll through the stocks.

7. The buttons at the bottom of the report window perform various actions with regard to the search report. Click the button or press the Alt key and initial letter key.

- *Save* (Alt+S) saves the report in the File Manager under the ProSearch File Type. Enter a filename when prompted.
- *Print* (Alt+P) prints the search report.
- *Text Save* (Alt+T) saves the report as a text file for importing into a word processing or other program.
- *IndFlag* (Alt+I) appears only with an industry group search. It automatically flags the industry groups found by the search. This enables you to run a stock search on just those industries.
- *AutoRun* (Alt+A) transfers the stock symbols to an AutoRun file, for retrieval of stock graphs.
- *Quote>Link* (Alt+Q) transfers the stock symbols to a QuoteLink file for the retrieval of stock quotes.

To Select Industry Groups

At the ProSearch main screen, click the IndGrp button or press Alt+I. Telescan's industry groups will be listed in a window. You may scroll through the window using the mouse, Arrow keys, or PgUp and PgDn keys. An asterisk (*) denotes a selected group. Use the option buttons on the right of the screen as follows:

- *All On/Off* (Alt+A) flags all groups or removes all flags.
- *Reverse On/Off* (Alt+R) reverses the current selections.
- *Find* (Alt+F) opens a Find window to allow you to search for a group by name or partial name.
- *Next/Find* (Alt+N) is used after the Find command to find the *next* group with the same word in the name.
- *Save* (Alt+S) saves the group selections and returns to the main screen. *Be sure to save your selections.*
- *Cancel* (Alt+C) cancels the selections and returns to the main screen.

USING MUTUAL FUND SEARCH OR OPTIONS SEARCH

Both Mutual Fund Search and Options Search operate similarly to Pro-Search. Mutual Fund Search uses Telescan's database of some 2,000 mutual funds; Options Search uses Telescan's database of some 35,000 options on stocks and indexes and more than 300,000 option combinations. The main differences in the program structure are these:

- The 82 search criteria in Mutual Fund Search are designed expressly for mutual funds; the 122 criteria in Options Search are designed expressly for options.
- 30 criteria may be used in a single search, rather than 40.
- The percentile rank is not shown on the mutual fund or options search report.
- The Objectives button at the bottom of the Mutual Fund Search corresponds to ProSearch's Industry Group button, allowing you to limit a search to funds with specific investment objectives.
- The search universes are program-specific.
- Backtesting does not work with mutual funds or options.

GENERAL KEYSTROKE AND MOUSE COMMANDS

The following general keystrokes and mouse commands are used in the Telescan program:

Action	Keystroke	Mouse
Open a menu:	Press the Right Arrow or Left Arrow key to highlight the menu. Then press the Down Arrow key to open it.	Click the menu with the left mouse button.
Select a menu item:	Press the Down Arrow key or Up Arrow key to highlight the item; then press Enter.	Double-click the menu item with the left mouse button.

Action	Keystroke	Mouse
Select a data field:	Press the Tab key or Enter to move the yellow cursor *down* one field. Press Shift and Tab simultaneously to move the yellow cursor *up* one field.	Click a field to activate it.
Choose an option button:	Press the Space bar to toggle the option on and off.	Click on an option button to select it.

Note: Option buttons are highlighted in red when selected.

Hot Keys

Hot keys initiate actions without opening a menu. Press and hold the (Ctrl) key while pressing the letter or F-key.

Ctrl+A	Opens QuoteLink.
Ctrl+E	Opens the AutoRun window.
Ctrl+F	Opens the File Manager window.
Ctrl+G	Opens graph window with stock prompt.
Ctrl+L	Opens the Log-on Setup window.
Ctrl+O	Log on or log off the database.
Ctrl+P	Deletes graphs marked for deletion, offline.
Ctrl+Q	Exits the Telescan program, online or offline.
Ctrl+R	Opens the Telescan Mail window, online.
Ctrl+S	Opens ProSearch.
Ctrl+V	Starts AutoRun online or AutoPrint offline.
Ctrl+F1	Opens one graph window.
Ctrl+F2	Opens two graph windows.
Ctrl+F4	Opens four graph windows.

Note: The above hot keys do not work if the Menu On/Off sign on the menu bar is off. Press Escape to turn the sign to Menu On.

SOURCE LIST FOR CYBER-INVESTING TOOLS

There are dozens of products and services that can be used for cyber-investing, and more are being introduced every day. What follows is a partial listing, by category, of those available in late 1996. Products and services are listed under their major function, although most perform a variety of cyber-investing tasks. The company is shown in parentheses. A cross-reference list of addresses, phone numbers, Internet addresses and other information starts on page 292.

An exhaustive list of computerized investing products may be found in *The Individual Investor's Guide to Computerized Investing* (Chicago: American Association of Individual Investors, 1995).

Asset Allocation & Portfolio Management

Most online trading services offer some form of portfolio tracking. These programs are designed specifically for asset allocation or portfolio management.

> CapTool (TechServe, Inc.)
>
> CompuServe Asset Manager (CompuServe, Inc.)
>
> Kiplinger's Simply Money (Computer Associates International, Inc.)
>
> Macro*World Investor (Macro*World Research Corp.)
>
> Portfolio Analyzer (Hamilton Software, Inc.)
>
> Portfolio Manager (Telescan, Inc.)
>
> Prosper (Ernst & Young)
>
> Quicken (Intuit, Inc.)
>
> Smart Money Interactive (Dow Jones & Company)
>
> WealthBuilder (Reality Technologies, Inc.)

Charting and Technical Analysis

Many programs and services offer price and volume charts and some form of technical analysis. The following are designed specifically for technical analysis.

AIQ MarketExpert and AIQ TradingExpert (Track Data Corp.)

Dow Jones News/Retrieval-Person Investor Edition (Dow Jones & Company, Inc.)

Metastock (Equis International, Inc.)

NavaPatterns (Nava Development Corp.)

OmniTrader (Nirvana)

SuperCharts (Omega Research)

TeleChart 2000 (Worden Brothers, Inc.)

Telescan Investment Platform and Telescan Analyzer (Telescan, Inc.)

TickerWatcher and Investex/RT (Linn Software, Inc.)

Windows on Wall Street (MarketArts, Inc.) (Also available through Dow Jones & Company, Inc.)

Mutual Funds

Although mutual fund information is available through many different services, the following are designed specifically for mutual funds.

Fund Master TC (Time Trend Software)

Morningstar Ascent (Morningstar, Inc.)

Mutual Fund Search (Telescan, Inc.)

Value Line Mutual Fund Reports (Value Line, Inc.)

Online Trading

Discount brokers who offer online trading via the Internet or their own proprietary software are listed in Chapter 16, along with full-service brokers who have a presence on the Web. All offer free quotes. Some of the discount brokers and all of the full-service brokers offer various research services to their customers.

Options

Option quotes are available from most of the sources that offer stock quotes. The following are search and analysis products designed specifically for options.

Option Master (Institute for Options Research, Inc.)

Options Search and Options Analyzer (Telescan, Inc.)

OptionVue IV (OptionVue Systems International, Inc.)

Quotes

Stock quotes are available through American Online, CompuServe, and Prodigy and most of the Internet websites mentioned in Chapter 16. Below are stand-alone products that offer online stock quotes and other financial services

BMI (BMI).

Dial/Data and Track/Online (Track Data Corporation)

Dow Jones News/Retrieval-Private Investor Edition (Dow Jones & Company, Inc.)

Reuters Money Network (Reality Technologies, Inc.)

Signal (Data Broadcasting Corporation)

Telemet Encore (Telemet America, Inc.)

Telescan Investment Platform and Telescan Analyzer (Telescan, Inc.)

Research and Fundamental Analysis

Company profiles and research reports are available through several independent companies. These companies also provide their reports through various online services, which are shown on the address list on pages 292–302.

Disclosure (Disclosure Incorporated)

I/B/E/S earnings reports (I/B/E/S International, Inc.)

M.A.I.D. global research reports (M.A.I.D.)

Market Guide (Market Guide, Inc.)

Multex research reports (Multex)

S&P MarketScope (Standard & Poor's, Inc.)

Thomson Research Reports (Thomson Financial Services & MarketEdge)

Trend Dynamics (CompuServe)

Value Line Reports (Value Line, Inc.)

Zacks Earnings Estimates (Zacks Investment Research)

Stock Search Programs

The following programs are designed specifically for screening stocks.

ProSearch (Telescan, Inc.)

U.S. Equities OnFloppy (Morningstar, Inc.)

Value/Screen III (Value Line Software)

ADDRESS LIST

Company	Products/Services
Accutrade, Inc. 4211 South 102nd Street Omaha, NE 68127 1-800-882-4887 402-331-7856 Email: info@accutrade.com Internet: http://www.accutrade.com	Accutrade for Windows Online trading
A.G. Edwards & Sons, Inc. One North Jefferson St. Louis, MO 63103 314-955-3000 Internet: http://www.agedwards.com	Full service broker
All American Brokers, Inc. P. O. Box 2226 Omaha, NE 63103-2226 Email: info@ebroker.com Internet: http://www.ebroker.com	eBroker Online trading
America Online 8619 Westwood Center Dr Vienna, VA 22182 1-800-827-6364 Internet: http://www.aol.com	A general online network offering a variety of financial services and access to individual providers
American Express Financial Direct P. O. Box 59196 Minneapolis, MN 55459-9801 1-800-658-4677 Internet: http://www.americanexpress/direct	Online trading and other financial services

Company	Products/Services
BMI 3 Triad Center, Suite 100 Salt Lake City, UT 84180 1-800-287-9519 Internet: http://www.dbc.com	Real time quotes
Ceres Securities, Inc. P. O. Box 2209 Omaha, NE 68103-2209 1-800-669-3900 Internet: http://www.ceres.com	Ceres Securities Online trading
Charles Schwab & Co., Inc. The Schwab Building 101 Montgomery Street San Francisco, CA 94104 1-800-648-5300 415-627-7000 Internet: http://www.schwab.com	StreetSmart eSchwab Online Investing Online trading, portfolio management, search programs
CompuServe P. O. Box 20212 5000 Arlington Center Blvd. Columbus, OH 43220-0212 1-800-848-8199 614-457-8600 Internet: http://world.compuserve.com	A general online network offering a variety of financial services and access to individual providers
Computer Aided Decisions, Inc. One Washington Mall, 10th Floor Boston, MA 02108 617-227-2288	Portfolio management and asset allocation Available through Telescan, Inc.
Computer Associates International, Inc. One Computer Associates Plaza Islandia, NY 11788 1-800-225-5224	Kiplinger's Simply Money Portfolio management
The Cyber-Investing Center Email: author@cyberinvest.com Internet: http://www.cyberinvest.com	Information on Investing Web sites
Data Broadcasting Corporation 1900 South Norfolk Street, Suite 150 San Mateo, CA 94403 1-800-367-4670 415-571-1800 Email: mwonline@dbc.com Internet: http://www.dbc.com	Signal MarketWatch Real time quotes, portfolio management, price and volume alerts, news

Company	Products/Services
Datek Securities Corp. 4522 Fort Hamilton Parkway Brooklyn, NY 11219 718-435-7100 Internet: http://www.datek.com	Datek Online Online trading
Disclosure, Incorporated 5161 River Road Bethesda, MD 20816 301-951-1300 Internet: http://www.disclosure.com	Global Access Research reports Also available through America Online, CompuServe, Investext, Reuters, and others.
Dow Jones & Company, Inc. P. O. Box 300 Princeton, NJ 08543 1-800-522-3567 609-520-8349 Internet: http://www.dowjones.com	Dow Jones News/Retrieval-Personal Investor Edition News, quotes and charts, fundamental and research data, portfolio management technical analysis via Windows on Wall Street
Equis International, Inc. 3950 South 700 East, Suite 100 Salt Lake City, UT 84107 1-800-882-3040 801-265-8886 Internet: http://www.equis.com	MetaStock The Downloader The Technician Technical analysis
Ernst & Young LLP 1225 Connecticut Avenue, N.W. Washington, D.C. 20036 1-800-2-PROSPER 202-327-6000 Email: prosper@ey.com Internet: http://www.ey.com/us/tax /prosper1.htm	Prosper Asset allocation, portfolio management, stock quotes
E*Trade Securities, Inc. 4 Embarcadero Place 2400 Geng Road Palo Alto, CA 94303 1-800-786-2575 415-842-8600 Internet: http://www.etrade.com	E*Trade Online trading Also available through America Online and CompuServe

Company	Products/Services
Fidelity Investments FMR Corporation 82 Devonshire Street Boston, MA 02109-3614 1-800-544-7272 617-563-7000 Internet: http://www.fid-inv.com	Fidelity On-line Xpress Online trading
Hamilton Software, Inc. 6432 East Mineral Place Englewood, CO 80112 1-800-733-9607 303-770-9607	Fundwatch Plus Investor's Accountant, Market Strategist, Market Watch Portfolio Analyzer Portfolio management, mutual fund analysis, technical analysis of stocks
Howe Barnes Investments, Inc. Chicago, IL 1-800-638-4250 312-655-3000 Email: invest@pawws.com Internet: http://pawws.com/Broker/How	The Net Investor Online trading
IDEA, a division of Independent Economic Analysis (Holdings) PTE Limited 8 Robinson Road, #14-00 Singapore 048544 U.S. 212-571-4332 London: 44-171-430-2888 Singapore: 65-536-7775 Internet: http://www.intermoney.com	Financial Markets Today FX Options Strategies Emerging Markets Today Emerging Markets-Asia Emerging Markets-Latin America Available via fax and through Telescan, Inc.
I/B/E/S International, Inc. 345 Hudson Street New York, NY 10014-4502 212-647-5700 Internet: http://www.ibes.com	Global earnings estimates and earnings surprises for US companies Available through CompuServe, NETworth, and others
Institute for Options Research, Inc. P. O. Box 6586 Lake Tahoe, NV 89449 1-800-334-0854 702-588-3590 Email: ior@sierra.net Internet: http://www.options-inc.com	Option Master Option analysis

Company	Products/Services
Intuit, Inc. 66 Willow Place P. O. Box 3014 Menlo Park, CA 94026 1-800-624-8742 415-322-0573 Internet: http://www.intuit.com	Quicken Investor Insight Portfolio management, stock quotes, company reports Quicken Financial Network: http://www.qfn.com
Investex Securities Group, Inc. 50 Broad Street New York, New York 10004 1-800-392-7192 Internet: http://www.investexpress.com	Investex Express On-line Online trading
INVESTools E-mail: feedback@tabula.com Internet: http://www.investools.com	A variety of financial informa- tion, including a collection of newsletters
Jack White & Company 9191 Towne Centre Drive, Second Floor San Diego, CA 92122 1-800-753-1700 E-mail: jwc@pawws.com Internet: http://pawws.com.Broker/Jwc	PATH Online Online trading
J.P. Morgan & Co., Inc. 60 Wall Street New York, NY 10260-0060 212-483-2323 Internet: http://www.jpmorgan.com	Full service broker
K. Aufhauser & Co., Inc. 53 Wall Street, Fifth Floor New York, NY I 10005 1-800-368-3668 E-mail: info@aufhauser.com Internet: http://www.aufhauser.com	WealthWEB Online trading
Linn Software, Inc. 1776 Peachtree Road NW, Suite 701 Atlanta, GA 30309 1-800-546-6842 404-733-5733 Internet: http://www.linnsoft.com	TicketWatcher (for MacIntosh only) Investor/RT Charting and technical analy- sis

Company	Products/Services
Lombard Institutional Brokerage, Inc. 595 Market Street, Suite 780 San Francisco, CA 94105-3407 1-800-688-6896 415-597-6500 Internet: http://www.lombard.com	Online trading
Macro*World Research Corporation 4265 Brownsboro Road, Suite 170 Winston Salem, NC 27106-3429 1-800-841-5398 910-759-0600 Internet: http://www.mworld.com	Macro*World Investor Also available through Telescan, Inc. and Security First Network Bank (http://www.sfnb.com)
M.A.I.D./Profound The Communications Building 48 Leicester Square London WC2H 7DB U.K. Tollfree: 1-800-201-3175 Internet: http://www.maid-plc.com	Company profiles and re- search reports on companies world-wide
MarketArts, Inc. 1820 N. Glenville Drive, Suite 100 Richardson, TX 75081 1-800-998-8439 214-783-6792 E-mail: wowinfo@wallstreet.net Internet: http://www.wallstreet.net	Window on Wall Street Technical analysis Window on Wall Street also available through Dow Jones & Company, Inc.
Market Guide, Inc. 2001 Marcus Avenue, Suite 200-S New Hyde Park, NY 11042 516-327-2400 Internet: http://www.marketguide.com	Corporate reports Also available through Teles- can, Inc., Prodigy, INVESTools, and others
Merrill Lynch & Co., Inc. World Financial Center North Tower New York, NY 10281-1332 212-449-1000 Internet: http://www.ml.com	Full service broker

Company	Products/Services
Morningstar, Inc., 225 West Wacker Drive Chicago, IL 60606 1-800-735-0700 312-696-6000	Morningstar Ascent (Mutual fund analysis) US Equities OnFloppy (Stock fundamental analysis) Morningstar mutual fund reports are available through America Online, CompuServe, Reuters Money Network, NETworth, INVESTools, Quick & Reilly, and others
Multex Systems, Inc. 33 Maiden Lane, 5th Floor New York, NY 10038 Toll-free: 1-888MULTEX 212-859-9890 E-mail: multexnet@multexsys.com Internet: http://www.multinet.com	Research reports Also available through Telescan, Inc., Reuters Money Network
National Discount Brokers 50 Broadway, 18th Floor New York, NY 10004 E-mail: ndb@secapl.com Internet: http://pawws.com/Broker/Ndb	NDB Online Online trading
Nava Development Corp. 251-A Portage Road Lewiston, NY 14092-1710 1-800-532-0041	NavaPatterns Technical analysis
NETWORTH Galt Technologies 4618 Henry Street Pittsburgh, PA 15213 412-681-6100 Internet: http://www.networth.galt.com	Information on mutual funds and equities, plus large collection of newsletters
Nirvana Systems, Inc. 3415 Greystone, Suite 205 Austin, TX 78731-2364 512-345-2566 1-800-880-0338	OmniTrader Charting and technical analysis
Notable Technologies, LLC 4122—128th Avenue S.E., Suite 305 Bellevue, WA 98006 1-800-814-4214 206-643-1610 Internet: http://www.notable.com	Septor on the Web Wireless stock alerts

Company	Products/Services
Omega Research Omega Research Building 9200 Sunset Drive Miami, FL 33173-3266 1-800-556-2022 305-270-1095 E-mail: service@omegaresearch.com Internet: http://www.omegaresearch.com	SuperCharts Wall Street Analyst TradeStation OptionStation Technical analysis, strategy testing, and option analysis
Oppenheimer & Co., Inc. Oppenheimer Tower World Financial Center New York, NY 10281 1-800-999-6726 212-776-7000 Internet: http://www.oppenheimer.com	Full service broker
OptionVue Systems International, Inc. 1117 South Milwaukee Avenue, #C10 Libertyville, IL 60048 1-800-733-6610 Internet: http://www.optionvue.com	OptionVue IV Options analysis
Pacific Brokerage Services, Inc. 5757 Wilshire Boulevard, Suite 3 Los Angeles, CA 909036 1-800-416-7113 310-273-2545 Internet: http://www.tradepbs.com	Online trading
PaineWebber 1285 Avenue of the Americas New York, NY 10019 212-713-2000 Internet: http://www.painewebber.com	Full Service Broker
PAWWS Financial Network 101 Hudson Street Jersey City, NJ 07302 201-432-3000 E-mail: pawws@pawws.com Internet: http://pawws.com	A network of online brokers and other financial service providers
PC Financial Network Donald, Lufkin, & Jenrette One Pershing Place Jersey City, NJ 07399 1-800-237-PCFN E-mail: info@pcfn.com Internet: http://www.pcfn.com	Online trading Also available through America Online, Prodigy, Reuters Money Network, and Sony Major Link Network

Company	Products/Services
PRARS 1-800-426-6825 E-mail: info@prars.com Internet: http://www.prars.com	Annual reports
Prodigy Services Company 22 North Plains Industrial Highway Wallingford, CT 06492 1-800-776-3449 Internet: http://www.prodigy.com	A general online network offering a variety of financial services and links to individual providers
Prudential Securities, Inc. One New York Plaza New York, NY 10292 212-214-1000 Internet: http://www.prusec.com	Full service broker
Quick & Reilly 26 Broadway New York, New York 10275 1-800-837-7220 212-748-6688 Internet: http://www.Quick-Reilly.com	QuickWay Plus Online trading, news, Standard & Poor's reports
Quote.com, Inc. 3375 Scott Boulevard, Suite 300 Santa Clara, CA 95054 408-327-0700 Internet: http://www.quote.com	Financial market data to Internet users, including stock quotes, S&P reports, Zacks earnings estimates
Reality Online, Inc., A Reuters Company 1000 Madison Avenue Norristown, PA 19403 1-800-346-2024 610-650-8600 Email: info@reality-tech.com Internet: http://www.moneynet.com	Reuters Money Network WealthBuilder Online trading, asset allocation, portfolio management, stock quotes, stock search programs, research reports
Smith Barney, Inc. 388 Greenwich Street New York, NY 10013 212-816-6000 Internet: http://www.smithbarney.com	Full service broker

Company	Products/Services
Standard & Poor's 25 Broadway New York, NY 15004 212-208-8702 Internet: http://www.stockinfo.standardpoor.com	S&P MarketScope MarketScope@Home Corporate reports also available through America Online, CompuServe, Telescan, Inc., Quick & Reilly, Dow Jones & Company, Inc., Reuters Money Network, Quote.com.
Stock Smart 2515 McKinney Avenue, Suite 1585 Dallas, TX 75201 Internet: http://www.stocksmart.com	Financial market data to Internet users for stocks and mutual funds
Techserve, Inc. P. O. Box 9 Issaquah, WA 98027 1-800-826-8082 206-391-4140 E-mail: sales@captools.com Internet: http://www.captools.com	CapTool Portfolio management
Telemet America, Inc. 325 First Street Alexandria VA 22314 1-800-368-2078 703-548-2042	Telemet Encore Telemet Radio Exchange Telemet Orion Stock quotes (delayed or real time)
Telescan, Inc. 5959 Corporate Drive, Suite 2000 Houston, TX 77036 1-800-281-4357 713-588-9700 Internet: http://www.telescan.com	Telescan Investment Platform ProSearch Mutual Fund Search Options Search Charting and technical analysis, quotes, fundamental data, S&P MarketScope, Market Guide, Zacks earnings estimates, insider trading. Search programs for stocks, mutual, funds and options
Thomson Financial Services 40 West 57th Street, Suite 1000 New York, NY 10019 1-800-929-3343 Internet: http://www.marketedge.com	MarketEdge Research reports and other investing information on the Internet

Company	Products/Services
Time Trend Software 337 Boston Road Billerica, MA 01821 508-250-3866	Fund Master TC Enhanced Optimizer Data Retriever FundPro Mutual fund pricing and analysis Also available through America Online and Prodigy.
Track Data Corporation 56 Pine St. New York, New York 10005 1-800-367-5968 702-831-2999 Internet for AIQ MarketExpert: http://www.aiq.com	AIQ TradingExpert for Windows AIQ MarketExpert for Windows Track/Online Dial/Data Technical analysis, delayed and real time quotes
Value Line Software 220 East 42nd Street New York, NY 10017-5891 1-800-833-0046	Value Line Reports Value/Screen III Corporate reports and stock search program
Wall Street City c/o Telescan, Inc. 5959 Corporate Drive, Suite 2000 Houston, TX 77036 1-800-324-4692 713-588-9700 Internet: http://www.wallstreetcity.com	An investing supersite sponsored by Telescan, Inc. offering extensive financial market data to Internet users with links to other investing sites.
Thomas F. White & Co., Inc. 1 Second Street, 5th Floor San Francisco, CA 94105 1-800-432-0327 Internet: http://www.rapidtrade.com	CompuTEL Securities Online trading
Worden Brothers, Inc. Five Oaks Office Park 4905 Pine Cone Drive Durham, NC 27707 1-800-776-4940 Internet: http://www.worden.com	Telechart 2000 Technical analysis
Zacks Investment Research, Inc. 155 North Wacker Drive Chicago, IL 60606 1-800-399-6659 312-630-9880 Internet: http://www.zacks.com	Earnings estimates reports Analyst Watch on the Internet Earnings estimates also available through Telescan, Inc., CompuServe, Dow Jones & Company, Quote.com, and others.

INDEX